CHEATED

T0243931

BILL WAISER *and* JENNIE HANSEN

CHEATED

The **LAURIER LIBERALS** *and*
the **THEFT** *of* **FIRST NATIONS**
RESERVE LAND

Copyright © Bill Waiser and Jennie Hansen, 2023

Published by ECW Press
665 Gerrard Street East
Toronto, Ontario, Canada M4M 1Y2
416-694-3348 / info@ecwpress.com

All rights reserved. No part of this publication may be reproduced, stored in a retrieval system, or transmitted in any form by any process — electronic, mechanical, photocopying, recording, or otherwise — without the prior written permission of the copyright owners and ECW Press. The scanning, uploading, and distribution of this book via the internet or via any other means without the permission of the publisher is illegal and punishable by law. Please purchase only authorized electronic editions, and do not participate in or encourage electronic piracy of copyrighted materials. Your support of the authors' rights is appreciated.

Cover design: Jessica Albert
Cover photograph: "Honourable David Laird explaining terms of Treaty #8, Fort Vermilion," 1899. The Glenbow Museum. Photograph is in the public domain.
Bill Waiser photo: Liam Richards
Jennie Hansen photo: Picture Perfect

LIBRARY AND ARCHIVES CANADA CATALOGUING
IN PUBLICATION

Title: Cheated : the Laurier Liberals and the theft of First Nations reserve land / Bill Waiser and Jennie Hansen.

Names: Waiser, Bill, 1953- author. | Hansen, Jennie (Historian), author.

Description: Includes index.

Identifiers: Canadiana (print) 20230237827 | Canadiana (ebook) 20230438814

ISBN 978-1-77041-748-9 (softcover)
ISBN 978-1-77852-224-6 (ePub)
ISBN 978-1-77852-225-3 (PDF)
ISBN 978-1-77852-226-0 (Kindle)

Subjects: LCSH: Land settlement—Government policy—Canada—History—20th century. | CSH: First Nations—Land tenure—History—20th century. | CSH: First Nations—Government relations—History—20th century. | CSH: First Nations—Claims—History—20th century. | CSH: First Nations reservations—History—20th century. | CSH: Canada—Politics and government—1896-1911.

Classification: LCC E92 .W35 2023 | DDC 333.2—dc23

This book is funded in part by the Government of Canada. *Ce livre est financé en partie par le gouvernement du Canada.* We also acknowledge the support of the Government of Ontario through the Ontario Book Publishing Tax Credit, and through Ontario Creates.

PRINTED AND BOUND IN CANADA

PRINTING: FRIESENS   5   4   3   2   1

MIX
Paper from
responsible sources
FSC
www.fsc.org   FSC® C016245

"The surrender was obtained not by the desire of the Indians, but by the strong wish of the Department."

INDIAN AFFAIRS INSPECTOR S.R. MARLATT

MANITOBA, MARCH 1903

"They [First Nations] are always averse to surrendering anything they have."

PRIME MINISTER WILFRID LAURIER

HOUSE OF COMMONS, OCTOBER 1903

FIRST NATIONS RESERVE SURRENDERS

For illustrative purposes only.

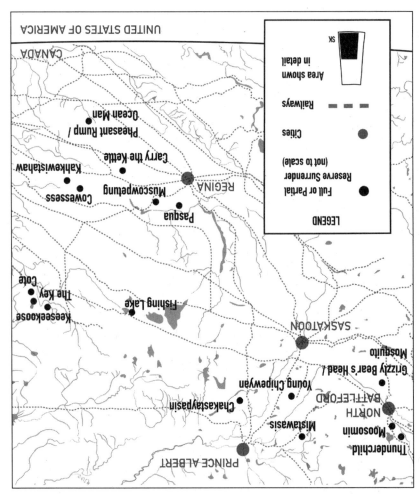

Saskatchewan

LEGEND

- Full or Partial Reserve Surrender (not to scale)
- Cities
- Railways
- Area shown in detail

UNITED STATES OF AMERICA

CANADA

Ocean Man
Pheasant Rump /
Carry the Kettle
Kahkewistahaw
Cowessess
Muscowpetung
REGINA
Pasqua
Côté
The Key
Keeseekoose
Fishing Lake
SASKATOON
Mosquito
Grizzly Bear's Head /
Young Chipewyan
NORTH BATTLEFORD
Chakastaypasin
Mistawasis
Moosomin
Thunderchild
PRINCE ALBERT

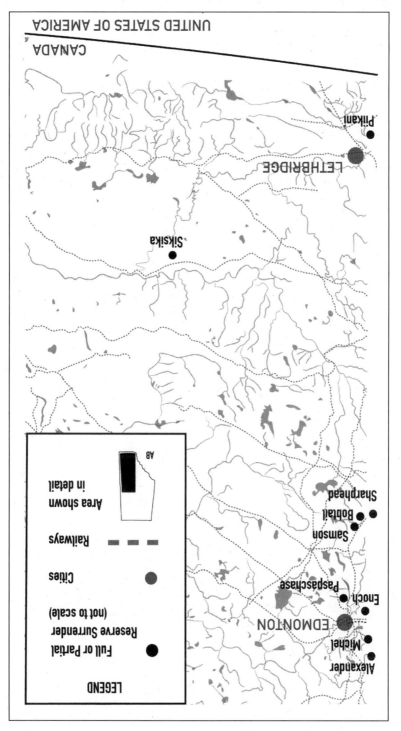

Alberta

UNITED STATES OF AMERICA

CANADA

Piikani

LETHBRIDGE

Siksika

LEGEND

Full or Partial
Reserve Surrender
(not to scale)

Cities

Railways

Area shown
in detail

AB

Sharphead

Bobtail

Samson

Paspaschase

Enoch

EDMONTON

Michel

Alexander

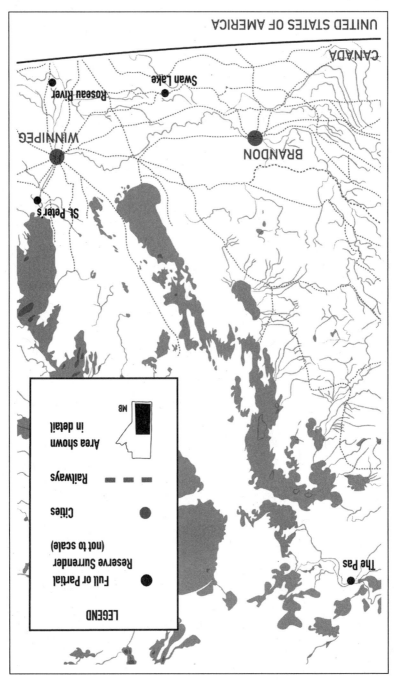

UNITED STATES OF AMERICA

CANADA

Swan Lake

Roseau River

WINNIPEG

BRANDON

St. Peter's

The Pas

LEGEND

● Full or Partial
Reserve Surrender
(not to scale)

● Cities

- - - Railways

Area shown
in detail

MB

First Nation Reserve	Year	Acreage Surrendered
Young Chippewyan	1897	23,040 acres (entire reserve)
Chacastaypasin	1897	13,360 acres (entire reserve)
Sharphead	1897	27,136 acres (entire reserve)
Pheasant Rump Ocean Man	1901	46,720 acres (entire reserves)
Enoch	1902	9,113 acres
Cumberland	1902	23,040 acres
Roseau River	1903	7,680 acres
Michel	1903	7,800 acres
Cote	1904	272 acres for townsite (Kamsack) 30 acres for railroad station
Carry the Kettle	1905	5,760 acres
Grizzly Bear's Head/ Lean Man	1905	14,400 acres
Cote	1905	18,043 acres (given 6,000 acres of hay lands in exchange)
Alexander	1905	9,518 acres
Pasqua	1906	16,077 acres
Michel	1906	2,400 acres
The Pas	1906	500 acres for townsite
Cowessess	1907	20,704 acres
Kahkewistahaw	1907	33,287 acres
Cote	1907	10,740 acres
Fishing Lake	1907	13,170 acres
St. Peter's (Peguis)	1907	48,000 acres (entire reserve)
Swan Lake	1908	2,880 acres plus 2,403 acres at Tramping Lake
Enoch	1908	6,300 acres
Thunderchild	1908	15,360 acres (entire reserve)
Moosomin	1909	15,360 acres (entire reserve)
Muscowpetung	1909	17,600 acres
The Key	1909	11,500 acres
Keeseekoose	1909	7,600 acres
Bobtail	1909	10,880 acres
Piikani	1909	23,500 acres
Siksika	1910	115,000 acres
Mistawasis	1911	1,607 acres

Surrender acreage found in P. Martin-McGuire, *First Nations Land Surrenders on the Prairies, 1896–1911* (Ottawa: Indian Claims Commission, 1998) and Indian Claims Commission reports.

↦ Contents ↤

YOU ARE NOT BEING CHEATED

I n January 1911, a handful of First Nations men, representing Treaty Four bands, travelled to Ottawa to speak directly to Prime Minister Wilfrid Laurier's Liberal government. Ever since treaties had been signed across western Canada in the 1870s, First Nations leaders had tried repeatedly to meet with the mysterious person or thing called government. Now, Treaty Four delegates were sitting down in Ottawa's Langevin Block with the country's two senior Indian Affairs officials: cabinet minister Frank Oliver and his deputy Frank Pedley.

The discussions stretched over five days as speaker after speaker talked openly about how their people had little control over their lives. Oliver and Pedley tried to be as reassuring as possible, insisting that the Laurier government always acted in their best interests. That led to pointed questions about why the Indian Affairs department had encouraged, if not forced, the surrender of some of their reserve land and what had happened to the promised benefits. To cut through the tension, a sanctimonious Oliver vowed, "We want you to know that you are not being cheated."[1] He was lying through his teeth.

++--++

Jump forward more than a century — to January 2021 — when Canada handed over $17 million to three Nakoda (Assiniboine) bands near

North Battleford, Saskatchewan, in compensation for an illegal land surrender. Even though the Grizzly Bear's Head/Lean Man First Nations had agreed in 1905 to forfeit 14,400 acres of their joint reserve, members of the neighbouring Mosquito First Nation participated in the vote — but it wasn't their reserve! The Crown had breached its treaty relationship with the Nakoda, and the surrender was ruled "invalid."[2] It was more polite than saying cheated.

Then, in June 2022, Liberal prime minister Justin Trudeau signed a staggering $1.3-billion land claim settlement with the Siksika First Nation. In 1910, they had been promised food for themselves and future generations if they surrendered 40 percent (115,000 acres) of their reserve in southern Alberta. Indian Affairs never honoured the agreement with the Siksika — in other words, they too were cheated. "We are gathered today to right a wrong from the past," an apologetic Trudeau said at the signing ceremony, "to start rebuilding trust between us."[3]

These two settlements, and others before them, are generally regarded as little more than a remedial footnote in the history of Indigenous/non-Indigenous relations in Canada. In fact, historical reserve surrenders tend to make news only when Canada announces a specific claims settlement. Even then, there are questions about why First Nations bands are being financially compensated for something that happened more than a century ago, especially when there were formal surrender agreements in place. But just as the terrible legacy of Canada's residential school system is being recognized today, so too must the Wilfrid Laurier government's determined push to secure the full or partial surrender of reserves promised in the treaty agreements.

Uncovering this land theft disguised as surrender didn't happen until the early 1970s, when First Nations bands and their organizations pursued specific claims through the new federal Office of Native Claims. These Indigenous claims, backed by federally funded research, dealt largely with Canada's failure to discharge its treaty obligations over land.[4] It quickly became apparent that lost reserve land was just as big an issue as securing land under treaty agreements. In 1976, the Federation of Saskatchewan Indians (now the Federation of Sovereign

Indigenous Nations) delved into reserve surrenders in the province with the assistance of the Ottawa-based research firm Tyler, Wright, and Daniel.

This work was guided by a forgotten 1913 federal inquiry, known as the Ferguson Commission, that had been established by Prime Minister Robert Borden's Conservative government to investigate alleged Liberal trafficking in western lands and natural resources, including First Nations reserves. The Ferguson report was never published. Nor did it apparently survive. All copies were supposedly lost when a February 1916 fire destroyed the Centre Block on Parliament Hill. The inquiry's findings, though, were heatedly debated in the House of Commons in April 1915, while shocking excerpts, together with damning commentary, were published in newspapers across the country.

Taking direction from these sources, researchers combed through old Indian Affairs files and discovered that three senior civil servants — Liberal patronage appointees — had orchestrated the surrender of the Ocean Man and Pheasant Rump reserves in 1901 and then rigged the tender process to secure most of the Nakoda land. In announcing its findings in March 1979, the Federation of Saskatchewan Indians described in detail how "the unholy trinity" conspired to commit "wholesale fraud" and suggested there were likely other "shadowy and unsavory" cases from that period.[5] Since then, there have been a number of specific claims investigations into questionable, if not unlawful, reserve surrenders.[6]

The Wilfrid Laurier government (1896–1911) is widely heralded for settling "the last best West." It encouraged tens of thousands of immigrant farmers to come to western Canada in the early 1900s and break the virgin prairie for grain production. That's only part of the Laurier legacy in western Canada, though. There were vast sums of money to be made from the great immigration and settlement boom — not only in land, but in exploiting resources and building infrastructure, such as rail lines, to meet settler needs. Nothing, not even First Nations reserve land, was immune from speculation and investment. Unlike the late

1870s and early 1880s, when the Canadian government wanted prairie First Nations settled on their reserves, the Laurier Liberals took hold of the Indian Affairs department and turned it into a machine for expropriating reserves, in whole or in part.

The Department of Indian Affairs justified this policy shift on the grounds that First Nations held "vacant lands out of proportion to their requirements." Because of the decline in band populations since the signing of the western treaties in the 1870s, many reserves were said to contain excess or surplus land. It didn't matter that the allotment of reserve land was a treaty right, based on the formula of one square mile (640 acres) for every family of five at the time of survey. The size of reserves, it was argued, had to be adjusted to match the reality on the ground around the turn of the century. This correction, moreover, was needed so that the potential of idle reserve lands was not wasted. Otherwise, continued First Nations occupation would "seriously imped[e] the growth of settlement."

The sale of surrendered lands, in turn, was presented by Indian Affairs as "in the best interest of all concerned." The proceeds would be used to benefit First Nations bands, while at the same time, "relieve . . . the country of the burden of their maintenance."[7] The use of the word "burden" betrayed just how the Laurier Liberals were determined to limit Canada's responsibilities to prairie First Nations by reducing the size and number of reserves, in violation of the treaties. It also perfectly fit with the Department of the Interior's role as a clearing house: ensure that as much land as possible was available for as many settlers as possible.

The sad irony was that there was no need to open up reserves to white settlement in the early twentieth century. Land could easily be secured elsewhere in the prairie west. Nor did First Nations have that much land to surrender. By 1913, 2,722,791 acres had been set aside for reserves. That was one-half of one percent of the total acreage of the three prairie provinces.[8] But there was opportunity for Liberal friends and associates, even patronage appointees, to make a small fortune in First Nations lands.

Reserve surrenders were largely initiated by elected parliamentarians and Indian Affairs officials, never by the bands themselves. Indeed, the loudest cheerleader was Frank Oliver, who believed, as if it were sacred gospel, that prairie reserves were "more valuable for the purposes of white men . . . they should be thrown open for settlement as soon as possible."⁹ Some of the individuals involved in this Liberal network went to great lengths to buy and hold surrendered reserve lands, even while payments to the bands were re-routed, delayed, or defaulted. They saw nothing wrong or dishonest with what they were doing, never worried how a surrender might affect the band's well-being. They were more interested in their own fortune — and that included Oliver. Choosing corruption over duty, he surreptitiously secured part of a reserve outside Edmonton. When the matter was raised during the 1915 House of Commons debate on the Ferguson report, Oliver didn't deny the secret land deal.

This rampant speculation in prairie reserves would never have happened without a co-operative and compliant Indian Affairs bureaucracy. First Nations could not simply be forced to give up any or all of their reserves. There were provisions in the federal Indian Act that clearly set out the rules and requirements for reserve surrenders. Other clauses specified how sale proceeds could be used and who could purchase surrendered land. These were legal imperatives, mandated by the Parliament of Canada. Yet over the course of the Laurier government, the legislation was significantly revised, narrowly interpreted, or plainly ignored. Department officials, for their part, actively pursued surrenders to the detriment of the bands, and in some cases, abused their position for personal gain. Their collective efforts resulted in the surrender of over half a million acres — 21 percent of reserve land. Put another way, one of every five acres set aside under treaty in western Canada was given up.¹⁰

Some sense of the number of surrenders during the Laurier years can be gleaned from Indian Claims Commission (ICC) reports that serve as the basis for First Nations surrender settlements with the Canadian government. There's also a major study, prepared at the request of the ICC, on the historical background of prairie reserve surrenders for the period 1896–1911.[11] But even though the report's surrender inventory, with accompanying documentation, is astonishing in its length, it's only a first step. What's needed is a comprehensive overview of why and how the Laurier government took reserve surrenders, what happened to the surrendered land, and who benefited.

Cheated tells the surrender story from the perspective of the Indian Affairs department. That's not to downplay or ignore First Nations agency. Prairie bands and their leaders determinedly resisted surrenders in the face of government connivance and coercion. It would be presumptuous, though, to speak for First Nations bands. Their oral history of the surrender experience can best be provided by the bands' Elders themselves, following protocol.

What follows, then, is a damning exposé of Liberal Indian Affairs ministers and their department staff, based largely on the meticulous and voluminous record-keeping of the Indian Affairs department. The irony is that these individuals, entrusted with the public good, incriminate themselves because of the paper trail. Their actions, moreover, are part of a larger, explosive narrative of single-minded politicians, uncompromising Indian Affairs officials, grasping government appointees, and well-connected Liberal speculators, set against a backdrop of politics, power, patronage, and profit. Indeed, the book provides a long-overdue appreciation of what prairie First Nations were up against because of the Laurier government's single-minded and almost relentless pursuit of surrenders. They had not failed to make reserves their home; the government failed them by taking away their land.

That was the message delivered in the House of Commons during the 1915 debate on the Ferguson report: the Laurier government had not honoured its treaty obligations and Indian Act commitments when it dispossessed prairie First Nations of their reserves. As Conservative backbencher and future prime minister R.B. Bennett argued at the time, it was "the poor Indians" who "must suffer," that they were "the victims" in this sorry episode. "If anything has ever in the annals of Parliament been placed upon the table of this House calculated to bring the blush of shame to the face of any Canadian," he sternly observed, "it is the revelation contained in the evidence that is here tonight."[12] William James Roche, Frank Oliver's successor as Indian Affairs minister, was equally censorious. With a theatrical flourish, he denounced "these nefarious transactions of such a villainous character."[13] Both men could have been more direct about the treatment of First Nations. They had been cheated.

Notes

1. *Library and Archives Canada (LAC)*, RG10, v. 4053, f. 379,203-1, "Notes of representation made by delegation of Indians from the West," January 1911.
2. "First Nation receives $127M to settle decades-long land claim," January 19, 2021, https://www.cbc.ca/news/canada/saskatchewan/land -claim-mosquito-grizzly-bear-s-head-lean-man-1.5879416.
3. "PM signs historic land claim settlement with Siksika First Nation," June 2, 2022, https://www.cbc.ca/news/canada/calgary/siksika-trudeau -signing-ceremony-1.6475167.
4. For background in the specific claims process see J.R. Miller, *Skyscrapers Hide the Heavens: A History of Native-Newcomer Relations in Canada* (Toronto: University of Toronto Press, 2018), pp. 279–80.
5. Regina *Leader-Post*, March 31, 1979.
6. Reserve surrender disputes are handled through the specific claims process and do not fall under Treaty Land Entitlement agreements. For information on specific claims settlements see https://geo.aandc .gc.ca/cirrp-scsim/index-eng.html.
7. Quoted in S. Carter, *Lost Harvests: Prairie Indian Reserve Farmers and Government Policy* (Montreal: McGill-Queen's University Press, 1990), p. 244.
8. P. Martin-McGuire, *First Nations Land Surrenders on the Prairies, 1896–1911* (Ottawa: Indian Claims Commission, 1998), pp. 27–8.

9. *LAC*, RG10, v. 3912, f. 111777-1, F. Oliver to C. Sifton, July 18, 1897.

10. Martin-McGuire, *First Nations Land Surrenders*, p. xiii.

11. Ibid.

12. House of Commons, *Debates*, April 14, 1915, p. 2593.

13. Ibid., p. 2567.

-← One →-

NO ONE WILL INTERFERE WITH YOU

Fort Carlton, August 1876. The treaty commissioner was stunned by an angry outburst. Treaty negotiations between the Plains Cree and the Crown's representative, Alexander Morris, had just resumed for another day. Assuming a reverential tone, Morris opened the morning meeting by explaining that the Queen, concerned about their future, wanted "to give each band that desires it a home of their own."[1]

This suggestion that reserves would be granted to the Cree people sparked a stinging rebuke from their headman, named Poundmaker. "This is our land," he vehemently interjected. "It isn't a piece of pemmican to be cut off and given in little pieces back to us. It is ours and we will take what we want."[2] Poundmaker's followers rose to their feet and roared their approval. It was some time before order was restored at the gathering. The young headman had made his point. Morris was deliberately emphasizing what the Cree would receive through the treaty when in fact they were giving up, in Poundmaker's words, "our land."

Once Morris recovered his composure, he advised the Cree that thousands of prospective homesteaders would soon invade the country and that the reserves would be held in trust by the Queen. "It is your own," Morris counselled, "and no one will interfere with you . . . as long as the Indians wish it . . . no one can take their homes."[3] It was one of many solemn promises that Morris made to reach the Treaty

Six agreement — promises that were backstopped by the honour of the Crown.

-<-<--〉->-

Federal responsibility for "Indians, and Lands reserved for the Indians" had been something of an afterthought at the time of Confederation. Colonial delegates never formally debated or discussed the question at the 1864 Charlottetown and Quebec conferences. It was simply suggested towards the end of the deliberations that jurisdiction over First Nations be listed as one of the powers of the general government (1867 BNA Act, section 91 [24]).

Responsibility for Indigenous peoples had traditionally been the domain of the British Crown, and it was in keeping with this practice that Canada's Parliament assumed this duty. It was also necessary because expansion into the western territory was a planned feature of

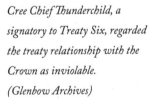

Cree Chief Thunderchild, a signatory to Treaty Six, regarded the treaty relationship with the Crown as inviolable. (Glenbow Archives)

Confederation (section 146). The new dominion government would have to negotiate treaty agreements with the First Nations of the region to secure access to their lands.[4] The alternative — fighting First Nations — was too costly. The United States spent more money on "Indian Wars" in 1870 than the entire Canadian budget for that year.[5]

In the latter half of the nineteenth century, First Nations affairs were largely secondary or peripheral to the day-to-day business of the Canadian government. It was not until May 1868, ten months after the first Canadian cabinet was sworn into office, that the Secretary of State for the provinces assumed responsibility for Indian Affairs. Then, in July 1873, when the Department of the Interior was created to administer the hundreds of millions of acres of western and northern lands that Canada had acquired from the Hudson's Bay Company, the new Interior minister also assumed the duties of superintendent general of Indian Affairs (more popularly known as the minister of Indian Affairs). The mandated pairing of two distinct areas of responsibility under one minister was unusual in Canadian federal governance, especially when cabinets of the day were relatively small. The arrangement remained in place — even after Indian Affairs was elevated in 1880 from a branch to a separate department — until 1935.

This one-minister, two-hats organization made some sense in the 1870s when the First Nations of western Canada were entering treaty agreements with the Crown and land had to be surveyed into homesteads in anticipation of the flood of white settlement. Interior matters, though, always enjoyed priority.

No sooner had Canada acquired its vast western empire than it put survey crews in the field measuring the land into townships and sections. By 1875, the dominion lands survey had subdivided 10.5 million acres. Thereafter, the pace quickened, and in just fifteen years, a whopping seventy million acres were carved into quarter-sections. Government surveys for the proposed transcontinental railway were equally impressive. From 1871 to 1877, field crews logged 46,000 miles, one-quarter of which had been painstakingly measured yard by yard. Then came the construction of the dominion telegraph and the Geological Survey of Canada's systematic mapping of the prairie west for natural resources.[6]

All of these activities were intended to facilitate the peaceful, orderly occupation of the land. Yet despite glowing reports about the soil fertility and the ready availability of homesteads, the expected flood of settlers was only a trickle in the 1870s. "When the treaty was made," First Nations farming instructor Robert Jefferson later recalled, "the Indians were told that the country would soon be full of white men, and, though several years had elapsed, the threatened influx had not materialized."[7]

Indian Affairs, by contrast, operated by a different timetable. In 1871, Canada began to negotiate the first of seven western treaty agreements — known as the numbered treaties — in present-day northwestern Ontario. These agreements, Treaties One to Seven, would eventually stretch across Manitoba and Saskatchewan to the Alberta foothills. Ottawa, though, had no immediate plans to deal with First Nations living west of present-day Manitoba, even though the Cree of the North Saskatchewan country had asked to meet with a Canadian representative at the beginning of the decade.[8]

"Our country is no longer able to support us," declared Sweetgrass, the leading Chief in the Fort Pitt district. "We invite you to come and see us and speak to us."[9] When no one came, the Cree took matters into their own hands: they stopped a telegraph construction crew and turned back a Geological Survey of Canada party in their traditional territory. Canada consequently had no choice. It sent Indian commissioner Alexander Morris to meet with the Cree of present-day central Saskatchewan and Alberta in the late summer of 1876. There was much at stake. The proposed treaty area covered some 120,000 square miles, lands crucial to Canada's westward expansion.

At the Treaty Six negotiations at Fort Carlton, commissioner Morris vowed that the Queen would not interfere with the Cree's traditional pursuits. He also offered agricultural tools and implements, seeds, and livestock, supplemented with farming instruction. And he promised famine assistance during times of severe hunger. These and

Cree Chief Pasqua made this pictograph of the Treaty Four meeting at Fort Qu'Appelle, North-West Territories, in 1874. (Royal Saskatchewan Museum)

other treaty terms, Morris assured the Cree, would be carried out with a "watchful eye and sympathetic hand."[10]

The Cree, in turn, regarded the treaty as the beginning of a long-term reciprocal relationship with the Crown, rooted in the concept of family and kin. They realized that they had to take up agriculture because of the rapid decline of the bison. And with Canada's help, they expected to successfully make the transition to farming and thereby ensure their future security and well-being. The treaty meant remaining an independent people, able to compete with newcomers to the region.

Under treaty, bands would take up reserves in places of their own choosing. Reserve acreage was to be determined by the band population at the time of survey. They were to remain that size even if band numbers went up or down. In other words, the reserve area was fixed in time — not to be adjusted or taken away, not even part of it.[11]

At Fort Carlton, Morris urged the Cree to select their reserves as soon as possible. "Now unless the places where you would like to live are secured soon," he counselled the Cree, "there might be difficulty. The white man might come and settle on the very place where you would like to be."[12] Reserved lands or iskomkan (Cree for "that which is kept back") also figured prominently in the next round of Treaty Six discussions at Fort Pitt. According to witness John McDougall, a Methodist missionary, Morris insisted that reserves would be "maintained for the Indians inviolate so long as the grass grows and the sun shines."[13]

This treaty commitment was contradicted by the Indian Act, ironically passed five months earlier in April 1876. Prime Minister Alexander Mackenzie's Liberal government called the legislation a housekeeping matter — bringing together and updating in a single piece of legislation all the existing laws and regulations regarding First Nations peoples and their land. The act, though, effectively defined First Nations as dependents and gave Indian Affairs the authority to regulate their lives through various means, including further legislation.[14]

Surprisingly, the act also contained provisions for the surrender of reserves, even though western treaty agreements had not yet been completed and lands were still being set aside for treaty bands. Canada seemed to be already preparing for the day when First Nations either assimilated or simply disappeared and no longer required separate reserves.

The apparent urgency to get treaty bands to select and take up reserve land never translated into action by Indian Affairs. During the 1870s, Canada seemed interested only in getting western First Nations to take treaty, even if it meant creating new bands and recognizing new chiefs. Beyond that, the federal government practised, as one Interior official put it, "the strictest possible economy."[15] There was only one Indian agent for the entire Treaty Six area in 1878. Incoming Indian commissioner Edgar Dewdney questioned how one person could deal with all Treaty Six bands, and in 1879, increased the number of agents to three. It was still unrealistically low, given the size of the treaty area, the number of bands under treaty, and the agents' responsibilities.[16]

The Canadian government also failed to devote adequate resources to surveying reserves to fulfill its treaty obligations. Commissioner Morris had promised during Treaty Six negotiations that Canada "would send next year [1877] a surveyor to agree with you as to the place you would like."[17] As of 1880, though, the Department of Indian Affairs had only two field surveyors — one who worked in Treaty Six territory, the other in Treaty Four and Treaty Seven territories combined. Many treaty bands did not have their reserves surveyed until the early to mid-1880s. By then, because band populations had declined since taking treaty, surveyors marked out smaller reserves.

The delay in getting treaty bands settled and actively farming left many prairie First Nations vulnerable when the bison disappeared from the northern plains in 1879. Indian commissioner Dewdney claimed in his first annual report that the "disappearance of the buffalo had taken the Government as much by surprise as the Indians."[18] It was quite an understatement. Dewdney toured the North-West during the summer of 1879, and according to his diary account, he was forever encountering First Nations anxious about how they were going to survive the coming winter.

The Cree and other Indigenous groups responded to the looming famine by travelling south across the international border in a desperate search for any remaining bison. Hunger took its toll. While on patrol in the Cypress Hills area, North-West Mounted Police sergeant Frank Fitzpatrick encountered a band of starving First Nations that he described as "a delegation from a graveyard."[19]

The Canadian government grudgingly fed First Nations over the winter of 1879–80, but did not want to make it an ongoing commitment. By the end of the 1870s, Ottawa was already regretting the financial commitment it had assumed in the western treaties. Eleven percent of all territorial expenditures went to meet treaty obligations, an amount that alarmed federal parliamentarians.[20]

NWT Indian commissioner Edgar Dewdney withheld rations from First Nations bands who remained outside treaty or had not settled on reserves. He called his policy "sheer compulsion." (McCord Museum)

Indian commissioner Dewdney's solution was to settle bands on their reserves once and for all so that they could become "self sup-porting," something he believed could be achieved "in a few years."[21] His plan had the backing of Prime Minister John A. Macdonald, who also served as superintendent general of Indian Affairs. The Conservative leader believed that it was "necessary" for the prime minister to have Indian matters "in his own hands" and consequently assumed the portfolio upon returning to power in 1878. He held it for nine years — the longest-serving superintendent general of Indian Affairs in Canadian history.[22]

Macdonald regarded First Nations as culturally inferior, though capable of being uplifted to embrace Euro-Canadian ways. If the Cree, Blackfoot, Saulteaux, and other First Nations people were to take their place in the new emerging West, they had to be educated, Christianized, and enfranchised. This transformation was possible, though, only if they gave up their nomadic ways and became self-reliant farmers.

That's why the Macdonald government decided to encourage on-reserve agriculture — what was known as the "home farm" system — so that First Nations could feed themselves. Agricultural assistance, though, did not come soon enough. Bands who tried working the land after taking treaty not only experienced lengthy delays in getting their reserves surveyed, but also found that equipment and supplies were defective or insufficient and arrived too late in the season to begin cultivation. When their first tentative crops failed, they were confronted with the harsh reality that large-scale farming in the northern prairies was anything but certain.

It would take years of experimentation and failure, by First Nations and newcomers alike, before the northern prairies could produce the bountiful harvests prophesied by Canadian expansionists. But unlike white settlers, who could abandon marginal homestead quarter-sections and try again someplace else or simply give up, bands had to stay and work their reserves regardless of the quality of the land.

The 1879 home farm program was supposed to transform First Nations into agriculturalists by teaching bands how to raise grain, vegetables, and livestock. Resident farm instructors, though, had little understanding, sympathy, or patience for bands under their guidance. They quickly learned that, until reserve lands could be successfully cultivated, their most important duty was to distribute food from on-reserve supply depots.

These relief provisions were not given freely. Some form of labour, no matter how demeaning or degrading, had to be performed before hungry First Nations were fed. This "work for rations" policy clearly violated the spirit and intent of the treaties. Government authorities countered that easy access to food would only encourage First Nations idleness.[23]

The Liberal Opposition in the House of Commons constantly rebuked the Macdonald government for spending too much on Indian Affairs administration, especially given the sluggish Canadian economy. During the budget debate in April 1882, former Liberal cabinet minister David Mills complained of "the largeness of the sum for annuities" and called for "some stringent check" on Indian Affairs expenditures. "It is pretty evident," Mills wryly added, "that the Indians have become pensioners upon the Public Treasury."[24]

These comments were part of parliamentary theatre — a way for the Opposition to enliven the otherwise dull chamber proceedings and score some political points. But they also resonated with the Canadian public, given the lowly place of First Nations in the national consciousness. Prime Minister Macdonald, stung by the criticism, gamely defended the costs, even admitting that his officials "are doing all they can, by refusing food until the First Nations are on the verge of starvation, to reduce expenses."[25]

Indian Affairs expenses continued to rise in the early 1880s as starving First Nations took up their reserves. Whereas there had been almost 8,500 treaty First Nations not on reserve in 1882, the number dropped to 1,307 the following year.[26] And the growing reserve population had to

Conservative prime minister Sir John A. Macdonald was constantly rebuked by the Liberal Opposition in the House of Commons for spending too much on Indian Affairs administration.
(Library and Archives Canada)

be fed until bands could support themselves. In his report for the fiscal year ending June 1883, Canada's auditor general found that $480,164 was being spent on provisions for destitute First Nations in Manitoba and the North-West Territories.[27] It was a staggering sum, one that likely surprised both sides of the House of Commons.

When the home farm program was initiated, Macdonald had naively predicted that, in making the transition to reserve agriculture, First Nations "will probably require some small supply of provisions each year."[28] The half-million-dollar figure provided more fodder for Opposition attacks. Liberal MP Philippe Casgrain charged that helping feed First Nations went against natural law. "They are a doomed race," he bluntly told the House, "and it is only a question of how soon they will disappear."[29] What Liberal MPs conveniently forgot, though, was that their party was in power (November 1873 to October 1878) when four of the seven western treaties were concluded — with their attendant obligations.

In the meantime, the mood on prairie reserves was one of disillusionment and betrayal. Hunger was always present because rations rarely met daily caloric needs and were generally unfit for human consumption, especially the salted pork that was shipped by barrel to reserve storehouses.

In January 1883, Edmonton-area Chiefs made a direct appeal to Prime Minister Macdonald about their dire situation. "We are reduced to the lowest stage of poverty," read their letter. "We were once a proud and independent people and now we [don't have] the means necessary to make a living for ourselves. . . . The government . . . can break every article of the treaty . . . and we have no redress."[30]

The other constant was sickness. By isolating bands on reserves, government officials sought to exercise greater control over their lives. But the weakened state of band populations, when combined with their wretched, crowded living conditions, made them extremely vulnerable to disease, especially tuberculosis. Mortality rates climbed as a deadly mix of malnutrition and infection carried away the aged, the healthy, even the very young. It was a far cry from the 1860s, when the protein-rich bison diet made the First Nations people of the plains some of the tallest humans in the world.[31]

Treaty bands might have been expected to lash out against government agents. Instead, Cree leaders sought to bring about change by peaceful means — by coming together, with other First Nations people if necessary, and lobbying the government for better support and assistance as promised in the treaties.

To that end, Chief Beardy called a council meeting at Duck Lake, Saskatchewan, in July 1884 to discuss a range of grievances — from the lack of schools and health care to poor farming equipment, clothing, and rations. Speaking with the force of years of bitterness and frustration, the chiefs affirmed their allegiance to the Queen and the treaty, contending it was Ottawa, not the Crown, which had created the current climate of ill will. "[I]t is almost too hard for them," reported sub-agent J.A. Macrae, "to bear the treatment received at the hands of the Government after its 'sweet promises' made in order to get the country from them."[32]

That senior Indian officials chose to downplay the growing sea of resentment and alienation was confirmed in a subsequent investigation by Hayter Reed, commissioner Dewdney's assistant. He dismissed the Duck Lake complainants as "ill-disposed and lazy . . . looking for extra aid."[33] Prime Minister Macdonald was anxious for any positive news and demanded that Dewdney deliver "a full *and favourable*" report on Indian settlement and agriculture — and the "prospect of *diminishing* expenditures."[34]

At the Duck Lake gathering, the Cree chiefs had expressed relief that their young men had managed to keep their anger in check. But when the Métis-provoked North-West Rebellion erupted in March 1885, violence flared at Fort Battleford and Fort Pitt along the North Saskatchewan River when several warriors decided to take advantage of the unrest to settle personal grudges.

First Nations involvement in the troubles was isolated, sporadic, and limited, certainly not part of a grand alliance with the Métis. Indian Affairs officials, however, deliberately used the rebellion to stamp out any

Deputy Superintendent General of Indian Affairs Hayter Reed reduced First Nations spending as much as possible in order to force treaty bands to become more self-supporting. (Library and Archives Canada)

remaining sense of independence, in particular the First Nations' diplomatic initiative to force the Canadian government to honour its treaty promises. Several leading Chiefs, such as Big Bear and Poundmaker, were imprisoned. More than twenty reserves were branded disloyal. Eight warriors were executed at Fort Battleford on November 27, 1885, in a public mass hanging that remains the largest in Canadian history.

The message was brutally clear: First Nations were to conform to government directives or feel an iron hand.[35]

After 1885, the Macdonald government introduced a number of coercive and interfering policies to bring prairie First Nations under Indian Affairs control and keep them separate from the white settler population. Perhaps the most controversial was the pass system, a way to regulate and restrict First Nations movement by requiring individuals to obtain approval from the local agent in writing before leaving their reserve. Then there was the permit system, which prohibited the off-reserve sale of First Nations farm produce unless first approved by the local Indian agent; settlers, meanwhile, could be fined for buying from First Nations farmers without a permit.

In 1895, Ottawa also banned religious dances and ceremonies that were at the heart of First Nations culture. Government officials maintained that First Nations would always remain unprogressive and corrupted as long as they adhered to traditional practices and beliefs. That included communal gatherings.

Prairie bands tried to resist or get around the new regulations in whatever way they could, albeit non-violently. This pushback — an attempt to loosen the government's grip on their lives — was interpreted by Prime Minister Macdonald as confirmation of First Nations' unwillingness to abandon their "lazy, indolent" ways and embrace a settled way of life. The reason for their sorry state, he argued, was not Indian Affairs policies, but rather their refusal to emulate white settlers. "Those are the real facts [about Indians]," he candidly told the House of Commons in May 1887, just months before he stepped down as superintendent general of Indian Affairs.[36] It was a telling commentary on how things had gone so terribly wrong only a decade after the last major western treaty was concluded.

The early 1890s brought no change in Indian Affairs policy or practice, just a greater emphasis on reducing department spending. That meant, for example, denying First Nations access to any new, steam-powered agricultural machinery. Instead, bands were made to do all the work by hand — seed their reserve fields, tend the crops, and bring in the harvest. This "peasant farming" policy had a stagnating impact on reserve agriculture. No matter how hard they laboured, bands found that their small subsistence plots were no match for white settler commercial agriculture, and they gave up in discouragement. Crop acreage and harvests — something carefully documented by voluminous, statistics-packed Indian Affairs annual reports — consequently declined in the early 1890s and led to the unfortunate conclusion that First Nations were not really committed to farming.[37]

Some bands, in fact, were worse off than at any other time under treaty. Because they had no stable reserve economy and could no longer count on government rations, First Nations people had to find other ways to survive. They had to go off-reserve in defiance of the government's restriction on such movement to hunt, trap, and gather, sometimes only a few rabbits or gophers.

Sickness also left a grim toll in band population ledgers. For the ten-year period from 1884 to 1894, the Crooked Lakes and File Hills reserves lost 41 and 46 percent of their population, respectively. Incredibly, the situation on the Battleford reserves was worse. Here, First Nations populations declined by more than half during the same period: deaths exceeded births by a two-to-one ratio.[38] White settler society concluded that prairie First Nations were a backward, impoverished, disease-ridden people, best isolated on their reserves.

That's where things stood when the Wilfrid Laurier Liberals assumed power in July 1896 and inherited the vexatious Indian Affairs portfolio. "The situation was in some ways chaotic," one western historian observed. "The government's policies were too frequently inconsistent, ill considered, and harshly administered."[39] To put it less elegantly, Indian Affairs policies were a train wreck. The overriding question

Liberal prime minister Sir Wilfrid Laurier assumed office at a time of unprecedented Canadian prosperity. (Library and Archives Canada)

was whether the new Laurier government would use the same track or head in a different direction.

Up to then, the Liberal Opposition had offered no alternative, apart from the repeated chorus that too much money was being spent for too few results. Just a year before the 1896 general election, the Liberals had introduced a motion — defeated on division — that First Nations matters had not been advanced by Conservative government "extravagance,"[40] and those expenses should be cut. Despite Canada's treaty obligations, they insisted that spending on First Nations was an ongoing expense that Canadians could ill afford.[41]

Clifford Sifton, the new Liberal minister of Interior and Indian Affairs, seemed ready — and willing — to take the axe to Indian Affairs. During a western speaking tour in early December 1896, before he officially took up his government duties, Sifton mused, "The Indians were the wards of the government," and when he settled down to work he would see that "we either had more Indians to look after or less officials, for at present there were nearly as many officials as Indians."[42]

On paper, the situation appeared to be most wasteful in the prairie west: nearly three-quarters of the Indian Affairs budget was spent there, even though the region's First Nations population represented only 25 percent of the Canadian total.[43] Sifton also publicly complained that the department headquarters in Ottawa, built by consecutive Conservative governments, was rife with pettiness and infighting.

These comments seemed to signal that the new minister was finally going to do what his Liberal predecessors had been demanding for almost two decades — reduce Indian Affairs spending by capping assistance, slashing staff, and streamlining the administrative apparatus. Sifton couldn't arrive in Ottawa soon enough.

Notes

1. A. Morris, *The Treaties of Canada with the Indians of Manitoba and the North-West Territories* (Toronto: Belfords, Clarke and Co., 1880), p. 204.
2. P. Erasmus, *Buffalo Days and Nights* (Calgary: Glenbow Museum, 1974), p. 244.
3. Morris, *The Treaties of Canada*, p. 205.
4. M. Martel et al., "Quebec and Confederation: Gains and Compromise" in D. Heidt, ed., *Reconsidering Confederation: Canada's Founding Debates, 1864–1999* (Calgary: University of Calgary Press, 2018), pp. 81–2.
5. R.C. Macleod, *The North-West Mounted Police and Law Enforcement* (Toronto: University of Toronto Press, 1976), p. 3.
6. B. Waiser, "The Government Explorer in Canada," in J.L. Allen, ed., *North American Exploration: A Continent Comprehended* (Lincoln: University of Nebraska Press, 1997), pp. 429, 443, 451.
7. R. Jefferson, "Fifty Years on the Saskatchewan," *Canadian North-West Historical Society Publications*, v. 1, n. 5, 1929, p. 51.
8. J.L. Tobias, "Canada's Subjugation of the Plains Cree, 1879–1885," *Canadian Historical Review*, v. LXIV, n. 4, 1983, pp. 520–1.
9. Quoted in J.R. Miller, *Compact, Contract, Covenant: Aboriginal Treaty-Making in Canada* (Toronto: University of Toronto Press, 2009), p. 154. Miller provides an excellent explanation of the First Nations' desire for treaty.
10. Morris, *The Treaties of Canada*, p. 212.
11. In September 1992, a Treaty Land Entitlement agreement was reached between the federal and provincial governments and the Federation of Saskatchewan Indian Nations. The deal provided Saskatchewan bands with funds to buy land that had been promised in the treaties but never awarded as reserve acreage.
12. Morris, *The Treaties of Canada*, pp. 204–5.
13. Quoted in S. Krasowski, *No Surrender: The Land Remains Indigenous* (Regina: University of Regina Press, 2019), p. 232.
14. During the debate on the Indian Act, David Laird, Superintendent General of Indian Affairs, told the House members "the Indians

must either be treated as minors or white men." House of Commons, *Debates*, March 30, 1876, p. 933.

15. Quoted in J.B.D. Larmour, "Edgar Dewdney, Commissioner of Indian Affairs and Lieutenant Governor of the North-West Territories, 1879–1888," unpublished M.A. thesis, University of Saskatchewan, 1969, p. 15.

16. D.J. Hall, *From Treaties to Reserves: The Federal Government and Native Peoples in Territorial Alberta, 1870–1905* (Montreal and Kingston: McGill-Queen's University Press, 2015), pp. 108–11.

17. Morris, *The Treaties of Canada*, pp. 204–5.

18. Canada. *Sessional Papers*, n. 4, 1880, "Annual Report of the Department of Interior for 1879," p. 79.

19. Quoted in J.F. Dunn, *The North-West Mounted Police, 1873–1885* (Calgary: Jack F. Dunn, 2017), p. 563.

20. A.J. Ray, *The Canadian Fur Trade in the Industrial Age* (Toronto: University of Toronto Press, 1990), pp. 34–40.

21. *Library and Archives Canada* (*LAC*), John A. Macdonald papers, v. 210, E. Dewdney to J.A. Macdonald, October 2, 1880, pp. 89361–9.

22. Quoted in J.R. Miller, "Macdonald as Minister of Indian Affairs: The Shaping of Canadian Indian Policy" in P. Dutil and R. Hall, eds., *Macdonald at 200: New Reflections and Legacies* (Toronto: Dundurn Press, 2014), p. 323. Macdonald also performed the duties of Interior minister, but gave them up in 1883. There was a separate Interior minister (from 1883 to 1887) until Macdonald ceased to handle Indian Affairs in 1887.

23. S. Carter, *Lost Harvests: Prairie Indian Reserve Farmers and Government Policy* (Montreal: McGill-Queen's University Press, 1990), pp. 79–95.

24. *Debates*, April 26, 1882, pp. 1184, 1186.

25. Ibid., p. 1186.

26. Larmour, "Edgar Dewdney," p. 74.

27. *Sessional Papers*, n. 6, 1884, "Auditor General's Report for the Year ended 30 June 1883," pp. 331–36.

28. *Sessional Papers*, n. 7, 1879, "Annual Report of the Department of the Interior for 1878," p. xi.

29. *Debates*, May 9, 1883, p. 1105.

30. The letter was reproduced in the *Edmonton Bulletin*, February 3, 1883.

31. See R.H. Steckel and J.M. Prince, "Tallest in the World: Native Americans of the Great Plains in the Nineteenth Century," *The American Economic Review*, v. 91, n. 1, March 2001, pp. 287–94. Among them was Ahtahkakoop, a future leader who stood six foot three inches with a muscular frame — he was sometimes called misi-minahik (tall pine). D. Christensen, *Ahtahkakoop* (Shell Lake: Ahtahkakoop Publishing, 2000), p. 62.

32. *LAC*, RG10, v. 3697, f. 15423, J.A. Macrae to E. Dewdney, August 25, 1884.

33. Ibid., H. Reed to J.A. Macdonald, January 23, 1885.

34. Larmour, "Edgar Dewdney," p. 82. Emphasis added.

35. B. Stonechild and B. Waiser, *Loyal till Death: Indians and the North-West Rebellion* (Calgary: Fifth House Publishers, 1997).

36. *Debates*, June 17, 1887, p. 1103.

37. Carter, *Lost Harvests*, pp. 193–236.

38. Grizzly Bear's Head, a Nakoda reserve, had the distinction of having the highest annual mortality rate during the rebellion era: an astounding 305 per 1,000. The next highest was Thunderchild at 233. Quebec City, by comparison, had a death rate of 31 per 1,000 in 1890, the highest among Canadian cities. M.K. Lux, *Medicine That Walks: Disease, Medicine, and Canadian Plains Native People, 1880–1940* (Toronto: University of Toronto Press, 2001), pp. 45, 51, 58.

39. Hall, *From Treaties to Reserves*, p. 195.

40. *Debates*, June 25, 1895, p. 3283.

41. See N.E. Dyck, "The Administration of Federal Indian Aid in the North-West Territories, 1879–1885," unpublished M.A. thesis, University of Saskatchewan, 1979.

42. Quoted in D.J. Hall, "Clifford Sifton and Canadian Indian Administration, 1896–1905," *Prairie Forum*, v. 2, n. 2, 1977, p. 127.

43. Ibid., pp. 130–1.

⊰ *Two* ⊱

POLITICAL BOSS

I n April 1902, Clifford Sifton, one of Canada's most powerful government ministers, crowed about "what is going on in the West
where we have turned dismal failure into a magnificent success."[1]

It was no idle boast. When the Wilfrid Laurier Liberals assumed
office in 1896, after eighteen years in the political wilderness, western
settlement and development remained the last great Confederation
project. It was widely believed that Canada's future prosperity — and
its independent existence on a continent dominated by the United
States — could not be assured until the northern prairies had been
settled and pioneer farms began producing crops for the international
market. The new Liberal government completed the task in only a
decade. By 1906, so many immigrants were pouring into the three
prairie provinces that Prime Minister Laurier ordered a special western census to document the phenomenal growth.

Sifton's boast, though, was really only half-right. Western settlement
might have been "a magnificent success" under his skillful direction as
Interior minister, but his other cabinet responsibility, Indian Affairs,
remained a "dismal failure." Those duties, because they did not measure up against the more pressing demands, were generally ignored or
narrowly met — to the detriment of Canada's treaty relationship with
prairie bands. Far from sharing in the largesse of the great Laurier
boom, First Nations were dismissed as an irrelevant minority — a

holdover from another time and place — and expected to disappear as more and more settlers arrived in the region.[2] At best, then, the Indian Affairs portfolio was "a responsibility to be lived with,"[3] occupying the corner of Sifton's desk in keeping with its peripheral importance.

◄◄--►►

Sifton, at just thirty-five, was the lone wolf in the Liberal cabinet. He probably wanted to be Liberal leader at one time, but that never happened because of Laurier's popularity and his hold on the party. He also struggled with hearing loss. Sifton was first and foremost "a political animal."[4] *Maclean's* magazine called him Canada's "political boss" in a March 1918 feature on his federal career.[5] Manitoba horse dealer and livery man Beecham Trotter was less kind, declaring Sifton "the greatest combination of cold-blooded businessman, machine politician, and statesman our country has produced."[6] Bob Edwards, editor and publisher of Calgary's satirical *Eye Opener* newspaper, went one better. He claimed that "the CPR, Clifford Sifton and the Almighty comprise the trinity of Canada, ranking in importance in the order named."[7] Sifton never commented on negative stories, but Edwards ranked high on his enemies list, especially after the *Eye Opener* suggested in 1905 that the minister was an unfaithful husband.

Sifton may have trained as a lawyer and had extensive business interests, but he thrived in the world of bare-knuckle politics. He instinctively wanted control and power, and his dual appointment in November 1896 as minister of both the Interior and Indian Affairs couldn't have been more to his liking. In fact, his arrival in Ottawa had been highly anticipated. Not only had his position in the new government been held for him until he entered the House after a special November by-election, but Laurier gave him a free hand and a blank cheque to get things done. Sifton was a highly talented individual with a brilliant mind, one of those rare elected officials absorbed with larger policy issues and the greater purpose of government.

Sifton had apprenticed in the bruising world of Manitoba provincial politics. Born in Ontario in 1861, he grew up in a family steeped

Liberal minister of Interior and Indian Affairs Clifford Sifton and his family.
His appointment to the Laurier cabinet came with great expectations.
(Library and Archives Canada)

in "Clear Grit" Liberalism, the Methodist church, and temperance. In his early teens, he moved to Winnipeg when his father secured a federal contract to build sections of the new telegraph and rail line. Sifton completed his education in Winnipeg and then Ontario, before studying law and being called to the Manitoba bar in 1882. Following his family to Brandon, Clifford opened a legal practice with his older brother, Arthur. Sifton had great business sense and made good money in real estate before seeking out other rewarding investments, including newspapers.

His interest in politics led to his election in 1888 as a member of Manitoba's first Liberal government, under Thomas Greenway. Sifton was a dominant presence as attorney general and minister of Education. He was also a formidable organizer and campaigner. The Liberal party machinery was geared to smite the Conservative foe.

He even paid operatives to keep track of political opponents and collect information, the more incriminating the better, to be used at election time. Sifton played a ruthless game of politics, where fair play was for losers.[8]

As head of both Interior and Indian Affairs, Sifton was expected to dispense jobs and award contracts to Liberal party supporters. This political work was doubly demanding because he also served as party organizer for areas west of Ontario. These government and political duties gave him an exceedingly large share of the patronage pie.

Sifton didn't see any contradiction between his duties as a Crown minister and filling government positions with Liberal associates or doling out government business at the constituency level. As he advised a friend after the ascension of the Laurier Liberals to office, "We must stop raising hell and raise something else. Now's our chance."[9]

Sifton's mixing of power and patronage was inspired by Canada's first prime minister, John A. Macdonald. The Conservative leader had adroitly used government jobs and contracts to reward loyal party supporters and win over others, who in return provided campaign contributions and other favours, such as editorial endorsement. Patronage helped keep the Conservatives in power, while maintaining discipline in party ranks.[10]

Sifton, in much the same way, became the Liberal kingpin who distributed rewards and benefits to a network of family, associates, and business people, many from the same social circles. Not surprisingly, most were Manitoba or territorial Liberals who had hitched their fortunes to his rising political star. These patronage recipients may not have been the best qualified for the positions offered or contracts awarded, but what mattered was loyalty to the Liberal party — and to Sifton, who always had his eye on the next election.[11]

Sifton's party machinery politics were no secret, and it was often claimed, based on his obvious wealth, that Sifton was himself involved in some shady dealings and kickback schemes. Conservatives delighted in substituting a dollar sign for the S in his last name ($ifton). Former prime minister Charles Tupper, a confirmed Sifton enemy, likened the cabinet minister's abuse of government patronage to a "carnival of crime."[12]

Then there was the story attributed to Richard Cartwright, minister of Trade and Commerce and one of Sifton's colleagues. After observing Sifton climb into his fine carriage, pulled by an exquisite team of horses, Cartwright apparently remarked to another Liberal: "Shall I tell you what Sir John Macdonald would have said to one of his ministers if he'd appeared thus? Sir John would have said, 'My dear fellow, it is bad enough to own it, but for heaven's sake don't advertise it.'"[13]

Despite the whiff of impropriety, political opponents and journalists were unable to produce any evidence of Sifton's supposed crimes. The "immensely able but deeply inscrutable" Sifton was careful in what he committed to writing.[14] His candour in some of his early letters as a cabinet minister soon petered out. Numerous telegrams were sent in cipher, and pages were ripped out of the letterbook he used as superintendent general of Indian Affairs. Ironically, his incoming correspondence often reveals more about the man and his activities.

One certainty is that Sifton had few friends in government, even in the Liberal caucus. He is said to have been "distantly formal, occasionally cordial, but too often abrupt and impatient" as an MP and cabinet minister.[15] Another certainty was that Sifton was in charge. Frederick White, who had served as comptroller of the North-West Mounted Police since 1880, complained to the Governor General that control of the force was "absolutely in Sifton's hands — that Sifton takes no advice whatever."[16]

One sure indication of Sifton's overriding desire to be in charge was his removal of A.M. Burgess and Hayter Reed as deputy ministers of the Interior and Indian Affairs, respectively. Both were long-serving civil servants and known Conservative sympathizers, but by March 1897, both were gone.[17] It was an unprecedented move, and Sifton came under fierce criticism in cabinet and government circles for acting so quickly and forgoing the two deputies' experience before getting his bearings in either department.

For Sifton, though, it was "impossible"[18] to keep Reed and Burgess in their positions if he was going to have a free hand to run the departments his way. Nor was he prepared to back down. "One rule I have in Department matters," Sifton told a Liberal territorial politician in mid-January 1897, "is that when I decide to do a thing — and do it — I never go back on it."[19] Still, it was not easy going for a new minister who expected people to bend to his will. In another letter around the same date, this time to fellow Manitoba politician John Donald Cameron, he confessed, "You cannot have much idea of the inertia of the body politic at Ottawa. It takes a great deal of pushing to get anything done."[20]

The dismissal of two senior bureaucrats signalled Sifton's emergence as a force in the new Liberal government. "Sifton has triumphed over Laurier," the deputy to the Secretary of State lamented. "Burgess and Reed are to be offered as propitiatory sacrifice to the new Minister."[21]

Territorial politician James Hamilton Ross, writing from Regina, offered a more nuanced assessment of Sifton's power play. Speaking on behalf of western Liberals, Ross congratulated Sifton for having "strength enough to withstand the pressure brought to bear by those who wish to allow things to run along in the old grooves and actually put their lives into the hands of their enemies."[22]

It was exactly the kind of support that Sifton cultivated — and rewarded. In 1901, Ross was named commissioner of the Yukon Territory, replacing William Ogilvie, who had balked at accepting one of Sifton's patronage appointees. Sifton answered Ogilvie's insolence with the brutal reminder that "all owe their positions to me."[23] Meanwhile Sifton's older and only brother, Arthur, took Ross's place as treasurer and commissioner of public works for the North-West Territories government.

Hardware merchant and Brandon mayor James Allan Smart benefited from his association with Sifton on many fronts. Born in 1858 in Brockville, Canada West (Ontario), Smart was one of thousands of Anglo-Canadians who moved to southwestern Manitoba in the early 1880s to cash in on the boom generated by the building of the Canadian Pacific Railway. Settling in Brandon in 1881, he used his successful hardware business as a springboard into other local business ventures. He also became involved in municipal politics, first as a city alderman and then mayor in 1885.

Smart and Sifton travelled in the same pack. Both helped found the Brandon Liberals Reform Association, both were investors in the *Brandon Sun* newspaper, and both dabbled in real estate. Coincidentally, both were also fathers of sons: Smart had four boys, Sifton five.

By the late 1880s, Smart and Sifton sat in the Manitoba legislature as members of the Greenway government. Smart served briefly as minister of Public Works before being demoted to provincial secretary and then losing his seat in the 1892 election. Smart was never the equal of Sifton, but had a knack for landing on his feet, thanks in no small part to his Brandon and Liberal connections. He acted as Manitoba commissioner at the 1893 Chicago World's Fair and was serving another term as Brandon mayor when Sifton asked him to come to Ottawa.

Sifton kept his intentions secret because he planned to replace both Burgess and Reed with Smart. That had never been done before. While there had only been one minister for Interior and Indian Affairs since 1873, there had always been two deputies. Sifton believed he could exercise greater control by rolling the two deputy ministers into one position. It also meant that there was no one who could specifically speak to First Nations interests and thereby made Indian Affairs even less of a priority for the new Laurier administration.

What certainly helped Sifton and his machinations was James Smart's reputation. In 1888, Conservative backbencher Thomas Mayne Daly had told Macdonald that Smart was "a man of integrity & worth & of great personal character."[24] It was high praise from the first mayor of Brandon (Smart had succeeded Daly) and the future minister of Interior and Indian Affairs (1892–1896).

Sifton was equally effusive in his March 1897 appointment letter, calling Smart "a gentleman whose acknowledged administrative capacity and practical experience of all matters pertaining to the development of those interests of the Dominion generally, and of . . . the North-West Territories particularly . . . specially qualify him to fill that office."[25]

It was something of a stretch to suggest that Smart had ever been much of an administrator or manager. Most of his past positions had been more modest leadership roles, including his work as a lay Baptist preacher. Smart was familiar with western land issues, given his real estate speculation, but he knew little about First Nations. Lord Minto, the Governor General of Canada from 1898 to 1904, probably came closest to understanding the connection between the two men when he said Smart was Sifton's "alter ego."[26]

Smart acted as Sifton's eyes and ears and could be relied upon to do his job with little direction. That was the real reason for his appointment as deputy minister to two departments; it had nothing to do with his apparent administrative talents, or even Sifton's search for efficiencies. As Sifton's biographer neatly summed up their relationship: "Sifton trusted him, and they worked well together."[27] It was inconsequential, then, whether Smart could play an instrument as long as the music was in the key of Sifton.

Sifton couldn't have been handed the task of getting the West settled at a more opportune time. The Laurier election victory coincided with a world economic boom, sparked by an unprecedented demand for Canadian commodities, lower shipping costs, and the discovery of gold in the Klondike and South Africa. The United States had also exhausted its homestead land and no longer captured the lion's share of immigrants who came to North America. Almost overnight, the Canadian prairies were transformed into "the last best West." An advertiser could not have asked for a more enticing image.

Sifton, in his capacity as federal Interior minister, made western Canada one of the most desired destinations for immigrants in search of land. Under his firm stewardship — Sifton was nicknamed the young Napoleon — a streamlined Interior department invested a substantial amount of time, energy, and money into the recruitment of experienced farmers. It circulated millions of promotional brochures, sponsored displays at exhibitions, and even financed western tours for journalists. Sifton expected results, not excuses, and results were

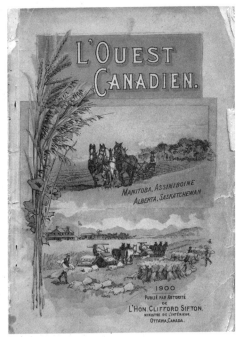

The Liberal government advertised western Canada as the land of opportunity. (University of Saskatchewan Archives and Special Collections)

measured in settlers on the land. One of the most gratifying statistics was that more homesteads were applied for in the first decade of the twentieth century than during the entire previous century. It was quite a turnaround.[28]

Given the fierce demand for land, Sifton could have simply relied on the free homestead system to get the prairie west settled. Tens of thousands of land-hungry homesteaders paid a $10 registration fee for their quarter-section, essentially free land, and were granted title after meeting specific residency and improvement requirements over a three-year period. Many settlers, though, had little practical farming experience and were defeated by the homestead regulations; two of every five homestead applications in the three prairie provinces were cancelled between 1871 and 1930.[29] Those who remained on the land struggled, sometimes over several years, to turn pioneer farms into commercial operations.

This process wasn't fast enough for Sifton, who was determined to accelerate occupation of the land so that the region could start

producing grain for the export market. His ready answer: corporations. Private businesses, with their size, capital assets, and market
connections, could do the job of exploiting western Canada's material
resources — everything from land and water to forests and minerals
— more expeditiously and efficiently. It was also an ideal way to profit
Liberal associates.

Theodore Arthur Burrows, a Manitoba lumberman, held more
timber berths in western Canada than any of his competitors in the
early twentieth century. He happened to be Sifton's brother-in-law.
He was also a long-time friend of dominion lands commissioner John
Gillanders Turriff, who was responsible for reviewing and accepting
bids for western timber limits. Somehow, Burrows managed to win
eighteen of nineteen tender competitions, including 500 square miles
of timber north of Prince Albert, Saskatchewan.[30]

Both Burrows and Turriff would be elected to the Liberal back-
benches in the House of Commons in the 1904 general election.
Burrows would later be named lieutenant governor of Manitoba, while
Turriff was appointed to the Senate.

Another beneficiary was James Duncan McGregor, a Brandon livestock dealer who secured a grazing lease to 47,600 acres of land between
the Bow and Belly Rivers in present-day southern Alberta. "J.D." or "Big
Jim," as he was known, was at one time Sifton's campaign manager.[31]
McGregor would succeed Burrows as Manitoba's lieutenant governor.

Colonization companies also became as much a part of the settlement project as individual homesteaders.[32] Sifton's Interior department
doled out large swaths of land on the understanding that colonization
syndicates had to place a prescribed number of settlers on each section
(640 acres) or township (36 sections). Whatever monies were made
from land sales were pocketed by the land companies. It was a speculator's dream.

It also lent itself to abuse. There was nothing preventing a syndicate from flipping part of its land grant and pocketing the proceeds.
Or small buyers could purchase several sections of company land and
wait a few years for land prices to rise before selling for a substantial
profit. Some syndicates engaged in what was known as "blanketing."

They would make bogus homestead applications in a district where they also held land and force prospective settlers to buy from them while homestead quarter-sections sat unoccupied.

More than a dozen land companies were operating in western Canada by the early twentieth century. The largest — in terms of land holdings — and most successful was the Saskatchewan Valley Land Company. Incorporated in 1902, it purchased close to one million acres of land that had been set aside for the Qu'Appelle, Long Lake, and Saskatchewan Railway along its line from Regina to Prince Albert. The company also secured another half million acres from the Laurier government.

These lands, particularly those south of Saskatoon, had been considered marginal and were skipped over by homesteaders. The Saskatchewan Valley syndicate, though, had ambitious plans. It ran advertisements in American newspapers and hired land agents scattered across the Midwest. It also arranged to have excursion trains bring prospective settlers and business people north to Canada, free of charge, and tour the company lands. Because the Americans had several decades' experience farming the semi-arid plains, they leapt at the opportunity before them and engaged in what was described as "a perfect orgy of land buying."³³ The syndicate made a fortune for its partners.

Other land companies were not as dominant, and certainly not as lucrative, but they employed similar promotion techniques, such as taking advantage of the lack of agricultural land south of the border to funnel settlers into western Canada. Many focused on placing religious or ethnic groups in so-called bloc settlements. One consistent purpose animated their operations, whatever their background, whether Canadian or American. They were all speculators, out to make as much money as they could from "the last best West."

None of the land companies would have existed and prospered without the active co-operation of the Interior department. Syndicate members all had good Liberal connections in one way or another and expected their investment in western lands to benefit from this association. The Western Land and Development Company, for example, included George Bulyea, a Liberal member of the North-West

Several members of the North-West Territories Council would later serve as Liberal Members of Parliament during Laurier's tenure as prime minister. (Glenbow Archives)

Territories government (and first lieutenant governor of Alberta); George Brown, a Liberal member of the NWT assembly (and second lieutenant governor of Saskatchewan); James Calder, another Liberal territorial politician (and future Saskatchewan and federal cabinet minister); and J.H. Ross, the Liberal territorial politician who had been named Yukon commissioner.

These men and the directors and shareholders of other companies expected Liberal patronage appointees in the Interior department to use their positions and influence whenever and wherever they could. There was even speculation that three of Sifton's patronage appointees — J.G. Turriff, commissioner of dominion lands; J. Obed Smith, commissioner of immigration; and C. Wesley (Wes) Speers, general colonization agent — were intimately involved with the Saskatchewan Valley Land Company.[34]

Sifton was also dissatisfied with the immigration side of Interior operations and decided that a more systematic, centralized approach was necessary to secure more settlers. The solution was a long-term contract, signed in November 1899, with the North Atlantic Trading Company (NATC). It was a remarkable business arrangement. Not only did the NATC secure a monopoly on — and get paid for — all Canadian promotional activities in Scandinavia and throughout continental Europe, but it also earned a bonus for every agricultural immigrant landed in Canada ($5 for anyone over twelve).

The contract also called for confidentiality, including names of syndicate members. This secrecy conveniently shielded William Thomas Rochester Preston, an Ontario Liberal operative whose reputation for gutter politics knew no depths. Preston had been named inspector of emigration for Europe in London — a new position created specifically for him as a political reward — and then used his influence with the government to float the NATC proposal. Preston's close association with the NATC, and the potential financial benefits of that association, did not become public until 1905.[35]

Sifton didn't approach his cabinet duty as Indian Affairs minister with the same alacrity. His biographer suggested that "the Indian administration was little more than a parenthetical concern" because of the heavy demands of the Interior portfolio. Sifton, though, was an extremely capable administrator with an appetite for big challenges. He didn't have to use the same "well-established [policy] grooves."[36] Nor was he handcuffed by the same budgetary constraints — something the Liberals in Opposition had harped about for years — because of the booming Canadian economy.

Sifton had the unprecedented opportunity to strike a new course, set a new tone, for federal Indian Affairs policy. Here was a talented, ambitious Member of Parliament who brought a western perspective to the cabinet table — although born in Ontario, he had lived and worked in Brandon, Manitoba, as a lawyer, businessman, and provincial politician. He may not have personally known any First Nations people, may not have had any dealings with them, but he certainly would have been aware of their situation. Given his reputation as a clear-sighted reformer, he was perfectly positioned to bring the same progressive zeal to the so-called Indian problem.

The Victorian way of thinking — that white, Christian society had a moral duty to uplift and civilize primitive peoples — had given way to a new reform impulse rooted in efficient, rational planning. Scientific management, not humanitarian sentiment, would best address the problems engendered by the emerging industrial society. It could also be applied to the day-to-day operations of Indian Affairs and its overall policy direction. This approach might even herald a new beginning for Canada's relationship with treaty First Nations.

Sifton, though, didn't see prairie First Nations as part of the new West of the new century. Racism — and the social Darwinism that justified it — went a long way in explaining this attitude. White settlers expected western Canada to be an Anglo-Canadian stronghold where the best features of British civilization were to take root and

WESTWARD AND NORTHERN HO!

THE GREATEST WAVE THAT EVER SWEPT ACROSS OUR GREAT PLAINS

The Toronto World, 14 November 1902

The great immigration and settlement boom at the beginning of the twentieth century dramatically remade the demographic map of western Canada.

(Toronto World, *November 14, 1902)*

flourish. There was to be no multicultural accommodation. Peasant immigrants from continental Europe would have to leave their cultural baggage at the border and accept and embrace the ways and traditions of their new country — to be "Canadianized," according to the popular terminology of the time. On the other hand, those who were considered incapable of integration, especially people of colour, were not welcome. The Canadian government deliberately discouraged the immigration of Asians, Blacks, Jews, and other peoples in the belief that their very presence threatened the white, Anglo-Canadian ideal for the region.

The same reasoning applied to prairie First Nations. They were viewed as an inferior people, standing in the way of the larger march of progress and the West's great future. One senior Indian Affairs official even hoped that, like the bison, they "must at no distant day become nearly extinct."[37] This attitude was reinforced in newspapers, especially in political cartoons which invariably portrayed Indian men, always heavily shaded, as either sinister or slovenly.[38]

That First Nations represented a dark, pre-modern past was also driven home at the September 1905 inauguration ceremonies for the new province of Saskatchewan. A group of First Nations in traditional regalia rode at the head of the parade as it made its way through the streets of downtown Regina. "There they were," lampooned the *Moose Jaw Times*, "the remnants of a departing race . . . a motley crowd."[39] If Saskatchewan were to fulfill its great destiny, then First Nations, like those in the inauguration parade, were expected to ride off into oblivion and never be heard from again.

Sifton also found prairie First Nations wanting when measured against homesteaders. He wanted sturdy, independent farmers who could largely make it on their own. As an official in his department put it, what western Canada needed was "men of good muscle who are willing to hustle."[40] Sifton genuinely believed that the best settlers were those who persevered on their land and steadily improved and expanded their operations by trying new methods and adopting new machinery. Once farmers had succeeded in turning the prairie wilderness into bountiful wheatfields, he expected wheat production to keep pace with the boom in manufacturing, industrialization, and resource exploitation in the early twentieth century. Prairie agriculture was a business, and Canadian grain a valuable commodity on the world market.

First Nations, by contrast, were depicted in popular media as a shiftless people, addicted to government assistance. That federal policies had been largely responsible for this dependence was never a consideration. Nor did it seem to matter that it was an unfair comparison — First Nations had been forced to practice subsistence farming with only basic tools, while their white counterparts ran mechanized operations. For Sifton and others, First Nations people had benefited from almost two decades of government support and encouragement — and squandered it.

By hunting, trapping, and gathering instead of working their lands, so the thinking went, prairie First Nations were failing to contribute to the material well-being of the region, failing to help realize western Canada's great agricultural future. Sifton outlined the government's position in a House of Commons speech in 1904: "We may as well be frank. The Indian has not the physical, mental or moral get-up to enable him to compete. He cannot do it."[41]

An underlying mistrust also stood in the way of Sifton and the Laurier government accepting prairie First Nations as participants in the settlement enterprise. During treaty negotiations in the 1870s, the various western First Nations had promised to remain peaceful and loyal to Queen Victoria. That vow, in the public memory, appeared to have been broken when several Cree and Nakoda bands were inexorably drawn into the 1885 North-West Rebellion. The white territorial community was thoroughly shaken by events that bloody spring and welcomed the repressive Indian Affairs measures introduced in the aftermath of the troubles. Confining First Nations to their reserves would reduce any potential threat to the settler population. When Almighty Voice, a young Willow Cree from the One Arrow reserve, murdered a mounted police sergeant in October 1895, several western newspapers raised the alarm, one questioning whether the region was "on the verge of another Indian uprising."[42] It was quite a leap, especially given the rarity of such crimes.

The Laurier government looked upon First Nations people, like this family camped near Saskatoon in 1908, as standing in the way of western Canada's great future. (Brock Silversides collection)

For white settlers, First Nations were a menacing presence in the West, seemingly one step away from a savage outburst if not for the mounted police presence and Indian Affairs management. Sifton himself alluded to this uneasiness about the prairie First Nations when he told the House of Commons that government policy was "based upon a belief that it is better . . . to bring Indians into a state of civilization or comparative civilization . . . than to take any chances of their becoming a disturbing fact in the community."[43] Such a statement portrayed a profound ignorance of the treaty relationship.

Sifton consequently eschewed any big, bold policy departures as Indian Affairs minister in favour of pursuing the same goal that the previous Macdonald government had set itself almost two decades earlier — getting First Nations self-supporting and thereby less reliant on government assistance, especially rationing. He wanted to do the minimum possible for treaty First Nations, while making noises about trying to help them. It was a way of evading Canada's treaty obligations when it was not possible to simply walk away from them. The irony was that westerners had mockingly called the Interior department the department of indifference before Sifton took over. That indifference now applied to Sifton's handling of Indian Affairs matters — except when it came to patronage.

Notes

1. Quoted in D.J. Hall, *Clifford Sifton, v. 2: A Lonely Eminence, 1901–1929* (Vancouver: University of British Columbia Press, 1985), p. 42.
2. B. Waiser, *Saskatchewan: A New History* (Calgary: Fifth House Publishers, 2005), pp. 163–83.
3. Quoted in D.J. Hall, "Clifford Sifton and Canadian Indian Administration, 1896–1905," *Prairie Forum*, v. 2, n. 2, 1977, p. 146.
4. P. Berton, *The Promised Land* (Toronto: Anchor Canada, 2002). Berton titles a subsection on Sifton "a political animal."
5. H.F. Gadsby, "Has Canada a Political Boss?" *Maclean's*, March 1918, p. 38.
6. Quoted in Berton, *The Promised Land*, p. 25.
7. Quoted in ibid., p. 266.
8. D.J. Hall, *Clifford Sifton, v. 1: The Young Napoleon, 1861–1900* (Vancouver: University of British Columbia Press, 1981), pp. 23–51.
9. Quoted in Gadsby, "Has Canada a Political Boss?" p. 39.
10. M. Bliss, *Right Honourable Men: The Descent of Canadian Politics from Macdonald to Mulroney* (Toronto: HarperCollins, 1994), p. 5.
11. Hall, *Clifford Sifton, v. 1*, pp. 124–6, 133.
12. Bliss, *Right Honourable Men*, p. 51.
13. Quoted in ibid., p. 52.
14. R. Graham, *Arthur Graham, v. 1: The Door of Opportunity* (Clarke, Irwin and Company, 1960), p. 51.
15. Hall, *Clifford Sifton, v. 1*, p. 133.
16. Quoted in Berton, *The Promised Land*, p. 27.
17. In July 1884, Sifton was a member of a two-person Brandon delegation that secured a meeting with Burgess to discuss local farmer

grievances. The pair were made to wait all day and then brusquely dismissed by the deputy minister. Sifton waited twelve years to get his revenge. Hall, *Clifford Sifton*, *v. 1*, p. 127.

18. *Library and Archives Canada (LAC)*, Clifford Sifton papers [reel C466], General Correspondence, C. Sifton to H. Reed, February 25, 1897.

19. Ibid., [reel C401], Ottawa letterbooks (January 13–February 1, 1897), C. Sifton to J.G. Turriff, January 14, 1897.

20. Ibid., C. Sifton to J.D. Cameron, January 15, 1897.

21. Quoted in Hall, *Clifford Sifton*, *v. 1*, p. 126.

22. Quoted in ibid., p. 126.

23. Quoted in ibid., p. 3.

24. Quoted in ibid., p.35.

25. *LAC*, Sifton papers [reel C404], Ottawa letterbooks (March 31–May 7, 1897), C. Sifton to Governor General in Council, March 1897, p. 272.

26. Hall, *Clifford Sifton*, *v. 2*, p. 64.

27. Hall, *Clifford Sifton*, *v. 1*, p. 126.

28. D.J. Hall, "Clifford Sifton: Immigration and Settlement Policy, 1896–1905" in H. Palmer, ed., *The Settlement of the West* (Calgary: University of Calgary 1977), pp. 60-85.

29. C. Martin, *"Dominion Lands" Policy* (Toronto: McClelland and Stewart, 1973), pp. 172–4. A major exhibit at Saskatoon's Western Development Museum calls settlement of the prairie west by homesteaders "Winning the Prairie Gamble."

30. J.E. Rea, "Burrows, Theodore Arthur" in R. Cook, ed., *Dictionary of Canadian Biography, v. XV, 1921–1930* (Toronto: University of Toronto Press, 2005) p. 172; Hall, *Clifford Sifton*, *v. 2*, pp. 188–9; Berton, *The Promised Land*, pp. 236–8.

31. Berton, *The Promised Land*, pp. 240–2; P. Hanlon, "McGregor, James Duncan" in *Dictionary of Canadian Biography, v. XVI, 1931–1940* accessed March 8, 2022, http://www.biographi.ca/en/bio/mcgregor _james_duncan_16E.html.

32. This corporate frontier prompted one western Canadian historian to claim that "the most successful era of land settlement" was actually the consequence of a "sales policy," not a "free homestead policy." Martin, *"Dominion Lands" Policy*, p. 95.

33. Quoted in T.D. Regehr, "Davidson, Andrew Duncan" in R. Cook, ed., *Dictionary of Canadian Biography, v. XIV, 1911–1920* (Toronto: University of Toronto Press, 1998), p. 271.

34. P. Martin-McGuire, *First Nations Land Surrenders on the Prairies, 1896–1911* (Ottawa: Indian Claims Commission, 1998), pp. 47–8, 60.

35. J. Petryshyn, "Canadian Immigration and the North Atlantic Trading Company 1899–1906: A Controversy Revisited," *Journal of Canadian Studies*, v. 32, n. 3, 1997, pp. 55–60.

36. Quoted in Hall, *Clifford Sifton, v. 2*, p. 43.

37. Quoted in M.K. Lux, *Medicine That Walks: Disease, Medicine, and Canadian Plains Native People, 1880–1940* (Toronto: University of Toronto Press, 2001), p. 159.

38. See C.J. Nielson, "Caricaturing Colonial Space: Indigenized, Feminized Bodies and Anglo-Canadian Identity, 1873–94," *Canadian Historical Review*, v. 96, n. 4, December 2015, pp. 473–506.

39. *Moose Jaw Times*, September 8, 1905.

40. Quoted in Hall, "Clifford Sifton: Immigration and Settlement Policy," p. 71.

41. Quoted in J.R. Miller, *Shingwauk's Vision: A History of Native Residential Schooling* (Toronto: University of Toronto Press, 1996), p. 135.

42. Regina *Standard*, October 31, 1895. See B. Waiser, *In Search of Almighty Voice Resistance and Reconciliation:* (Markham: Fifth House Publishers, 2020).

43. Quoted in Hall, *Clifford Sifton, v. 2*, p. 43.

◂ Three ▸

THE NEW MINISTER HAS GONE TOO FAR

O n September 22, 1896, just weeks into the new parliamentary session, Nicholas Flood Davin, the Conservative MP for Assiniboia West, was at his theatrical best. Rising from his House of Commons seat, Davin feigned shock, then disbelief, that the Indian commissioner for the North-West Territories was telling his officials to only "deal with friends of the Government."[1]

This dig at the newly elected Wilfrid Laurier Liberals was a charade — nothing more than needling the new government about its blatant use of patronage. Davin and his fellow Conservatives knew all too well that the incoming Liberals would never do business with so-called enemy Indian Affairs contractors or, for that matter, leave enemy appointees in place. Indeed, there was a widespread belief in Liberal ranks that the Indian Affairs outside service was "stuffed from the beginning to end . . . with nominees of the late Administration."[2]

This was a grievance that rankled Clifford Sifton — a powerful reminder of the influence that Conservatives once wielded. As the new Indian Affairs minister, he would fix that. Sifton may have talked about the onerous challenge of dealing with western Canada's First Nations, but he worked harder to ensure that Indian Affairs positions, including the list of suppliers, were "stuffed" with good Liberals.[3]

John Douglas McLean, the new Indian Affairs secretary, directed department patronage for the Laurier government. The New Brunswick–born McLean had joined Indian Affairs in 1882, at age twenty-seven, as the deputy minister's private secretary. Before that, he served six years with the dominion lands side of Interior operations. In 1889, McLean had been placed in charge of the department's Land and Timber branch, but craved advancement. He even appealed to Sifton during the government changeover, playing up his party affiliation; he had always remained true to his "principles as a Liberal" during the dark days of Conservative rule.[4] Sifton might have dismissed McLean's entreaties if not for the fact that McLean was an experienced civil servant — and a Liberal — with an intimate knowledge of the Indian Affairs inside service in Ottawa.

Sifton recognized McLean as someone who could help James Smart run the department, while the new deputy minister grappled

Indian Affairs secretary J.D. McLean was a driving force in the department bureaucracy. (McCord Museum)

with the greater, and more important, demands of the Interior portfolio. That Smart's priorities were immigration and settlement was confirmed when the deputy minister played no role in the reorganizing and downsizing of the Indian Affairs department in early 1897.

McLean could also be expected — given that he served as department secretary at Sifton's discretion — to put the new government's interests above those of First Nations. Little is known, though, about McLean the person beyond his official correspondence. He was the epitome of the public servant, faithfully carrying out government duties and never attracting attention. Even though he kept to the background, he was a constant presence, always with a hand in some issue or topic. Maybe that's why Sifton put his faith in him and promoted him. It would also explain why he managed to survive several governments of both political stripes and retire in 1930 after half a century with the department.[5]

McLean immediately took charge of the Indian Affairs office and its operations. He was painstakingly officious. Nothing escaped his

The Indian Affairs department was located in the Langevin Block, immediately east of Parliament Hill, in Ottawa. (Library and Archives Canada)

attention — from high-level summaries for the minister to setting working hours and deciding smoking policy. He also looked after several more pressing needs. McLean oversaw the movement of the Indian Affairs offices to the second floor of the Langevin Block so that the department was consolidated with Interior under one roof. One urgent concern was getting department documents and files out of old wooden filing cabinets and stored in a more secure place.

McLean also handled patronage distribution, compiling and working from lists of good Liberals who, for example, were awarded contracts as suppliers and provisioners for First Nations reserves. He regularly sent out memoranda identifying those who had been added or struck off the local patronage schedule. As one Liberal acknowledged, "There is always a little to make in any supplies."[6]

McLean assisted Sifton in his evaluation of Indian Affairs personnel, providing information about who might be expendable. These dismissals excluded several senior personnel in the Ottawa office — what was known as the inside service — with the notable exception of Hayter Reed. Sifton divided the department into three branches, each with its own chief clerk. Duncan Campbell Scott remained accountant, Samuel Bray continued as chief surveyor, and W.A. Orr looked after lands and timber.

That these three civil servants retained their positions meant that the department would likely continue along the same grooves. It also appears that Sifton wanted some consistency — and corporate memory — in department operations, if only to ensure that Smart did not flounder as the new deputy minister.

That same need for consistency and experience also applied to Sifton. In late January 1897, Sifton appointed clerk James A.J. McKenna as his private secretary for Indian Affairs business. McKenna had acted in the same capacity a decade earlier for another superintendent general of Indian Affairs — namely, Prime Minister John A. Macdonald.

Even with Sifton's reforms, the relatively small size of the Indian Affairs inside service was not unusual for Ottawa at the time. On the

J.A.J. McKenna, Sifton's private secretary, was vitally involved in Indian Affairs matters. (Library and Archives Canada)

eve of the twentieth century, government was limited in scope and much of a department's business was normally handled by the minister and a handful of staff. Sifton actually preferred it that way.

Senior Indian Affairs officials were expected to run the reorganized department, making decisions that, in many instances, Sifton simply endorsed. His greater concern was filling the endless patronage demands — what Prime Minister Laurier regarded as "the most important single function of government" across all departments.[7] Sifton, though, took the centralization of power one step further by embarking on a major overhaul of the department's operations in western Canada.

Since the early 1880s, the Indian commissioner of the North-West Territories had made his home in the territorial capital in Regina, along Canadian Pacific's main railway line. A large building on Dewdney Avenue, not far from the North-West Mounted Police headquarters and training depot on the west side of town, served as the nerve centre for Indian Affairs operations. Sifton did not see a need for the office,

The western office of the Indian Affairs department in Regina.
(Provincial Archives of Saskatchewan)

especially since its existence went against his desire to keep the locus of power and control in Ottawa. He also wanted to reduce the number of outside service employees, especially those who owed their jobs to Conservative party connections.

In deciding where and how much to cut, Sifton turned to Indian commissioner Amédée Forget, an unlikely survivor in the world of partisan politics. Despite his Liberal party affiliation, Forget had been the first and only clerk to the North-West Territories Council (1876–1888) before being appointed assistant Indian commissioner and then commissioner in 1893.

Forget would oversee the neutering of his own powers and the dismantling of his office. The Regina headquarters were to be relocated to Winnipeg, while the downsized staff largely attended to inspections.[8] Indian Affairs field officials were to communicate directly with Ottawa. That correspondence, in turn, would be handled by McLean, thereby giving the department secretary tremendous influence over department operations and practices.

Forget also provided advice about the reorganization of western Indian agencies and the staff to be assigned to them. Over fifty department employees were fired or forced to retire, while many of those who escaped the cuts had their salaries reduced.[9]

This purge had more to do with placing Liberals in many of the vacated positions — something that Forget gladly handled, based on names put forward by western Liberal political figures. In the end, there were twenty-nine fewer Indian Affairs employees in the 1897–98 department budget (115) than the year before (144). The number of officials, though, would steadily creep up the next few years to 133 in 1904–05, a difference of only eleven from the start of Sifton's term as minister.[10]

Overall Indian Affairs spending also increased under Sifton. Despite the minister's "slash and burn" rhetoric, the department budget for Manitoba and the North-West Territories in the first year of Liberal rule ($734,920) was slightly higher than the previous year under the Conservatives ($701,504). It rose almost every year thereafter, reaching $869,981 in 1904–05.[11] This spending included lucrative patronage contracts and the rewarding of Forget for his Liberal party service. In October 1898, he was named lieutenant governor for the North-West Territories, and seven years later he became Saskatchewan's first lieutenant governor.

The retooling of Indian Affairs was well underway by the time James Smart arrived in Ottawa in the late winter of 1897, ready to assume his new duties. For the past few months, at Sifton's insistence, Smart had been on a small inspection tour of federal immigration offices in prairie communities. By early March, though, Sifton finally showed his hand and submitted separate recommendations to cabinet that Smart be appointed deputy minister to Interior and Indian Affairs, effective April 1, 1897.

Smart was immediately embroiled in a turf war with McLean at Indian Affairs. The new deputy minister did not know how things worked and bumbled along as best he could, trying to deal with the myriad of demands from MPs and business people while also acting upon Sifton's short, almost cryptic requests for information or action.

McLean seemed to resent Smart's intervention in department affairs and formally told him by memorandum in early May "that a great many matters that come to you might be referred to me" and that it would be more efficient if McLean drafted responses on behalf of the deputy minister.[12] Smart sent a stinging note in response, prompting McLean to assure his boss that his intent was only to supply information "on matters purely routine and official."[13] A few days later, in a fit of pique, McLean suggested obliquely that Smart do his homework. The deputy minister was to read the material supplied to him and stop stuffing McLean's department mailbox with unsubstantiated complaints about procedure and policy.

The real clincher that Smart was adrift and out of the loop, however, was his discovery in late May that the Indian commissioner's western office was being reorganized and moved without his knowledge. When Smart asked McLean what was going on, the secretary said that Forget had consulted directly with Sifton and had his "sanction for all that has been done."[14] Smart had to deal with the fallout from this and other changes. Several dismissed employees from across the country appealed to the deputy minister for help saving their jobs.

Smart and McLean eventually reached an understanding. Maybe Sifton had a few quiet words with Smart about McLean's value to the department, especially when the minister's own time was being gobbled up by more urgent matters. In the early spring of 1897, Prime Minister Laurier had asked Sifton to negotiate a deal with the Canadian Pacific Railway to help finance a new line through the Crow's Nest Pass, from Lethbridge to Nelson, in order to access promising mineral deposits in southeastern British Columbia.

Smart would also have been increasingly busy with his own Interior responsibilities and probably came to the realization, albeit grudgingly, that McLean was a good person to keep a steady and careful watch over his Indian Affairs duties, especially during his absences on government business. Whatever the reason, by mid-June 1897, McLean was running the department as if it were his own bailiwick — even quietly amending Smart's correspondence — and communicating directly with Sifton's private Indian Affairs secretary McKenna.

That McLean and McKenna worked around Smart was undoubtedly known to Sifton, perhaps even encouraged by him. The minister either knew that his Brandon friend could not manage two departments or, to be less charitable, that he would be ineffective at Indian Affairs. Whatever the reason, Sifton seemed content to shake up the department and then step back and let McLean and McKenna run things.

Sifton's workload, in the meantime, became impossibly heavier when news of the August 1896 Klondike gold discovery reached the outside world — and Ottawa — in mid-July 1897. The placer gold discovery in Canada's remote northwest caught the Laurier government flat-footed, all the more so because of the tens of thousands of stampeders who madly headed to the Yukon to strike it rich. It fell to Sifton, as minister responsible for the North-West Territories, to deal with the Klondike gold rush — he called it an "avalanche of responsibility." He had to ensure, among other challenges, that Canadian sovereignty was respected and the Canadian treasury benefited from the rich find. The isolation of the region only compounded his task.

Sifton assumed the Yukon assignment just as the shakedown in the Indian Affairs outside service was finalized. His work wasn't done though. Sifton sought an overview of the department, in particular outstanding issues and current problem areas. It might appear to have been a backwards way of dealing with his new ministry — dismiss staff first, then consider the department situation — but his first priority upon taking up his cabinet post was centralizing control and consolidating power in Ottawa.

Once these changes had been effected, Sifton asked McLean for a synoptic report. The document he put together included maps and tables of First Nations reserves prepared by the Lands branch. He also compiled a list of outstanding reference cases that were still awaiting an opinion from the Department of Justice. This backlog might explain why McLean recommended to Smart that the department have its own in-office legal clerk who could guide senior Indian Affairs officials in their interpretation and application of policy. Sifton agreed and recruited Regina lawyer Reginald Rimmer, legal advisor to the lieutenant governor of the North-West Territories, and not surprisingly a Liberal.

Department responsibilities under the Indian Act and the associated legal questions assumed greater importance in the late 1890s, largely because of constant requests about access to Indian lands and resources, especially after Laurier took office. That First Nations had treaty rights — or that Canada had treaty obligations — was never a consideration to Liberals seeking some regulatory favour or inside advantage.

Several letter writers asked Indian Affairs whether Indian reserves were to be sold now that there had been a change of government. Others wanted to lease Indian lands — from New Brunswick (Tobique First Nation) to Vancouver Island (Snuneymuxw First Nation). The

Sifton was a dominant force in the Laurier cabinet, but his Interior workload took priority over his Indian Affairs duties. (McCord Museum)

mayor of Gananoque, Ontario, for example, was interested in some of the Thousand Islands. There were also unsolicited applications to cut timber on reserves. Someone from Toronto even wanted to haul gravel from a nearby reserve.

All of these requests can be found today, tucked here and there throughout the department's 1897 correspondence, next to memos dealing with the reorganization and patronage considerations. Smart, for the most part, fielded any queries from MPs and senators, while ensuring that any letters from Brandon-area residents found their way to Sifton's desk.

There is no documentary evidence that the Indian Affairs department under Sifton wanted to make reserve surrenders a new priority — especially with the minister knee-deep in other policy issues. Senior Indian Affairs officials were more concerned with department structure and personnel than policy in the first half of 1897. If there was a plan to initiate reserve surrenders, it was a discussion officials held among themselves.

What apparently pushed the department into not only taking but actively encouraging surrenders was the existence of two Treaty Six reserves in the Saskatchewan district that had been unoccupied for a number of years: Young Chipewyan and Chakastaypasin. They presented Sifton with an unexpected opportunity to add the reserves to his inventory of settlement land.

Conservative T.M. Daly, Sifton's immediate predecessor as Interior and Indian Affairs minister, had tried to initiate the surrender of the two reserves in the fall of 1895. After attending the Regina Territorial Exhibition in August 1895, Daly made a special trip with Prime Minister Mackenzie Bowell to Duck Lake to visit some of the North-West Rebellion battle sites. That's when he learned about the Young Chipewyan and Chakastaypasin reserves and their "fine tracts of land."[15]

According to the Indian Act, the Indian Affairs department could not unilaterally take over any reserve set aside as part of the treaty agreement. A deputized representative had to convene a special meeting of the adult male members of the band, supervise a vote, and keep a record of the proceedings. One sentence of the act, though, was particularly ambiguous, even problematic: "The release or surrender shall be assented to by a majority of the male members . . . at a meeting." It was not clear from the wording of the legislation whether a surrender had to be approved by the majority of the band's male population or simply approved by the male majority at the meeting. Former Liberal prime minister Alexander Mackenzie had maintained that a majority of male band members was needed, but his government never initiated a reserve surrender.[16]

Indian Affairs, for its part, adopted a narrow interpretation of what constituted a majority. On November 19, 1888, a surrender meeting was held for the Papaschase reserve on the south side of the North Saskatchewan River, directly across from Edmonton. It was the first time that a surrender was taken in the prairie west. Three former Papaschase band members, then living at the Enoch reserve, agreed to turn over forty square miles to the Crown. No attempt was made to summon other former Papaschase men living on other reserves in the area and thereby ensure that the majority of former band members participated in the vote.

In 1893, Amédée Forget cautioned Indian Affairs deputy minister Hayter Reed that the department's surrender practice was possibly invalid. But the Conservatives took no action to bring clarity to the matter, even though the Department of Justice said it would be best to amend the Indian Act to remove any ambiguity about the word "majority."[17]

In the case of the Young Chipewyan and Chakastaypasin reserves, Reed didn't see "any necessity . . . for taking a surrender at all" because of what Reed described as "the circumstances" of the two reserves.[18]

The thirty-square-mile Young Chipewyan reserve (also known as Stoney Knoll) had been surveyed in 1879 along the north branch of the Saskatchewan River near present-day Laird, Saskatchewan. The band chose not take up the reserve, but continued to follow a seasonal subsistence round in the region. When a dominion lands survey crew arrived in the area in 1883, it never realized that the land had been

A.E. Forget (with his pet monkey) served as Indian commissioner for the North-West Territories before being named lieutenant governor for the new province of Saskatchewan in 1905. (Provincial Archives of Saskatchewan)

set aside, so it subdivided the reserve into townships. By 1888, Indian Affairs no longer paid the Young Chipewyan people as a separate band and considered the reserve "abandoned."

Indian Affairs also listed the Chakastaypasin reserve as abandoned, but for a different reason. The twenty-four-square-mile reserve was located on the south branch of the Saskatchewan River, southeast of Prince Albert. In the aftermath of the rebellion, Indian Affairs considered Chakastaypasin and his people to be rebels — even though they had left their reserve out of fear of being dragged into the troubles. The department deposed the Chief and deliberately broke up the band. By 1890, the Chakastaypasin reserve was officially considered vacated, while former members found a new home with the Cumberland, James Smith, and One Arrow bands.

Because the Young Chipewyan and Chakastaypasin people had joined other bands, Reed believed they had forfeited any claim to the reserves. There was no need for surrender meetings, he reasoned, because no one lived there anymore, if they ever did. But his seemingly straightforward reasoning was derailed by a technicality.

Up until 1895, treaty First Nations were informally transferred from one band to another by adding or subtracting names from the annuity lists. Then, section 140 was added to the Indian Act: anyone seeking to join another community had to secure formal approval from the absorbing band and the superintendent general of Indian Affairs. This amendment suggested that Young Chipewyan and Chakastaypasin people still held an interest in their reserves — until formal transfer applications were completed.

Forget was at a loss about what to do in the case of the Young Chipewyan band. On February 3, 1896, he complained to Reed that finding "the few remaining members" would be "a most difficult matter" and asked whether it was "absolutely necessary" to try to secure formal transfers.[19] Reed admitted that "it is probably hardly worthwhile to make any great exertion."[20]

Forget had better luck determining the whereabouts of former Chakastaypasin band members, but they wanted compensation for their reserve before signing any forms. This delay meant that nothing was done about securing the two reserve surrenders before the June 1896 general election that brought Laurier to power.

In fact, Sifton probably did not learn about the vacant reserves until early January 1897 when a settler applied to cut logs on Sugar Island, part of the Chakastaypasin reserve, because "the Indians have left."[21] Prince Albert merchant Thomas Osborne Davis also contacted Sifton about the status of the reserve, noting that the Conservatives had planned to open both the Chakastaypasin and Young Chipewyan reserves and encouraging the new minister to "have it done as early as possible."[22]

Sifton turned to Forget for some background information — and a way forward. The Indian commissioner suggested that "nothing should hinder" the opening of the Young Chipewyan reserve because it had "never been settled by them [band]." But he also believed — contrary to Reed's opinion — that "the necessity of taking a surrender" for the Chakastaypasin reserve trumped any formal transfer agreements.[23]

McLean decided to seek a Department of Justice opinion about the matter in mid-April. Sifton's impatience was clearly evident in his marginal notation on the covering memo — he just wanted to know whether a Chakastaypasin surrender meeting had to be convened.[24] The pressure to do something only intensified when Richard Cook, the future mayor of Prince Albert, submitted a petition claiming the "idle" and "vacant" reserve was holding back settlement.[25]

Sifton chose not to wait, but to grab what he could. In early May, in his capacity as Indian Affairs minister, he asked that the lands of the Young Chipewyan reserve be turned over to Interior, his other area of responsibility. Young Chipewyan became only the second prairie reserve to be surrendered to the Crown, albeit by order-in-council on May 11, 1897.

Three days later, E.L. Newcombe, the deputy minister of Justice, pointedly informed McLean that his reading of the Indian Act determined that the Chakastaypasin reserve could be released only by taking a surrender.[26] McLean took the ruling in stride and quickly made arrangements — with Sifton's concurrence — to have Duck Lake Indian agent Robert McKenzie convene a surrender meeting. It didn't seem to matter that the order should officially have come from the minister or his deputy.

On June 23, 1897, nine former Chakastaypasin members who had formally transferred to the Cumberland band voted to surrender the twenty-four-square-mile reserve. When the reserve was surveyed nineteen years earlier, the band population was 121. McKenzie forwarded the surrender documents to Ottawa on July 1, 1897. He provided no report about the meeting itself or whether he had made any effort to involve Chakastaypasin people who had joined other bands. The surrender was approved by order-in-council three weeks later.[27]

Sifton's acquisition of abandoned reserve land for Interior purposes didn't end there. Reed had also been scheming to take Sharphead, another Treaty Six reserve, without a surrender. Located at Wolf Creek (near present-day Ponoka, Alberta) and part of Indian Affairs' Hobbema agency, the forty-two-square-mile reserve had been surveyed for the Stoney (Nakoda) band in 1885. Five years later, the Sharphead people, who had once numbered 200, were nearly wiped out by a measles epidemic.

Those who survived joined other local bands, especially the Paul reserve at White Whale Lake, west of Edmonton. By 1895, the abandoned Sharphead reserve was in Reed's crosshairs. But like Young Chipewyan and Chakastaypasin, he wasn't able to pull the trigger before the change in government.

The vacant Sharphead reserve soon came to the attention of the new Laurier administration. In late June 1897, a local rancher asked the Interior department for a grazing lease there. His request was forwarded to W.A. Orr of Indian Affairs, who in his capacity as head of the Lands and Timber branch recommended that the reserve be handled the same way as Young Chipewyan and Chakastaypasin.

McLean ordered the taking of a surrender on July 21 — even though, once again, he didn't have the authority to do so. Indian agent Charles de Cazes, assisted by Forget, convened a meeting on September 11 and secured a surrender vote from nine former Sharphead band members living at White Whale Lake. That Indian Affairs officials were little concerned about procedure was plainly evident when the affidavit confirming the authenticity of the surrender documents was sworn before Forget instead of an independent third party.[28] The Interior department wanted the land back, and its counterpart Indian Affairs was willing to oblige.

Deputy minister Smart hadn't been directly involved in the arrangements to secure the surrender of the three western reserves. Nor apparently had he been consulted. These were largely matters between Sifton and McLean. But Smart would have been well aware of how Indian land had become available for settlement and sensed an opportunity. He had seen how relatively easy it was for Indian Affairs to secure the surrender of the three vacant reserves.

Why couldn't the department push for other surrenders, pressuring bands to give up some, if not all, of their reserves, to satisfy the growing white settler demand for farm land? He could use his position as Indian Affairs deputy minister to secretly manipulate the land sales arrangements so that he and a few Liberal friends acquired most of the

First Nations lands. Smart could then put on his other hat, as Interior deputy minister, and use his connections to market the land directly to speculators. It seemed a fail-safe scheme.

What wasn't appreciated, though, was how prairie reserves had become the one constant for First Nations bands by the late 1890s. Cree headman Poundmaker may have complained at the Treaty Six negotiations about "our land" being given back in "little pieces," but Indian commissioner Alexander Morris's assertion that reserves offered "a home of their own" proved prescient.[29]

Past Conservative administrations had interfered in the lives of prairie First Nations in a number of ways, but they had left reserves alone because they wanted bands to remain in place, settled and confined. And over the years, reserves assumed an importance to First Nations that few probably appreciated at treaty time. They provided security of tenure, sanctuary in the face of white encroachment, and above all a sense of identity and community. Reserves were places where First Nations always returned, where families gathered to share stories, where traditional cultural and spiritual practices were observed, and where the dead were buried.[30]

Even though reserves were an inviolate treaty right, they now came under intense and unrelenting attack. Not only had First Nations failed to become self-supporting agriculturalists, according to the Laurier Liberals, but reserves themselves were an impediment to western development and the region's great future. The reasoning was seductively simple: because First Nations didn't make proper use of their reserve land, it should be taken over and occupied by actual settlers, especially if the soil was good. It didn't matter that reserves were only a very small percentage of prairie lands.

The Indian Affairs bureaucracy also believed that reserves were "backward" enclaves — not fulfilling their purpose as a stepping stone to assimilation and civilization. Being a "home of their own" for prairie bands was not good enough. "Experience does not favour the view," Sifton's private secretary observed in April 1898, "that the system [reserves] makes for the advancement of Indians."[31]

Opening up reserves seemed the right thing to do, especially for speculators like Smart, masquerading as public servants. Smart had no qualms about abusing his government position for private benefit, no qualms about making official decisions for criminal gain. Nor did some of Sifton's other political appointees. Their freedom to act with few constraints led to outright graft and corruption. For them, sharing in the spoils of office meant speculating in reserve lands — illegally if necessary, and at Indian expense if possible.

Notes

1. House of Commons, *Debates*, September 22, 1896, p. 1683.
2. *Debates*, September 25, 1896, p. 2030.
3. The new Laurier government was determined to avoid the "principled" mistake of the last Liberal administration — that of Alexander Mackenzie in the mid-1870s — which failed to purge Tory appointees from the civil service. Now, after eighteen years of Tory rule, the Liberal faithful wanted their turn and assailed the new government with hundreds of requests for jobs or other personal favours.
4. *Library and Archives Canada* (*LAC*), Clifford Sifton papers [reel C452], General Correspondence, J.D. McLean to SGIA, July 15, 1896.
5. That McLean was faithfully reliable, to the point of doing whatever was asked of him, was underscored when he made a hurried presentation on behalf of the Six Nations Haudenosaunee Chiefs to visiting British prime minister Stanley Baldwin in his private rail car when the train stopped briefly in the Ottawa station in 1927. *Ottawa Journal*, February 17, 1939.
6. Quoted in Tyler and Wright Research Consultants, "The Alienation of Indian Reserve Lands during the Administration of Sir Wilfrid Laurier, 1896–1911: Pheasant's Rump Reserve #68, Ocean Man #69," unpublished report for the Federation of Saskatchewan Indians, 1978, p. 69.

7. J. English, *The Decline of Politics: The Conservatives and the Party System, 1901–1920* (Oakville: Rock's Mills Press, 2016), p. 17. See also pp. 12–13.

8. The report on the reorganization of Indian Affairs operations in the North-West Territories is found in the Sifton papers as part of a memoranda series. B. Titley, *The Indian Commissioners: Agents of the Canadian State and Indian Policy in Canada's Prairie West, 1873–1832* (Edmonton: University of Alberta Press, 2009), pp. 137–8.

9. Titley, *The Indian Commissioners*, pp. 138–9. The Moosomin *Spectator*, in an editorial headlined "The Slaughter in the Indian Department," charged that "the new minister has gone too far . . . the result in the end will be a loss instead of a gain." Moosomin *Spectator*, May 13, 1897.

10. D.J. Hall, "Clifford Sifton and Canadian Indian Administration, 1896–1905," *Prairie Forum*, v. 2, n. 2, 1977, p. 131.

11. Ibid., p. 147, note 11.

12. *LAC*, RG10, v. 1120, DSGIA letterbooks [reel C9001], J.D. McLean to J.A. Smart, n.d.

13. Ibid., May 10, 1897.

14. Ibid., May 22, 1897.

15. *LAC*, RG15, v. 274, f. 390906, J. McTaggart to T.M. Daly, October 12, 1895.

16. This "majority" question arose during the House of Commons debate on the Indian Act in March 1876. When Hector Langevin, a former Conservative superintendent of General Affairs, sought clarification, Indian Affairs minister David Laird simply replied, "Of course the majority at the meeting." Langevin countered, "There should be a certain proportion of the band present." Laird then assured Langevin that "the Department took good care in their practice not to allow these surrenders unless the Indians were at home at the time." Langevin was still not satisfied and advised the Liberal government that "for the protection of the Indians . . . little as possible [be] left to chance." (*Debates*, March 21, 1876, p. 752.) The matter came up again only a few days later. This time, Langevin put his questions directly to Prime Minister Alexander Mackenzie and wanted to know if "the majority of the band should be required to be present when this

[reserve surrender] was in consideration." Mackenzie vowed, "That is required." (*Debates*, March 30, 1876, pp. 928–9.) Treaty Six later specified that the disposition of reserves could only be done "with their [First Nations] consent first." There was no such clause in Treaty Seven.

17. *LAC*, RG10, v. 3574, f. 197, A.E. Forget to H. Reed, December 29, 1893; H. Reed to A.E. Forget, January 14, 1894; v. 3729, f. 26,137, E.L. Newcombe to H. Reed, November 30, 1894; P. Martin-McGuire, *First Nations Land Surrenders on the Prairies, 1896–1911* (Ottawa: Indian Claims Commission, 1998), pp. xxxii, 20–1, 90.

18. *LAC*, RG10, v. 6663, f. 109A-3-1, part 1, H. Reed to A.M. Burgess, November 8, 1895.

19. Ibid., A.E. Forget to H. Reed, February 3, 1896.

20. Ibid., H. Reed to A.E. Forget, February 8, 1896.

21. Ibid., C. Sifton to H. Reed, January 13, 1897.

22. Ibid., T.O. Davis to C. Sifton, March 31, 1897.

23. A.E. Forget to C. Sifton, April 3, 1897, quoted in Indian Claims Commission, "Young Chipewyan Inquiry," December 1994, p. 17.

24. *LAC*, RG10, v. 6663, f. 109A-3-1, part 1, J.D. McLean to Department of Justice, April 14, 1897.

25. Ibid., R. Cook to C. Sifton, April 17, 1897.

26. Ibid., E.L. Newcombe to J.D. McLean, May 14, 1897.

27. See "James Smith Cree Nation Chakastaypasin IR 98 Inquiry," unpublished Indian Claims Commission Report, March 2005.

28. Martin-McGuire, *First Nations Land Surrenders*, pp. 246–7.

29. P. Erasmus, *Buffalo Days and Nights* (Calgary: Glenbow Museum, 1974), p. 244; A. Morris, *The Treaties of Canada with the Indians of Manitoba and the North-West Territories* (Toronto: Belfords, Clarke and Co., 1880), p. 204.

30. M. Abley, *Conversations with a Dead Man: The Legacy of Duncan Campbell Scott* (Vancouver: Douglas and McIntyre, 2013), p. 140; D.J. Hall, *From Treaties to Reserves: The Federal Government and Native Peoples in Territorial Alberta, 1870–1905* (Montreal and Kingston: McGill Queen's University Press, 2015), p. 136.

31. Hall, "Clifford Sifton and Canadian Indian Administration," p. 145.

Four

SPECULATORS AND BOODLERS

They were crooks. Or as the *Brandon Independence* derisively called them, "speculators and boodlers." What the Manitoba newspaper didn't know in February 1900 was who they were — only that they were said to be an American syndicate that had reached an agreement with the Wilfrid Laurier government to buy the Ocean Man and Pheasant Rump reserves in the Moose Mountain region of present-day southeastern Saskatchewan. That the contiguous reserves hadn't been surrendered by the two Nakoda bands made "the whole affair . . . so mysterious and improbable."

Even more "alarming [and] astonishing" was the price that the syndicate was offering for the 47,000-acre parcel of land. The Interior department had apparently agreed to sell the reserves for only ninety cents per acre when land in the area easily fetched an average of $3 per acre. If the rumour was true and the reserves were to be opened to settlement, then sell the land directly to settlers, the *Independence* insisted. "There is no reason," the paper thundered, "why third parties should be enriched at the nation's expense."[1]

But that's exactly what happened. Three federal civil servants — James Smart, Frank Pedley, and William White — concocted a scheme to secretly acquire the two reserves and then sell the lands to American speculators for a handsome profit. They were able to get away with it, not simply because of their positions, but because the interests and well-being of two Nakoda bands didn't matter to the Department of Indian Affairs. Treaty rights were sacrificed on the altar of greed.

⋖⋖⋗⋗

James Smart, the new deputy minister for Interior and Indian Affairs, was often away from Ottawa on government business. Starting in the spring of 1897, he travelled throughout North America and to western Europe — places like Montreal, Chicago, New York, and London — promoting Canadian immigration and settlement. It was appealing work, certainly far better than being desk-bound and file-laden in the capital.

Smart seemed bored in his new job as a bureaucrat and not willing to put in the work overseeing two departments unless there was something in it for him. He was also restless, jumping from idea to idea, unable to fully commit to anything.

That's probably why he headed off for many weeks at a time, doing what he liked best. As a senior representative of the Liberal government, Smart enjoyed a travel budget that matched the importance of his mission. It was a good gig, making connections at meetings or

Deputy minister of the Interior and Indian Affairs James Smart sought to benefit from his dual position, including speculating in surrendered First Nations lands. (Library and Archives Canada)

promotional fairs, talking up western Canada as the land of opportunity. He also realized that there was money to be made from Canada's settlement boom and that he could use his position to advantage.

Smart was a major player in an immigration scheme that bilked the Canadian government of tens of thousands of dollars. In September 1899, Interior and Indian Affairs minister Clifford Sifton sent his deputy to London to finalize a contract with the North Atlantic Trading Company (NATC). W.T.R. Preston, Canada's inspector of emigration for Europe, had reached a tentative deal with the company to advertise "the last best West" in Scandinavia and western Europe.

It's not known whether Smart and Preston had worked out their plan before the deputy minister was dispatched to London. But the pair quickly concocted an agreement with the NATC that made them primary beneficiaries. Indeed, Smart, Preston and a few other Liberal associates likely constituted the NATC syndicate. It'll never be known because of the secrecy of the deal and the destruction of records. And there was no formal contract — just an exchange of letters between the company and Preston, signing on behalf of the Canadian government.

The NATC soon began claiming bonuses for all immigrants landed in Canada, even if the immigrants hadn't actually been recruited by the company. It also collected bonuses for children, even though anyone under twelve wasn't intended to be part of the bonus plan. The company essentially wanted to be paid "on nothing more than a head count."[2]

There was also no financial accounting of what the company supposedly spent on promotion, only what it apparently cost to run its London office. The NATC regularly invoiced the immigration branch, and on the recommendation of Smart and Preston, cheques were issued. Where the money went remains a mystery, but it was a substantial sum. The Laurier government paid $367,246 to the NATC for 70,953 immigrants.[3]

Smart also speculated in prairie lands. He could have parlayed his insider position into a silent partnership in a colonization company, as did several other Liberal government officials. But there was greater opportunity trading in First Nations lands. Smart could sanction the surrender of a reserve, quietly acquire it, and then flip the land to American investors for a tidy sum.

He couldn't do it alone, though. He needed connections and a network to make the plan work and avoid possible complications that might lead to uncomfortable questions.

Smart recruited two Liberal friends who, like him, had been appointed by Sifton. One was William J. White, inspector of United States immigration agencies, the other Frank Pedley, the superintendent of immigration. Together, the trio pulled off the biggest grab of Indian reserve land in Canadian history.

William (Will) White was an old Sifton business associate from Brandon — and a natural partner for Smart's scam. Born in Ontario in 1853, White was editing the Exeter newspaper when another local young man, Tom Greenway, the future Liberal premier of Manitoba, convinced him to seek his fortune in the booming West. White settled in Brandon in 1882 and started the weekly *Sun* the same year. The newspaper prospered and was soon incorporated as the Brandon Sun Printing and Publishing Company. Investors included Sifton and Smart. The *Sun* served as a Liberal party organ in the province, and it was said that Sifton wrote many of the editorials. In 1897, White sold the newspaper to a Sifton-backed press consortium.

But White wasn't done in the "news" business. Since Confederation, Canada had lost a steady stream of people to the United States. Sifton now wanted to reverse that flow and people the Canadian prairies with settlers from the American Midwest. He relocated the Canadian immigration office from Chicago to St. Paul, Minnesota, and dramatically increased the number of full-time immigration agents, and especially the commissioned sub-agents, to several hundred.

White, in his new capacity as inspector of United States immigration agencies, was to run the propaganda campaign. It was his job to prepare publicity materials, including pamphlets and lantern slides, that would convince Americans that western Canada was a perfect place to settle.[4] White consequently oversaw a network of dominion agents, and these connections would be exploited by the three co-conspirators.

Frank Pedley, on the other hand, was one of the few patronage appointees to the Interior department who wasn't a colleague of Sifton at the time he became superintendent of immigration. Born in Newfoundland in 1858, Pedley was the son of a Congregationalist minister; three of his six brothers were also ministers. Eschewing religion for law, he trained at Toronto's Osgoode Hall and then ran a practice in the city for the better part of the 1890s, first on his own and then in partnership with Alban Cartwright Bedford-Jones. Pedley was a Liberal stalwart and a frequent speaker at party events, in addition to serving as president of the Toronto Young Men's Liberal Association.

Given his high regard within the party, it's surprising he never ran as a candidate. In July 1897, Pedley's name was put forward as a possible candidate for a job with the new Laurier government. After being personally interviewed by Sifton in Ottawa, he was appointed the first superintendent of immigration.[5]

Pedley was responsible for Canada's immigration program and answerable to Smart. The pair were in constant communication and often on the road together. But even though Smart may have had greater authority, Pedley was more skilled and often served as a fixer. He was once dispatched, for example, to quell a Doukhobor protest march in the Yorkton area.

Pedley had likely been a participant in the NATC boondoggle. There's no way that the superintendent of immigration wouldn't have known about the scheme, and he was probably compensated for his acquiescence.

Smart set the plan in motion in early November 1898 while on an inspection tour of southeastern Assiniboia (present-day southeastern Saskatchewan) on the lookout for a place to settle several hundred Galician immigrants who had recently arrived in the West. From his home in Brandon, he took the train to Moosomin and then travelled by wagon south to Moose Mountain district. Here he visited district farms and the White Bear reserve on the east side of the mountain and Pheasant Rump and Ocean Man on the west side.

On November 12, Smart advised Sifton that he had found "an excellent location for Galicians." According to the plan appended to his letter, Smart recommended that the Pheasant Rump and Ocean Man bands be placed on the White Bear reserve and that their former 60,000 acres be opened to settlement. "It seems ridiculous," he griped, "to lock up such a splendid piece of land for so very few people."[6]

Taken at face value, Smart's proposal didn't add up when measured against the situation on the ground. The two Nakoda bands, Pheasant Rump and Ocean Man, entered Treaty Four in 1875 and had their reserves surveyed, side-by-side, six years later.[7] The Nakoda had little affinity with the White Bear reserve, a Cree-Saulteaux band, some fifteen miles away on the other side of Moose Mountain, whose partially wooded land was better suited to a more traditional hunting and gathering lifestyle.

While the White Bear people pursued a more traditional livelihood into the new century, agriculture on the Pheasant Rump and Ocean Man lands was a stellar success, in part because of the first-class soil but also because of the adoption of machinery and the careful tending of cattle. Indian Affairs inspector Alexander McGibbon enthused that the Nakoda were "nearer the point of . . . supporting themselves than anyone I have yet visited."[8]

Department secretary J.D. McLean was equally impressed, but in a backhanded way. In November 1898, the same month that Smart visited the reserves, McLean complained that the "per capita amount of assistance given to White Bear's is much larger" and that it would be "better" if the band followed the Nakoda lead and "extend their agricultural . . . operations."[9] The two Nakoda bands should consequently have been left in place — "contented and comfortable," in the words of McGibbon.[10]

Moving them to the White Bear reserve was nonsensical, if not deleterious. All their hard work making a new life for themselves as agriculturalists, something that had been elusive for many bands, would be undone. There was plenty of land elsewhere in the territories to accommodate the 500 Galician families.

Once back in Ottawa in early December 1898, Smart presented a different explanation for pursuing the amalgamation of the three Moose Mountain reserves. In a memorandum to McLean, he instructed the

Indian Affairs secretary to "take immediate steps to see upon what terms the two Indian reserves . . . can revert to the Government for use of the Department of the Interior." Smart suggested it would be "much more convenient" if the three bands were brought together on the White Bear reserve.[11]

It was a curious intervention by the deputy minister. Smart had never shown any interest in the administration of prairie reserves. His ignorance in such matters was underscored by his mistaken belief that the Laurier government could simply negotiate "terms" for acquiring the two reserves.

Samuel Bray, head of the Indian Affairs surveys branch, reported favourably on proposed amalgamation — on the understanding that the surrender provisions of the Indian Act had to be followed and that the White Bear band agreed to take in the Pheasant Rump and Ocean Man people. The two Nakoda bands, Bray maintained, could easily be accommodated at White Bear because of the decline in reserve population since the band entered treaty. In other words, White Bear had more land than it needed.

Bray's justification of Smart's proposal went against the treaty agreement. Reserve size was determined by the band population at time of survey. Elected and government officials often used this groundless "surplus" land argument to call for reserve surrenders. Nor did the larger interests of the Nakoda bands come into consideration.

McLean didn't question the wisdom of relocating the two bands, let alone wonder why they would willingly abandon their successful farming operations and give up their land. He simply reinforced Bray's reminder that a surrender vote was necessary — the reserves "belong to them . . . they might be induced to surrender for a fixed sum."

Smart was all for that. "Have steps taken," he urged. "This ought to be attended to at once."[12]

It fell to Indian commissioner David Laird to determine what it would take for the Pheasant Rump and Ocean Man bands to walk away from their successful farming operations and move in with the White Bear band. Laird, a Liberal journalist from Prince Edward Island and former cabinet minister in the Alexander Mackenzie government, had served as commissioner almost a quarter century earlier. He hated the duties, especially dealing with First Nations, and resigned after only a few years on the job. His sole achievement as commissioner was the Treaty Seven agreement with the Blackfoot in 1877.

Laird returned to Charlottetown to edit the *Patriot* newspaper but hoped for better fortune when the Laurier Liberals were elected in 1896. His preferred patronage plum was the lieutenant governorship of the North-West Territories, but when Interior minister Sifton gave the vice-regal position to Indian commissioner Amédée Forget in 1898, Laird was named commissioner as a consolation prize.

Laird was once described as "sober, pious, high-minded, energetic, and capable . . . act[ing] always with the conviction that he was on the side of right and progress."[13] What mattered to Sifton was that he was a safe choice as Indian commissioner, especially since Ottawa had already taken steps to limit the role and responsibilities of the Indian Affairs office in Winnipeg.

Laird would grumble about his restricted duties, but like his new political masters, he believed that prairie settlement trumped treaty rights. He shared the view that bands had excess reserve land and that these acres should be turned over to the Interior department.[14] The surrender mechanism, though, had to be respected. "The Indians should not be deprived of their occupancy rights," he observed during his 1905 presidential address to the Historical and Scientific Society of Manitoba, "without compensation and their formal consent."[15]

Just days before Christmas 1898, Laird reported to Ottawa that the Pheasant Rump and Ocean Man bands were open — "favourable" was the word he used — to the department offer.[16] That news in itself might seem suspect, but what was more suspicious was the additional information that Henry R. Halpin, the farmer for the Moose Mountain agency, had already discussed the matter with the two bands even before Laird asked him to ascertain their position.

In November, Halpin had apparently met with Smart in Winnipeg after the deputy minister had visited the Moose Mountain reserves and come up with his plan. The Moosomin *Spectator* claimed at the time that the farm instructor had been to the city on Indian department business and returned home with a "satisfied smile."[17] Perhaps he had agreed to do a favour for Smart. It would certainly explain why Halpin managed to hang on to his position, even though he was a known drinker who fudged his department accounts.[18]

McLean, given his boss's orders, was more interested in knowing exactly what the two Nakoda bands wanted for their reserves and pressed Laird to set the terms. Halpin held a "very satisfactory" meeting with the bands in mid-January 1899 and reported that, in exchange for their lands, they wanted an annual cash payment and assistance in resuming their farming efforts at White Bear. The agency farmer downplayed the resistance of older members, suggesting that they could be forced to go along with the surrender.[19]

Laird forwarded Halpin's report to McLean at the end of the month, adding that the land of the two reserves was at least worth "$1.00 per acre en bloc." A lower price, the Indian commissioner warned, would "soon be noised abroad."[20]

Smart didn't ask about the price the Pheasant Rump and Ocean Man bands wanted for their lands until six months later. He had been busy plotting. At some point, Smart spoke to Will White about getting their hands on the two Moose Mountain reserves — probably when the pair were travelling together on government business in the United States in late 1898. Frank Pedley was likely brought into the scheme in Ottawa over the winter.

Smart's June 1899 query about the price of the Indian lands — and his insistence before he even got a reply that the land should be worth no more than $1 per acre — signalled that the trio were finally in a position to act. Something was afoot. Why else would Pedley make the unusual request that Wilbur Van Horn Bennett, the Canadian immigration agent in Omaha, Nebraska, come to the capital for a meeting later that summer? And when Bennett couldn't travel to Ottawa, why did Pedley make a special trip to see him later that fall?

Wilbur Bennett was the linchpin in the Moose Mountain land deal. Once a small-time real estate operator in Omaha, Bennett had supplemented his income by flogging Canadian Pacific Railway lands to Nebraska clients. His success attracted the attention of the Interior department when it wanted to amplify its operations in the United States, and Bennett was hired as a commissioned Canadian immigration agent in March 1897. He was promoted, on the recommendation of Smart and White, to a full-time salaried agent by the end of the year.

Bennett had a well-earned reputation as one of the most adept, well-connected agents in the American Midwest, a canny salesman and shameless promoter who counted influential business figures among his close friends. If someone wanted to find buyers or settlers for Canadian lands, Bennett was the one who could arrange the deal. He was so good at it that the Canadian Pacific Railway secretly retained his services, even though such work conflicted with his official government duties.[21] Smart, White, and Pedley wanted to work with him too.

In late September 1899, Pedley embarked on a trip to western Canada as part of his immigration work. Despite the demands of his job, he found time to visit the Moose Mountain reserves — probably to see first-hand the lands that Smart had been touting. Pedley then slipped across the border to confer with Wilbur Bennett in the immigration agent's Omaha office.

By early November, Bennett was in Canada, travelling with Wes Speers, a general colonization agent, at the request of the Immigration branch. He was there to familiarize himself with several prospective settlement areas and then report directly to Ottawa. Like Pedley, Bennett included the Moose Mountain reserves on his western itinerary. He then made a quick trip to Ottawa and was back in Omaha before month's end.[22] It was time to put the scheme into play.

An offer letter, addressed to Sifton, arrived in Ottawa before the end of the year. It came with a personal endorsement by Wilbur Bennett, appended as a covering note. Two Omaha men — George F. West, an employee of the Chicago and Northwestern Railway and coincidentally Bennett's brother-in-law, and Joseph G. Armstrong, a well-to-do banker — wanted to buy the Pheasant Rump and Ocean Man reserves. They said they represented "a number of gentlemen" who wished to pursue "a scheme of settlement."

What they had in mind was purchasing the 47,000 acres of the two Nakoda reserves for ninety cents per acre, in addition to providing another $4,000 for moving expenses to the White Bear reserve. The opportunity to purchase the land had fallen into their lap. A "gentleman," never identified in the letter, had recently met with the two Nakoda bands during a recent land-hunting trip to the Assiniboia district and was told that "they were desirous of moving to the Eastern Reserve . . . they were quite willing to move at any time."

In exchange for the reserve land, said to be "of a mixed character," West and Armstrong promised to place a minimum of twenty-five settlers on the entire parcel. If the government acted quickly, two settlers could be on the land by the spring of 1900.[23]

The West and Armstrong "offer" was handled in the first instance by J.A.J. McKenna, Sifton's private secretary, before being passed to Indian Affairs secretary J.D. McLean. It should have raised eyebrows.

Even though co-conspirator White had reviewed the letter before it was mailed, the five-page, typewritten offer was riddled with errors, hand corrections, and scribbled additions. That it would be sent was cocky. That Bennett had secretly forged Armstrong's signature on the document smacked of hubris.

Then there was the offer itself. The suggestion that the soil varied in quality contradicted Smart's earlier assertion that it was "a splendid piece of land." Smart had also complained that "so very few people" lived on the two reserves, and yet the Nebraska offer was only going to put twenty-five settlers on 47,000 acres — that was 1,880 acres per settler, the equivalent of 1,400 football fields!

Ninety cents per acre was also an unrealistically low price, especially given the land boom in the Assiniboia district. Most incredible, though, was the self-possessed assertion — attributed to some unknown gentleman — that the Pheasant Rump and Ocean Man bands were so anxious and ready to move that they were willing to surrender their home reserves for an uncertain future.

McLean asked long-serving Indian Affairs surveyor Archibald W. Ponton to review and comment on the Nebraska proposal. Ponton offered no substantive objections, but recommended that the Nebraska syndicate be asked to put more settlers on the land and pay for the subdividing of the reserves.

He also cautioned that it might be difficult to secure a surrender unless the department was willing to "grant any reasonable demands made by the Indians." Or put another way, inducements "would lead to an early settlement of the matter."[24] McKenna agreed with Ponton's suggestions, adding only that the Nebraska men be asked to put down a deposit of $1,000 as "an evidence of good faith."[25]

That "good faith" didn't extend to the Pheasant Rump and Ocean Man bands. At no point did Ponton, McKenna, or any other government official question whether the proposal was worth considering. Nor did they consider the Crown's treaty relationship with the Nakoda, or whether any of the agricultural items, to be offered during the surrender meeting, were actually part of Canada's obligations to the bands. They expected the Nakoda to give up one treaty right (their reserves) to secure access to another treaty right (agricultural assistance).

With the tacit acceptance of the Nebraska offer, Smart, in his capacity as deputy minister of Indian Affairs, called for the surrender of the Pheasant Rump and Ocean Man reserves in early February 1900. But Laird, whose views were required on the sale price being proposed, was away from his Winnipeg office for several weeks on department business. This delay coincided with a query from George West, one of the Nebraska letter writers, who innocently asked Sifton, "We are anxious to know if the proposition . . . will be accepted."[26]

Smart was also not pleased with the pace of things, and with West's letter in hand he commanded McLean, "Push this."[27]

He was upset, if not angry, when Laird finally responded that the Nebraska syndicate was paying too little and putting too few settlers on the land. Most disquieting, though, was the Indian commissioner's suggestion to "open the land for sale to actual settlers, whether Canadian or U.S. immigrants" instead of making it "possible for Messrs. West and Armstrong to hold back . . . the land for speculative purposes."[28] McLean tried to blunt Laird's criticism of the proposed sale price of the two reserves by pointing out to him that the Nebraska syndicate was prepared to purchase all of the land at once.

Smart, meanwhile, asked homestead inspector W.B. Underhill, based in Melita, Manitoba, for an "independent" opinion of the quality of the reserve lands. The Liberal patronage appointee didn't disappoint his political master. Underhill insisted that the price per acre was justified, all the while praising the syndicate and its offer.[29]

Smart also realized that Laird had to be neutralized and made a special trip to Winnipeg on government business in early April 1900. Laird got the message and thereafter posed no threat to Smart's plan. Nor did senior Indian Affairs officials in Ottawa. They understood that the deputy minister would brook no opposition to the surrender and sale of the two Nakoda reserves, so they did what was expected of them, without a word of protest.

Smart, Pedley and White were counting on keeping the sale of the two Moose Mountain reserves confidential until the deal with the

William White, inspector of United States immigration agencies, used his connections to market surrendered reserve land and pocket the proceeds. (Library and Archives Canada)

Nebraska syndicate was closed. Someone talked, though, and a few Manitoba newspapers reported the story in the late winter of 1900. That got the attention of Nicholas Flood Davin, the Conservative Member of Parliament for Assiniboia West, and he formally submitted several questions to the minister of Indian Affairs in mid-March 1900. The government response was at best vague, only confirming that the sale of the Pheasant Rump and Ocean Man reserves was under consideration, but that no buyer or acreage price had been settled upon.[30]

This unwanted attention prompted Smart to ask in late April what, if anything, had been done to secure the surrender of the two reserves. When Laird replied that he was still awaiting instructions in keeping with the provisions of the Indian Act, Smart jotted "Let Stand" on the letter.[31]

This pause didn't mean that the deputy minister and his partners had been spooked by the publicity. Rather, they sought to take advantage of another opportunity to acquire even more Indian land for speculative purposes.

Even though the Chakastaypasin reserve had been surrendered to the Crown in July 1897, the Indian Affairs department dithered for more than a year and a half before deciding to market the lands to individual buyers through a dominion lands agent.

These sales were to be governed by the 1888 Land Regulations (more properly known as the Regulations for the Disposal of Surrendered Indian Lands), which set out the amount of land that could be secured by a single buyer, the payment schedule (including interest), the residency period on the land, and required improvements (such as breaking land and building a shelter). These regulations were meant to discourage speculation. No single person or syndicate could amass or control large chunks of former reserve land.

Then, in the spring of 1899, the Prince Albert Board of Trade put forward another option for the former reserve — setting it aside for a group of Hungarian settlers looking for land in the region. Negotiations with Indian Affairs were personally handled by T.O. Davis, the recently elected Liberal MP for the sprawling Saskatchewan riding, and somewhat surprisingly the agent for Hungarian colonists.

Davis owed his seat to Prime Minister Laurier and Sifton. In the June 1896 general election, Laurier had run in Quebec East and Saskatchewan — in those days it was possible to run in more than one constituency in the same election. Laurier won both seats and chose to represent his home riding. That left the Saskatchewan seat vacant. The likely Liberal candidate for the December 1896 by-election was Davis, who was personally endorsed by Laurier.

Davis was despised by the Prince Albert Liberal organization for "his rough and ready politics," however, and Sifton had to dispatch his older brother, Arthur, to Prince Albert in an effort to bring the local Liberals to heel. Davis won, but his only opponent, the Independent Liberal J.R. McPhail, charged that Davis had "bought his seat" and threatened to overturn the result in court. Sifton had to use all of his authority and influence to quash the local Liberal revolt — even though Davis didn't deny his corrupt practices in private correspondence with the minister.[32]

Davis remained ever thankful of Sifton's support, even naming one of his sons Clifford Sifton Davis. The Saskatchewan MP would be called to the Senate in September 1904.

Davis, like many other Anglo-Canadians who had settled in Prince Albert in the early 1880s, had speculated in land in and around the community. It wasn't until the immigration boom of the late 1890s, though, that the great hopes for the Prince Albert district seemed about to be realized. Davis expected to use his new status as a member of the Laurier government to his advantage, and was forever making demands. At one point, Sifton quipped in frustration, "I thought T.O. [Davis] had asked for everything he has seen around this office, but apparently not."[33]

Davis had his eye on the abandoned Chakastaypasin reserve, and had even asked Sifton in March 1897 when it was going to be opened to settlement. Now, in June 1899, he met with Indian Affairs secretary McLean to hammer out a deal for the land on behalf of his Hungarian clients. The self-important Davis pushed for a quick resolution of the matter. An August 1899 government order sanctioned the sale of the land for only $1.50 per acre, with the stipulation that one settler had to be placed on each section of land (twenty-four settlers in total). Davis would have made a small windfall.

By the spring of 1900, though, the Hungarian settlers had never materialized, and Davis had failed to provide the down payment for the land. Anxious to get his hands on at least some of the Chakastaypasin reserve, Davis called for the land to be put up for sale, in keeping with the initial plan of Indian Affairs.[34]

That's when Smart pounced. Knowing that the Davis deal was dead, the deputy minister alerted Pedley and White, and together they hatched a new plan. A clandestine meeting was arranged in St. Paul, Minnesota, between White and Wilbur Bennett, the Omaha immigration agent. They were joined by N. Bartholomew, the Canadian immigration sub-agent from Des Moines, Iowa — and, more importantly, one of Bennett's men.

The upshot of this meeting was a letter to Smart, sent by J.W. Mitchell and John C. Neeley of Council Bluffs, Iowa, on April 28, 1900. The pair claimed to represent "a large number of well-to-do farmers in Iowa and bordering states" who were seeking to establish a colony on the former

Frank Pedley, superintendent of immigration, also engaged in illegal activity. He later replaced James Smart as deputy minister of Indian Affairs.
(Library and Archives Canada)

Chakastaypasin reserve.[35] They proposed a set of terms identical to those reached by Davis and Indian Affairs for the sale of the reserve lands.

Reading between the lines, it was clearly evident that someone had tipped off Mitchell and Neeley that Davis couldn't honour his agreement and gave the pair a copy of the order-in-council authorizing the sale. What wasn't so apparent, though, was that the letter, including the signatures of Mitchell and Neeley, was likely prepared in the Omaha office of Wilbur Bennett, directly across the Missouri River from Council Bluffs.

The Iowa offer reached Indian Affairs just as W.A. Orr, head of the Lands branch, was preparing to sell the Chakastaypasin lands in individual quarter-section parcels. He suggested that the proposal be turned down. Smart, however, put the matter on hold for the time being, probably to Davis's consternation.

Nothing was done about the fate of the two Nakoda reserves or the Chakastaypasin reserve through the late summer and fall of 1900 while the Liberal government concentrated its efforts on securing re-election that November. Manitoba was a fiercely contested battleground. Smart and other Liberal appointees were called home for the local campaign.

Sifton's provincial foe in the national election was Robert Rogers, a powerful cabinet minister and "dominant star in the Manitoba Conservative galaxy." Once described as his party's "organizing mastermind," Rogers was "never in his true element unless an election impended." He was a skilled manipulator "to whom the higher art of statecraft was quite unknown."[36] Rogers exploited local disgruntlement over federal policies, effectively blaming Sifton for holding back Manitoba.

Sifton, in turn, did everything necessary to retain his Brandon constituency, such as hiring a small team including J. Obed Smith and R.E.A. Leech to do "special work." "You have to get down into the same place where the other people are," he'd counselled the year before, "and fight."[37]

The Liberals won a larger national majority, thanks in part to a strong showing in the North-West Territories and British Columbia. Manitoba, though, was effectively a draw —the Liberals won four seats (including Sifton's) and the Conservatives, three. Smith and Leech weren't forgotten: the first was named Winnipeg immigration commissioner, the other a census officer for the 1901 enumeration.[38]

Secure in their government positions, Smart and his two partners lost no time resurrecting the two bogus land schemes. In a forged letter dated November 28, 1900, Mitchell and Neeley asked whether the Indian Affairs department had reached a decision about their offer to buy the Chakastaypasin reserve. A second letter, dated only two days later, inquired about the two Moose Mountain reserves and the status of the Nebraska proposal.

This time, though, both letters were addressed to Smart instead of Sifton and gave their return address as Omaha.[39] They even appeared to have been prepared on the same office paper using the same typewriter.

Smart decided to deal first with the Pheasant Rump and Ocean Man reserves. In early December 1900, he instructed Laird to negotiate directly with the Nebraska syndicate, encouraging him to request a larger cash outlay for the transfer of the two bands to the White Bear reserve. Smart was attempting to distance himself from any eventual sale agreement — as if his unusual interest in the matter hadn't already raised suspicions. At least he could count on Laird to finalize the sale terms in his favour, especially after his little tête-à-tête with the Indian commissioner in Winnipeg earlier that year.

Laird dutifully contacted George West of the Nebraska group and asked for a greater amount for resettling the two bands, as well as a higher price per acre for the two reserves. West balked at paying more than $1 per acre for the land, but eventually agreed to provide $4,080 for the resettlement of the bands once they agreed to give up their reserve land. These inducements, in advance of a surrender vote, violated the Indian Act.

By way of a memorandum on March 5, 1901, Smart sought the approval of Sifton, the Indian Affairs minister, to proceed with a surrender meeting. He insisted that the Pheasant Rump and Ocean

Man bands aspired to move to the White Bear reserve — incorrectly identifying them as Cree — and that the mixed quality of the land justified the price to be paid by the Nebraska group.

Across the bottom of the memo below his signature, Smart wrote, "This will be a splendid arrangement . . . for the Indians."[40]

The recommendation couldn't have come across Sifton's desk at a more demanding, stressful time. He had spent more than two years developing and implementing the Laurier government's policies for the Yukon — including posting the North-West Mounted Police at the summits of the Chilkoot and White passes to bring some order to the chaotic gold rush, introducing new mining regulations, and establishing the district as a separate territory. It was extra work, piled on top of his other Interior and Indian Affairs duties, and Sifton was worn out. "I would as soon spend my life in a treadmill," he confided to a fellow Manitoba Liberal, "as carrying the load of work I have to do now."[41]

Sifton was also being held personally responsible for all that had gone wrong with the administration of the new territory, including the revelation that officials were not only speculating in gold claims, but using their government positions to leverage bribes. His most vociferous critic was Governor General Lord Minto, who penned an incendiary memo after a trip to Dawson City in August 1900: "My verdict is — criminal administration by the Min. of the Interior."[42]

These distractions meant that the minister relied on Smart's advice about the Pheasant Rump and Ocean Man reserves. He penned his approval, and the surrender documents were sent immediately to Laird, including a letter granting authority to take the surrenders.

David Laird had never handled a surrender meeting before. If his account is to be believed, it was a rather simple and straightforward process. He met with the bands on March 20, and the next afternoon, the Pheasant Rump and Ocean Man representatives agreed to surrender their reserves, and then, together with the White Bear band, they

Indian commissioner David Laird acted on behalf of the Laurier government at several reserve surrender meetings. (Library and Archives Canada)

all signed an amalgamation agreement. It was all done in violation of the Indian Act.

Laird provided no formal account of who attended the meeting, what was discussed, or how the vote proceeded. His only comment was that the Nakoda bands wanted their graveyards protected. He later added in his annual department report that "the move is a good one."[43]

Xavier James McArthur, the Nakoda interpreter, provided a much different account of the meeting. He recounted how Laird offered to buy the two reserves the first day, holding out the prospect of cash for the bands' consent. The Ocean Man group agreed to the surrender, but the Pheasant Rump men repeatedly said no.

On the fourth day, an irate Laird brusquely ended negotiations with the threat that the North-West Mounted Police would be called to forcibly take the band to the White Bear reserve. McArthur claimed that the Pheasant Rump band never agreed to a surrender, but fearful for their future, they reluctantly abandoned their reserve.[44]

With the completed surrender documents in hand, Smart arranged for the submission of an order-in-council, dated April 3, 1901, and endorsed by Sifton, that confirmed both the reserve surrenders and the sales agreement with the Nebraska syndicate. All that was needed was cabinet approval and the Governor General's signature.

Smart also took it upon himself — again, uncharacteristically — to impress upon department surveyor J. Lestock Reid that the subdivision of the two Nakoda reserves was to be completed as soon as the field season would allow. Reid was in Winnipeg by the end of the month, ready to proceed to Moose Mountain.

That left one other outstanding matter — flipping the surrendered land for a sizeable profit. Canadian immigration agent Wilbur Bennett had forged the name of Joseph G. Armstrong, the well-off Omaha banker, on all correspondence with the Canadian government. Now, Bennett told Armstrong about a wonderful opportunity to buy 47,000 acres of prime agricultural land north of the border.

Little did Armstrong know that the difference between the price already agreed upon with the government and what he would be asked to pay would be pocketed by the three co-conspirators and their accomplices. To sweeten the deal, Bennett also promised Armstrong a steady stream of immigrant farmers for the land.[45]

In late April, Armstrong travelled north to the Canadian border, where he was met by Speers, the colonization agent, and taken to see the Moose Mountain reserves. The pair then continued on to the Leland Hotel in Winnipeg, where another guest, surveyor Reid, confirmed that the bands had surrendered the reserves and that he was about to measure the land into quarter-sections. Armstrong was won over, but he didn't want to invest in the land on his own and brought in some partners — two business friends from Souris, Manitoba, who were prominent Conservatives.

Smart's carefully orchestrated scheme began to unravel. The pending sale of the two reserves was leaked to the local paper, the Souris *Plaindealer*, and quickly picked up by other Manitoba newspapers in early May 1901.[46] Local Liberals were incredulous. If the Laurier government was going to dispose of the reserve land, then Liberals — not Conservatives, let alone an American — were entitled to it, especially

Liberals who were Sifton's constituents and had just helped the minister win re-election.

A two-person delegation hurriedly set off for Ottawa to see Sifton about their egregious treatment — and in their words, "claim first consideration" as their right as Liberals.[47] On the same train was one of Armstrong's Souris partners, headed to Ottawa to settle on a price for the two reserves. It's amazing there were no fisticuffs once the Souris men discovered their competing interest in the land. What made things worse for Smart was that the government order authorizing the sale to the Nebraska syndicate hadn't yet been approved.

The Souris delegation didn't get any satisfaction from Sifton, who insisted that the two men should really be meeting with his deputy. Smart was equally coy, confiding that the sales arrangement was about to be finalized, but refusing to divulge any of the terms. Returning to Souris in a huff, the pair didn't give up, submitting their own application for the purchase of the Moose Mountain reserves.

And that wasn't the only offer. Other Liberal faithful in Manitoba heard about the opportunity and began making inquiries. The Smart group was losing control of the situation.

At the end of May 1901, the order-in-council authorizing the sale was quietly withdrawn. A subsequent Winnipeg newspaper report, submitted anonymously, said that the Armstrong deal had collapsed and that the land in question was to be made available for homesteading.

What got lost in this kerfuffle over the sale of the land was that the Pheasant Rump and Ocean Man bands had moved to the White Bear reserve in the spring of 1901. The cancellation of the sales agreement seemed to put the relocation in limbo. Commissioner Laird wondered who was now going to pay the promised compensation, while Secretary McLean wondered if the bands should return to their reserves.[48]

Smart had no intention of either opening the Nakoda reserves to homesteading or allowing the two bands to go back to their former homes. In July 1901, Smart directed the Indian Affairs office in Winnipeg to conduct a valuation of the lands so that they might be sold by public auction. The task fell to J.B. Lash, Laird's secretary, who was confronted by members of the Pheasant Rump and Ocean Man bands who felt betrayed and angry over the failure to secure lumber and other supplies as part of the relocation agreement.

Laird was also perturbed and suggested that the right thing to do was to provide a cash advance, and the sale of the lands would be carried out at a later date. Smart replied that he couldn't find any department funds for this purpose. Instead, he insisted that surveyor Reid's delayed subdivision of the reserves be completed as soon as possible.

It was only after the deputy minister received Reid's survey notes and Lash's valuation that he approved money for the bands. In the meantime, a new order-in-council accepting the surrenders was signed by the Governor General on September 28, 1901. The two reserves were to be sold "in such a manner as may be considered in the best interests of the Indians."[49]

Smart played his hand in early October. He announced that the sales regulations for surrendered reserves were to be set aside in favour of marketing the land by tender. He also oversaw the wording of the sales poster, such that prospector bidders weren't provided with any information about the land and had to submit individual tenders for the 308 full and partial quarter-sections. Each tender had to be accompanied by 5 percent (cash or cheque) of the bid amount.

These conditions were designed to discourage people from bidding. So was the distribution of the sale poster in the third week of October. It left little time for interested parties to meet the November 15 tender deadline — and only if they knew about it.

Advertising was deliberately limited in Assiniboia so that local settlers, who knew the value of the land, were shut out of the sale. Some of the local Liberals disqualified themselves by submitting a single application for a block of reserve land and then expecting Sifton to use his influence to override the tender provisions.[50]

Seven days before the tender deadline, Smart, Pedley and White secretly started work on their own bids for the Pheasant Rump and

Ocean Man lands. They struck an agreement with Pedley's former law partner A.C. Bedford-Jones to submit tenders on their behalf, though Bedford-Jones would not use his own name on the bids. To ensure that no one could link the trio to the bids, three other Toronto lawyers — R.B. Beaumont, J.W. Marsh, and E.C. Mackenzie — would have their signatures forged on the documents.

The tenders were typed on government stationery in Pedley's Ottawa office over several nights. Bids were crafted for each quarter-section based on the otherwise confidential land assessment information gathered by surveyors Reid and Lash. The completed forms were sent to Bedford-Jones at his Canada Permanent Building office, where he signed and dated them, appended the deposits, and then sorted them by name into three bundles before mailing them to Ottawa.[51]

Smart, Pedley, and White must have been pleased with their handiwork, even smug about how all their scheming was about to pay dividends. Not only were they about to commit fraud, they were also about to defy the Indian Act, which forbade department employees from buying any land that had been surrendered by a band.

This prohibition was part of the original Indian Act, passed in April 1876 by the Alexander Mackenzie government, and remained in force through amendments to the act. Smart might have insisted that he wasn't actually the "agent for the sale of Indian lands," as specified in the legislation, but he was the one who decided how the Moose Mountain reserves were to be marketed and how the sale was to be advertised and where. If caught, Smart faced the loss of his job and a fine. His land purchase would also be voided.

Secretary McLean and Lands branch chief Orr opened the tenders together. It was the first time that former Indian land had been put up for sale in such a manner, and the results were nothing short of remarkable. Three Toronto lawyers, who likely had never travelled to western Canada and probably couldn't even locate Moose Mountain on a map, successfully bid for 298 of the 308 quarter-sections. They secured 45,000 acres (about seventy square miles) for only $1.23 per acre. The average price for prairie lands that year was $3.36 per acre.[52]

Bedford-Jones, acting on behalf of Smart, Pedley, and White, handled the sale of the Moose Mountain quarter-sections. He had the three lawyers whose names had been forged on the tenders conveniently assign control of their lands to him. He then entered into negotiations with Alfred S. Porter and Eugene S. Case, both of Minneapolis, Minnesota, who agreed in April 1902 to buy the 45,000 acres for $112,500 (about $2.50 per acre, more than double the tender amount).[53]

These American buyers had been found through White's cross-border connections. He had put the word out about the availability of the land among his many agents operating in the United States — and probably promised a healthy bonus.

This quick sale of the Nakoda lands put a nice bit of cash into the pockets of the three senior civil servants and saved them from possible exposure. Porter and Case also profited from their investment. They had no trouble finding settlers and quickly resold the land at prices more reflective of the value of farm land in the district.

A trainload of immigrants leaves Mountain Lake, Minnesota, for western Canada.
(Library and Archives Canada)

Indian Affairs, for its part, didn't see its money for the two reserves for several years. Bedford-Jones repeatedly missed payment deadlines and was constantly hounded by the department to pay his overdue instalments. He formed his own company, Canada National Land and Development, in 1903 and apparently used his share of the money from the Moose Mountain swindle to speculate in other First Nations lands.[54]

Smart and his partners also managed to get their hands on a large portion of the Chakastaypasin lands. Smart had temporarily set aside the sale of the former reserve in April 1900 while the bogus Iowa syndicate offer was still on the table. Then, in October 1901, Smart turned to the same rigged tender process that was being used to market the Moose Mountain reserves. The sale arrangements were consequently identical to those for the former Nakoda lands, including the short notice and minimal advertising.

Smart prepared 129 tenders, drawing on confidential valuation information to set a price for each quarter-section. Bedford-Jones then completed the bids, this time forging the name of salesman J.W. Smith, who lived in the same boarding house as the Toronto lawyer.

When the tenders were opened on November 22, just one week after the awarding of the Moose Mountain lands, Smith laid claim to 8,638 acres, more than one-half of the Chakastaypasin reserve (14,864 acres).[55] The subsequent bulk sale of these quarter-sections — again through the Canadian immigration agent network — netted another windfall for the three senior government officials.

The Indian Affairs department justified the tendering of the former Moose Mountain reserves as being in "the best interests" of the Nakoda. Determining those best interests never included any consultation with the bands, though, let alone any consideration of whether the Nakoda treaty rights might be adversely affected.

The Pheasant Rump and Ocean Man bands were bullied by Indian commissioner Laird's threat — forced to abandon their successful

A Nakoda family before their tipi in the Moose Mountains in 1911. (Adrian Paton collection)

farming operations and move to the White Bear reserve, where they were expected to start over again under less than ideal conditions. It made a mockery of the government's "best interests" argument.

Senior Indian Affairs officials should have recognized that Smart's behaviour in the whole affair betrayed a sinister purpose. Yet they looked the other way, not necessarily because they countenanced what the deputy minister was doing, but because they were more concerned with protecting their jobs. That a group of First Nations was cheated in the end was unfortunate, but apparently acceptable.

Sifton's role in the sorry episode is also subject to conjecture. During a House of Commons debate over the cost of Indian provisions, Sifton slyly suggested that "the political friends of the government do not profit very much."[56] He might have been more evasive, even feigned temporary amnesia, if asked about Indian lands, especially given what he likely knew about Smart's activities.

Secretary McLean carried on a back-channel communication with Sifton's private secretary, McKenna. If McLean, who liked to know everything that was going on in the department, sensed that Smart's actions were potentially harmful to the ministry and the government, he would have informed McKenna.

Why, then, didn't Sifton act on the information and put a stop to the land sale and reprimand Smart and his colleagues or even seek their resignation? Here was a powerful minister who once told a party supporter, "Experience shows that in the past the most guilty and rascally officials have been kept in place by political influence."[57]

In Sifton's political world, only Conservatives were called out for wrongdoing and corruption. Liberal office-holders and patronage appointees, no matter how "guilty and rascally," were spared public exposure and censure — if only to protect the party. And according to the norms of the time, they may have been simply unethical rather than criminals.

Sifton's silence also doesn't mean that he was secretly involved. There's no evidence that the minister personally benefited from the Moose Mountain plot. Sifton was guilty in other ways, though. He created the conditions in which these kinds of shady deals could happen, even flourish under the Liberal administration. He also wilfully ignored what was going on. The alternative was opening a box of snakes.

Sifton probably chose to do nothing because prairie First Nations just didn't matter to him, and if Liberal friends could benefit from the sale of reserve lands, all the better. It was as if Smart, Pedley, and White's acquisition of over 53,000 acres of former Indian lands were a collateral cost of the Laurier government's settlement of the West.

Whatever the explanation, surrenders would gain momentum in the early twentieth century as the demand to open reserves to white settlement intensified. The forfeiture of the Pheasant Rump and Ocean Man reserves for suspect reasons was just the beginning.

Notes

1. Quoted in Tyler and Wright Research Consultants, "The Alienation of Indian Reserve Lands during the Administration of Sir Wilfrid Laurier, 1896–1911: Pheasant's Rump Reserve #68, Ocean Man #69," unpublished report for Federation of Saskatchewan Indians, 1978, pp. 130, 132.

2. J. Petryshyn, "Canadian Immigration and the North Atlantic Trading Company 1899–1906: A Controversy Revisited," *Journal of Canadian Studies*, v. 32, n. 3, 1997, p. 62.

3. Ibid., pp. 58–64.

4. D.J. Hall, *Clifford Sifton, v. 1: The Young Napoleon, 1861–1900* (Vancouver: University of British Columbia Press, 1981), pp. 24, 259; P. Berton, *The Promised Land: Settling the West, 1896–1914* (Toronto: Anchor Canada, 2002), pp. 170–1.

5. Tyler and Wright, "Pheasant's Rump Reserve #68, Ocean Man #69," pp. 69–70.

6. *Library and Archives Canada* (*LAC*), Clifford Sifton papers [reel C479], General Correspondence, J.A. Smart to C. Sifton, November 12, 1898.

7. Nearby was a medicine wheel that was some 2,000 years old and one of the largest on the northern plains (near present-day Kisbey, Saskatchewan).

8. *LAC*, RG10, v. 3899, f. 98974, A. McGibbon report for A.E. Forget, November 23, 1896, p. 51.

9. Quoted in Tyler and Wright, "Pheasant's Rump Reserve #68, Ocean Man #69," p. 82.

10. McGibbon report for Forget, November 23, 1896, p. 51.

11. *LAC*, RG10, v. 3839, f. 69244, pt. 1, DSGIA letterbooks, J.A. Smart to J.D. McLean, December 3, 1898.

12. Ibid., S. Bray to J.A. Smart, J.D. McLean marginal note, Smart marginal note, December 6, 1896.

13. A. Robb, "Laird, David" in R. Cook, ed., *Dictionary of Canadian Biography, v. XIV, 1911–1920* (Toronto: University of Toronto Press, 1998), p. 578.

14. B. Titley, *The Indian Commissioners: Agents of the State and Indian Policy in Canada's Prairie West, 1873–1932* (Edmonton: University of Alberta Press, 2009), pp. 59–61, 146–55, 174–6.

15. Quoted in ibid., p. 153.

16. *LAC*, RG10, v. 3839, f. 69244, pt. 1, D. Laird to J.D. McLean, December 22, 1898.

17. Quoted in Tyler and Wright, "Pheasant's Rump Reserve #68, Ocean Man #69," p. 96.

18. Ibid., p. 79.

19. *LAC*, RG10, v. 3839, f. 69244, pt. 1, H.R. Halpin to D. Laird, January 25, 1899.

20. Ibid., D. Laird to J.D. McLean, January 30, 1899.

21. Tyler and Wright, "Pheasant's Rump Reserve #68, Ocean Man #69," pp. 106–9.

22. Ibid., p. 112.

23. *LAC*, RG10, v. 3839, f. 69244, pt. 1, J.G. Armstrong and G.F. West to C. Sifton, December 4, 1899. Both signatures are in the same handwriting.

24. Ibid., A.W. Ponton to J.D. McLean, January 22, 1900.

25. Ibid., J.A.J. McKenna to J.A. Smart, February 5, 1900.

26. Ibid., G.F. West to C. Sifton, February 14, 1900.

27. Ibid., J.A. Smart to J.D. McLean, marginal note on West to Sifton, February 14, 1900.

28. Ibid., D. Laird to J.D. McLean, February 27, 1900.

29. Ibid., W.B. Underhill to J.A. Smart, March 20, 1900.

30. Ibid., "Notes on a Question Asked in House of Commons on Moose Mountain Lands," March 16, 1900.

31. Ibid., J.A. Smart marginal note on D. Laird to J.D. McLean, April 30, 1900.

32. Hall, *Clifford Sifton*, v. 1, pp. 136–8. See also G. Abrams, *Prince Albert: The First Century, 1866–1966* (Saskatoon: Modern Press, 1966), pp. 104–7.

33. Quoted in T.D. Regehr, *The Canadian Northern Railway: Pioneer Road of the Northern Prairies* (Toronto: Macmillan, 1976), p. 168.

34. Tyler and Wright, "Pheasant's Rump Reserve #68, Ocean Man #69," pp. 136–7.

35. *LAC*, RG10, v. 3839, f. 69244, pt. 1, J.W. Mitchell and J.C. Neeley to J.A. Smart, April 28, 1900.

36. R. Graham, *Arthur Meighen, v. 1: The Door of Opportunity* (Clarke, Irwin and Company, 1960), pp. 46, 68, 87, 90.

37. Quoted in W.L.R. Clark, "Politics in Brandon City, 1899–1949," unpublished Ph.D. thesis, University of Alberta, 1976, p. 34.

38. Ibid., pp. 32, 34–5.

39. *LAC*, RG10, v. 3839, f. 69244, pt. 1, J.W. Mitchell and J.C. Neeley to J.A. Smart, November 28, 1900; G.F. West to J.A. Smart, November 30, 1900.

40. Ibid., J.A. Smart to C. Sifton, March 5, 1901.

41. Quoted in Hall, *Clifford Sifton, v. 1*, p. 252.

42. Quoted in D.J. Hall, *Clifford Sifton, v. 2: A Lonely Eminence, 1901–1929* (Vancouver: University of British Columbia Press, 1985), p. 1.

43. *Sessional Papers*, 1902, n. 27, "Annual Report of the Department of Indian Affairs for 1901," p. 211.

44. Tyler and Wright, "Pheasant's Rump Reserve #68, Ocean Man #69," pp. 164–6.

45. Ibid., pp. 179–80.

46. Ibid., p. 182 (Souris *Plaindealer*, May 19, 1901).

47. *LAC*, RG10, v. 3839, f. 69244, pt. 1, J.Y. Bambidge and J. Medill to C. Sifton, May 10, 1901.

48. Tyler and Wright, "Pheasant's Rump Reserve #68, Ocean Man #69," pp. 188–9.

49. *LAC*, RG10, v. 3839, f. 69244, pt. 1, C. Sifton to Governor General in council, September 14, 1901.

50. Tyler and Wright, "Pheasant's Rump Reserve #68, Ocean Man #69," pp. 203–18.

51. Ibid., pp. 218–21.

52. House of Commons, *Debates*, April 14, 1914, p. 2550.

53. Tyler and Wright, "Pheasant's Rump Reserve #68, Ocean Man #69," pp. 221, 224–5.

54. P. Martin-McGuire, *First Nations Land Surrenders on the Prairies, 1896–1911* (Ottawa: Indian Claims Commission, 1998), p. 62.

55. Tyler and Wright, "Pheasant's Rump Reserve #68, Ocean Man #69," pp. 223–4.

56. *Debates*, July 10, 1903, p. 6424.

57. *LAC*, Sifton papers [C4030], Ottawa letterbooks (March 6–31, 1897), C. Sifton to E.C. Arthur, March 19, 1897.

-+- *Five* -»-

AMPLE LAND LEFT

n January 1899, farmer Richard S. Lake, a Conservative member of
the North-West Territories assembly, travelled to Ottawa to meet
with the minister of Interior and Indian Affairs. He wanted to talk
to Clifford Sifton about the partial surrender of three Crooked Lakes
reserves on the north side of the Canadian Pacific Railway main line.

Lake spoke from notes, prepared just before the meeting at Ottawa's
exclusive Rideau Club. On a page of club stationery, the former British
civil servant had calculated that the Ochapowace, Kahkewistahaw, and
Cowessess bands held "surplus" land. Their 1898 populations had dwin-
dled since the 1879 survey of their reserves. Lake proposed that several
square miles along the bottom of each reserve be sold, leaving them
still with more land than they needed.[1]

Lake's Rideau Club jottings aligned with the Indian Affairs
department's attitude about surrenders, but officials decided to defer
the matter because of expected resistance.[2] This government hesitancy
soon evaporated, though, as a network of competing rail lines spread
across western Canada in the early twentieth century. Settlers on the
land and in dozens of new towns complained about the presence of
First Nations reserves, saying they had no place in the new West or
its future.

But it was their political leaders, especially Frank Oliver, who led
the charge to get reserves surrendered and the land sold. The Edmonton

Liberal believed that prairie bands represented "a drawback to the country"[3] and wanted their reserves relocated as far away as possible, preferably to remote areas.

⦁⦁⦁

Twenty years earlier, several thousand First Nations people had been evicted from the Cypress Hills in what is now southwestern Saskatchewan and southeastern Alberta. The Canadian Pacific Railway main line was to be built across the southern prairies,[4] and the federal government was worried about the threat posed by a large First Nations population so close to the transcontinental link. Edgar Dewdney, the Indian commissioner for the North-West Territories, consequently ordered Cree and Nakoda leaders to move elsewhere — even though it was a breach of their treaty rights. He closed Fort Walsh in 1882, eliminating the only source of provisions, and forced bands to leave under police escort.[5] The Cypress Hills dispersal ensured there would be no reserves near the CPR main line between present-day Indian Head in southern Saskatchewan and Brooks in southern Alberta.

Many of the bands forcibly removed from the Cypress Hills were sent to the North Saskatchewan country. Their reserves were now 200 miles north, and not at the heart, of the western settlement frontier. So too were the towns of Prince Albert, Battleford, Edmonton. They may have continued to serve as important regional centres, but their growth stalled without a railway connection.

As long as settlement lagged in North Saskatchewan, there was generally no demand for reserve land in the district. White communities were more likely — especially after the 1885 North-West Rebellion — to want First Nations to remain on their reserves, away from the white population.

Other bands dispatched from the Cypress Hills were settled to the east in the Qu'Appelle Valley.[6] Their reserves were much closer to the CPR main line, but again, sluggish development meant they were more or less left alone in the 1880s and 1890s. The laying of steel from Winnipeg to Calgary in 1882–83 had sparked a temporary town-building frenzy, especially in southwestern Manitoba and eastern Assiniboia. Places like Virden, Moosomin, Whitewood, and Grenfell appeared on the map seemingly overnight, while a large number of homestead entries were taken out along both sides of the CPR line.

Before farmers could get established, though, the Canadian economy went into recession and remained in the doldrums for the better part of the next decade. Homestead applications stalled. There were fewer applications for homesteads for Manitoba and the North-West Territories in 1884 (3,333) than there had been in 1879 (3,470) — and that was *after* the construction of the main line across the prairies.[7] Those settlers already on the land struggled to get established and harvest a decent crop through several rough years, particularly in the late 1880s and early 1890s.

This dismal situation was turned on its head with the great settlement rush of the late nineteenth and early twentieth centuries. Most homesteaders couldn't find land in established districts — unless they could afford to purchase it — and turned to the North Saskatchewan country to make their new homes. The new settlement wave rolled northwestward from southwestern Manitoba/southeastern Saskatchewan in a sweeping arc towards Edmonton.

It's a pattern borne out by the homestead statistics. In the Battleford district, for example, only 506 homestead applications had been made from the program's inception in 1872 to 1902 (seventeen per year). Then, in the early 1900s, settlement took off in west-central Saskatchewan. There were 1,198 homestead applications in the Battleford district in 1903; 1,704 in 1904; 3,608 in 1905; and 7,900 in 1906. The 1,650 homestead applications in April 1906 at the Battleford dominion lands office was the highest one-month total for the entire province of Saskatchewan.[8] The story was much the same in other districts across the northern prairies.

The sheer number of settlers created a seemingly insatiable demand for rail service and rural delivery points. Pioneer homesteads would never be transformed into viable commercial operations without nearby grain-handling and marketing facilities. Two new transcontinental railways, the Canadian Northern and the Grand Trunk Pacific, pushed across the North Saskatchewan country in the early 1900s. A proliferation of branch lines followed in their wake. The rival CPR scrambled to keep pace and solidify its hold on its territory.

The railways, in turn, were the major engine of a town-building phenomenon that was nothing short of extraordinary. No less than 600 towns and villages with a population of at least a hundred found their way onto the map of the three prairie provinces by the start of the Great War in 1914.[9] Most had at least one elevator, some several in a row, for storing grain for shipment.

These years also marked the emergence of the large prairie city. Western Canada's booming wheat economy demanded central shipping points that also doubled as major wholesale and distribution centres for the rapidly growing rural population. There was also a related need for food processing, manufacturing, and light industry, in addition to retail trade, commercial, and financial facilities.

In the future province of Saskatchewan, Regina enjoyed a head start because of its role as territorial capital, but faced tough competition from Moose Jaw, a divisional point on the CPR main line. Saskatoon on the South Saskatchewan River was a sleepy village of 113 in 1901, but became known as the wonder city when the population topped 12,000 ten years later.

Next door in Alberta, Calgary seemed destined to be the dominant city. But Edmonton proved a worthy contender for the metropolitan crown. Once a backwater town on the North Saskatchewan River, the community's fortunes picked up with the arrival of the Calgary and Edmonton Railway in 1891. Settlers looking for land used Edmonton as their jumping-off point. So did hundreds of stampeders who opted for the "back door" or all-Canadian route to the Klondike goldfields over the winter of 1897–98.

Over the ten-year period from 1891 to 1901, Edmonton's population surged from 300 to 2,626. The town reached city status in 1904 (8,350) and continued to grow by leaps and bounds with the arrival of the Canadian Northern Railway main line in 1905, followed by the

Grand Trunk Pacific four years later. Along the way, it laid claim to the title of provincial capital and home to the provincial university.

This spectacular western growth translated into demands for reserve surrenders. In fact, Richard S. Lake's 1899 request to reduce the size of the Crooked Lakes reserves was resurrected.

By the early twentieth century, the wheat economy in eastern Assiniboia was flourishing. New farming methods and new crop varieties, especially an earlier maturing wheat (Marquis), enabled farmers to cultivate more acres and produce larger harvests. In the fall of 1901, the volume of wheat was so incredibly large that it overwhelmed the grain-handling system throughout Assiniboia. Half the record crop was lost to spoilage. The grain bottleneck angered farmers, and at Indian Head, where the situation had been particularly bad, they held a protest meeting in mid-December to talk about the formation of an agrarian organization to promote their collective interests.

Conservative R.S. Lake frequently called for the opening of First Nations reserves to white settlement. He would later serve as Saskatchewan lieutenant governor. (Provincial Archives of Saskatchewan)

Later in the evening at that same gathering, nearly a thousand people watched territorial Premier Frederick Haultain debate Manitoba Premier Rodmond Roblin on whether Manitoba should annex the thriving district of Assiniboia. The five-hour clash between two western heavyweights had been precipitated by a Manitoba resolution calling on the federal government to extend the province's boundaries west and north.

The matter was a long-festering one, dating back to 1870 when Ottawa created a small, rectangular-shaped Manitoba — hence the nickname "the postage stamp province." Manitoba leaders had forever claimed that the restrictive boundaries had compromised the province's future. It was Roblin, though, premier since December 1900, who wrapped himself in the Manitoba flag and made the boundary question one of the defining issues of his government's province-building agenda. He argued that acquisition of agricultural lands to the west would allow Manitoba to take its rightful place in Confederation.

Roblin, a Conservative, also denounced the Laurier Liberals and their western lieutenant Sifton for thwarting Manitoba's destiny. According to Premier Roblin, they had deliberately "cabined, cribbed, and confined" the province.[10] These kinds of arguments may have played well back home in Manitoba, but they failed to sway the residents of Assiniboia, as evidenced by the their cool reception to Roblin's speech.

Lake, who represented the constituency, was a platform guest during the Indian Head debate. He had never lost interest in securing the surrender of Crooked Lakes reserves. The fact that eastern Assiniboia was finally producing some of the finest crops in the North-West, while railway and elevator companies strained to keep up with the volume, only strengthened his call to open First Nations land to white settlement.

Lake could also point to the surrender of the two Nakoda reserves at Moose Mountain, immediately south of Grenfell, in April 1901 and their subsequent sale by tender in November. He was dismayed, though, by the limited and last-minute distribution of the Moose Mountain sales notice. It was as if Indian Affairs were trying to deter local people from bidding for some of the 47,000 acres of prime agricultural land.

Lake was determined to find out why there was almost no competition when the sale took place. He would later reveal his findings on the floor of the House of Commons after he had been elected as the Conservative federal representative for Assiniboia East in 1904.

In response to a government declaration that reserve land sales were well advertised, Lake countered that disposition of the two Moose Mountain reserves had been announced in the local Moosomin *Spectator* only eight days before tenders were due in Ottawa. He then described to the House how "three gentlemen," acting through a Toronto law firm, had inexplicably secured all but ten of the 308 quarter-sections. The prices paid for the land, he continued with obvious disdain, were "well below its value . . . practically given away."[11]

Lake didn't seem to know who bought the land — or if he did, he said nothing that day, only that it was another example of Liberal patronage at its worst.

The surrender of the Moose Mountain reserves generated another attempt to secure settler access to the Crooked Lakes lands. In early 1902, just weeks after the sale of the former Nakoda lands, a petition made the rounds in the Broadview, Whitewood, and surrounding districts. Some 200 citizens signed their name.

The petition, sponsored by Welsh-born J.G. Stevens, a Broadview minister, called on the minister of Indian Affairs to secure the bands' consent to sell a three-mile strip along the bottom of their reserves next to the CPR. It claimed that the proximity of the reserves "seriously retard[ed] the development" of local communities, that the allotted land was "much in excess of the requirements" of the bands, and in a thinly veiled swipe at reserve agriculture, that the land was needed for "actual settlers."[12]

The petition was favourably received. Not only were the Assiniboia settlers told in March 1902 that the "minister appreciates the desirability of acceding to their prayer," but that his department would "do its best to procure the consent of the Indians" to the surrender.[13] To that end, an official from the Indian Affairs office in Winnipeg was to meet with the bands to discuss a possible surrender. The speed of the response signalled that reserve surrenders would now be actively pursued by the Liberal government.

Indian commissioner David Laird had a personal stake in the Crooked Lakes surrender. In 1874, while serving as minister of the Interior and Indian Affairs in the Alexander Mackenzie Liberal government, he had agreed to be one of three treaty commissioners for Treaty Four and made the cross-country trip to meet with the Cree and Saulteaux at Fort Qu'Appelle. Now, twenty-eight years later, another Liberal government was seeking to backtrack on the treaty promise that reserves would be inviolate band territory.

Laird chose to handle the matter himself and arranged a council with the Chiefs and headmen of the bands on April 26, 1902. Maybe he believed that the leaders would be more welcoming and co-operative given his past association with them. He was known to them as Tall White Man, his long frame accentuated by his trademark black stovepipe top hat.

Laird's mission met with stiff resistance, though. The band representatives remembered how he had told them at the Fort Qu'Appelle treaty meeting to take up their reserve land and settle down. They couldn't now, as one councillor politely but firmly informed Laird, "consent to part with any of it." Others were just as gracious, pleased that the Indian commissioner had come to see them, but resoundingly said no.

Only the aged Chief Kahkewistahaw, who had signed the treaty in 1874, dispensed with the niceties for a withering harangue. "Did I not tell you a long time ago," he said, angrily pointing at Laird, "that you would come some time, that you would come and ask me to sell you this land back again, but I told you at that time, No." When, in exasperation, Laird asked whether anyone present was in favour of his request, "there was no response whatever."

Laird advised Ottawa that there was no hope of the two bands "surrendering any portion of their reserves."[14] It's not clear how the department took the news. Laird's report about the meeting is the last document in the file for the next two years; there's not even a marginal notation on the letter.

Chief Kahkewistahaw (centre front) who had signed treaty in 1874, was incensed when asked to surrender part of his band's reserve in 1902. (Kahkewistahaw First Nation)

Indian Affairs had better luck securing a surrender from the Enoch reserve. It was largely the handiwork of Liberal MP Frank Oliver, who considered himself Alberta's biggest booster.

Back in 1876, the twenty-three-year-old had staked his future on the old fur trade community, claiming decades later that he believed that "the place . . . was particularly worked by the star of Empire."[15] Oliver, with his wiry frame, piercing eyes, and heavy moustache, more like a thick-bristled brush covering his mouth, became a fixture in Edmonton, particularly after he launched his *Bulletin* newspaper at the start of the 1880s. It gave him an editorial pulpit from which he "argued, cajoled, bargained, and bullied."[16] The rival, pro-Conservative *Calgary Herald* slagged the *Bulletin* as "the meanest paper published by the meanest man in Canada."[17]

Oliver was a firm prohibitionist and anti-smoker who touted the restorative value of public spaces and community sports, including the fledgling bicycle club.[18] But he could hold grudges, especially against those he believed had wronged western settlers. At the top of his list were the CPR and the Conservative Party, both largely responsible for Edmonton's "slow and lean years."[19]

Once Oliver became a member of the Laurier government in 1896, he lost no time peppering Interior and Indian Affairs with an assortment of requests and queries. It was as if the two departments answered only to him. At one point, in the early new year, Sifton got so tired of yet another Oliver letter that he refused to respond to any more and suggested that Oliver come around to his office when the backbencher arrived in Ottawa in late March 1897.

Oliver could be brazen, if not petulant, about what he wanted done and was never completely satisfied unless he got his way. Renowned for his "wild talk,"[20] he was never one to let party affiliation put a brake on what he said or who he went after. It's easy to understand why he proved such a thorn in the side of his own government. While Sifton may have been criticized for going too far in putting the Liberal stamp on the new administration, Oliver and his newspaper constantly complained that he never went far enough. "I cannot make anything at all out of Oliver," Sifton confessed to a Portage la Prairie friend and fellow Manitoba MP, "and I do not care to say much upon the subject upon paper."[21]

Liberal Edmonton MP Frank Oliver believed that First Nations had no place in the new West of the late nineteenth century. (City of Edmonton Archives)

Other Liberal caucus members might reasonably have wondered whose side Oliver was on. The answer was obvious — his own.

Oliver was a blatant racist, even allowing for the standards of his time. He regarded First Nations as an inferior race, a backward, primitive people who had no place in the new society taking shape on the western plains. Oliver said repeatedly that any attempt to uplift and civilize them, let alone turn them into agriculturalists, was a colossal waste of time and money, and that federal policies had actually made them dependent on the government for their survival and well-being.

He also questioned Canada's treaty relationships and the commitments made on behalf of the Crown. "This bargain [Treaty Six]," he once grumbled, was "a great mistake, as every one must acknowledge, and the sooner the mistake is rectified the better."[22] The only sensible course of action, according to Oliver, was to break up reserves, especially those near white communities, and force bands to fend for themselves. "Now is the time," he ranted in one of his heated editorials, "for the government to declare . . . whether the country is to be run in the interests of the settlers or the Indians."[23]

Oliver was hell-bent on getting rid of all reserves in the Edmonton district. He went about it methodically, convinced that once one fell, the others would follow in succession like dominoes. He started in the early 1880s with an all-out lobbying assault against the Papaschase reserve on the south side of the North Saskatchewan River, directly across from Edmonton. That reserve was surrendered in November 1888.

Next on his hit list was the Enoch reserve. In January 1898, the residents of Stony Plain, west of the reserve, petitioned the Laurier government to open a right-of-way through the reserve to Edmonton. It was a backhanded attempt to secure a surrender. At the very moment that Stony Plain settlers were complaining that the reserve was hindering local development, territorial work crews were improving and upgrading the baseline (survey road) across the top of the reserve to provide a direct route to Edmonton. There was no need for another road.

Oliver seized on the resolution to call for the elimination of the reserve. As he told Sifton, the Enoch band members "could be better accommodated elsewhere," especially when the reserve held some of "choicest" land in the district.[24] Oliver put forward a mind-boggling proposal: to give Stony Plain farmers access to Edmonton, Indian Affairs should seek a surrender of any land immediately north of the proposed right-of-way through the reserve. The audacious Oliver called the removal of the fourteen square miles "the best solution."[25]

In late March 1898, senior Indian Affairs officials pursued the surrender of a two-mile strip from the top of the Enoch reserve, amounting to more than 9,000 acres. In justifying the action, department secretary J.D. McLean reasoned, "There would be ample land left for these Indians."[26] He also arranged with department surveyor A.W. Ponton, as his first priority that coming field season, to subdivide the released Enoch land into quarter-sections so that the lands could be placed on the market.

The Enoch people, though, voted against giving up any land at the surrender meeting on April 22. Agent Charles de Cazes communicated the unanimous decision to Ottawa, along with the suggestion that a partial surrender was not needed if a right-of-way through the reserve could be negotiated. The department was forced to concede, given the band's resolve, that the agent was right. Not even a direct personal appeal to Sifton — Oliver ambushed the minister at the end of the parliamentary session — made any difference.

Oliver had been snookered, but that's when fate intervened. De Cazes died July 10, 1898, at his agency residence at Stony Plain. His replacement — at Oliver's repeated urging — was Edmonton trader and liquor merchant James Gibbons. It was no coincidence that he was also president of the local Liberal association and had helped Oliver get elected to the House of Commons in 1896.

These Liberal connections glossed over Gibbons's lack of qualifications, including serious reservations about his character. As a friend of Oliver, the new Indian agent could be counted upon to support the wishes of the Edmonton MP over the interests of the Enoch band.

Deputy Minister James Smart would later complain to McLean that someone was feeding Oliver confidential information.[27]

Oliver lost little time in using Gibbons to secure a surrender at Enoch. In April 1899, he raised the matter again, subtly suggesting to Smart that "if the new agent made the proposition to them they would agree to it."[28] Smart, who was busy at the time trying to stickhandle the surrender of two Moose Mountain reserves for his personal benefit, ordered a review of the file.

McLean delivered the verdict: there was no need to seek a surrender because the reserve road was going ahead. The Indian Affairs department might have hoped that was the end of the matter. But as Sifton once said about dealing with Oliver, "It is quite impossible to convince him permanently and my judgment is that any time that is spent on him will simply be wasted."[29]

Enoch came up again in December 1900 when Thomas Page Wadsworth, inspector of Indian agencies, reported that settler cattle and horses were wandering onto the reserve and grazing there. The obvious answer was to encourage local settlers to fence their land. McLean decided that it might be easier to put a fence around the reserve, charging the cost against the band's capital account (roughly $42,000 at the time).[30]

Oliver chose this moment to strike, probably in response to the recent surrender and pending sale of the two Moose Mountain reserves. In a hard-hitting editorial in the *Bulletin* in October 1901, Oliver asserted that Indians had no place in a settled and developing West but should be shunted to the margins of white society. "A township in a good hunting country and near a fishing lake," he asserted, "is more valuable to the Indians than a township of fine agricultural land near a railway station."

Oliver also chastised Indian Affairs for not showing more "effort . . . at displacing the Indians" and suggested that "the proper . . . business arrangement" would dissolve their opposition to giving up their reserve lands.[31] Any such inducements went against Canada's Treaty Six obligations and Indian Act regulations, but Oliver didn't care.

Sifton's former private secretary arrived in Edmonton on the heels of Oliver's latest salvo against the Enoch reserve. Now serving as assistant Indian commissioner, James McKenna was officially there to take applications for Métis scrip. But the larger import of his new posting, apart from assisting the elderly Laird, was to bring some much-needed backbone to the Indian Affairs Winnipeg office and energize its work in the prairie west.

McKenna sympathized with Oliver's position on reserve surrenders. Any differences were more a matter of how they were handled.[32] Perhaps that's why McKenna found time to meet privately with Gibbons, the Indian agent. A little more than a month later, just before Christmas 1901, Gibbons wrote a long, rambling letter to Secretary McLean that suggested the stalemate over fencing the Enoch reserve could be ended if the band surrendered fourteen square miles from the northern half of the reserve (north of the road allowance) and then fenced the remainder.

As if by previous agreement, McKenna followed Gibbons's lead and recommended the partial surrender of the Enoch reserve in a January 3, 1902, memorandum to Sifton. McKenna was serving as acting deputy minister at the time, while Smart was absent for several months in Europe on Interior business. The memo rehashed many of the same arguments that had been put forward by Oliver, including the possible use of inducements.[33]

McKenna made no attempt to find another solution — in particular, using funds from the Enoch Cree capital account to fence the reserve. Nor did anyone consult with the band beforehand to determine its wishes.

Sifton immediately approved the McKenna note, triggering a surrender meeting less than three weeks later on January 23, 1902. There are no minutes or any other record of the council, and consequently no information about what Gibbons told the band or what exactly was discussed. The Indian agent simply reported that fourteen men had approved the surrender — nothing more, not even if they represented the majority at the meeting.

The only clue to how past band resistance had been overcome was a list, appended to the completed surrender documents, that named those male band members who were to receive farming outfits. This spending was allowable under the Indian Act, but it could not exceed 10 percent of the proceeds from the future land sale. Nor was it to be used as an inducement, effectively a bribe to encourage a yes vote at a surrender meeting.

There was a surreal side to the agreement. The band was being asked to surrender 9,113 acres of first-rate farm land so that members could get farming outfits. The irony was probably lost on Indian Affairs: that the Enoch Cree had to give up one treaty right (part of their reserve) to secure access to another treaty right (agricultural assistance).

The department seemed more concerned with getting the deal finalized as quickly as possible. That occurred on April 1, 1902, with the approval of Privy Council Order 515. Even the impatient Oliver was probably amazed by the speed at which the surrender came about once the government machinery was in motion.

McKenna expected the Enoch surrender to be followed by others. They would no longer be exceptional or infrequent. "We are going to have pressure," he warned Sifton, "from many quarters for the throwing open of reserves."[34]

One such appeal came from C.S. Lowrie of Kinistino, Saskatchewan, in January 1902. He asked about opening up the lower half of the Cumberland reserve, east of Prince Albert. The request was endorsed by local Liberal MP T.O. Davis, who remained vitally interested in speculating in western lands.

It was a curious request. While the northern prairies were on the cusp of a settlement boom, soon to be home to tens of thousands of immigrant farmers, the rolling, bush-covered Carrot River country, reaching south from the Saskatchewan River, existed in relative isolation. There was little settlement here, and little threat of any homesteading rush, because of the rough, gravelly terrain blanketed by a wall of aspen forest.[35] It was the same territory where the Willow Cree fugitive Almighty Voice had successfully eluded the North-West Mounted Police for nineteen months in the mid-1890s.[36]

"The Willows" home of Liberal T.O. Davis and his family. Davis, an MP and later senator, sought surrendered First Nations land in the Prince Albert district. (Prince Albert Historical Society)

The possible routing of a Canadian Northern Railway branch line through the district, though, dazzled pioneer farmers and held out great hopes for the future. Lowrie slammed the southern half of the Cumberland reserve as "a great eyesore," while touting the "great benefit" of placing white settlers there.[37]

In early March 1902, with the Enoch surrender awaiting final government approval, secretary McLean asked Laird to look into the Cumberland matter, adding what would become standard reasoning: "it [the reserve] is much larger than necessary."[38] Shaken by his rebuke at the Crooked Lakes reserves, Laird recommended that inducements be offered to the Cumberland band — an advance of 10 percent of the projected sale proceeds.

Laird met with the Cumberland band at Fort à la Corne, the local Hudson's Bay Company post, on July 24, 1902, and managed to obtain the release of township 46 (thirty-six square miles). How he convinced the band to accept the surrender is an unanswered question. Laird's report to the department provided not a single word about the proceedings, only that he had been successful.[39] That was all that mattered to Indian Affairs. Before the Cumberland surrender was formally approved by order-in-council in mid-October 1902, a surveyor subdivided the township so that the land could be marketed in the coming months.

The most anticipated reserve sale at the time was the Enoch parcel. Oliver called the surrendered fourteen square miles a "magnificent" opportunity.[40] Throughout the summer of 1902, Indian Affairs repeatedly told prospective buyers that details about the Enoch sale would have to wait until after the land was surveyed into quarter-sections. But Deputy Minister Smart was already angling to purchase the land using the same process that he had engineered for Moose Mountain. On April 21, 1902, he informed Secretary McLean that he intended to set aside the federal Regulations for the Disposal of Surrendered Indian Lands and sell the Enoch reserve "in the same way" as the two Moose Mountain reserves — in other words, by private tender.[41]

Oliver and Indian agent Gibbons, on the other hand, continued to push for the lands to be sold by public auction, expecting "the competition will be very keen."[42] Surveyor A.W. Ponton, in forwarding his Enoch survey plan and notes to Ottawa in July 1902, also observed that it was "the hope of the actual farming community . . . that they will be allowed a chance to bid at open auction."[43] Smart, though, would have his way.

Indian Affairs announced in late October that the Enoch lands were to be sold by secret tender and that bids for the fifty-six quarter-sections were due in Ottawa by December 3, 1902. That left about a month for interested parties to put together their submissions.

As in the case of the sale of the two Moose Mountain reserves, Smart deliberately tried to restrict competition for the lands. The sale poster was only inserted in the *Edmonton Bulletin* and the *Winnipeg Free Press*, both Liberal newspapers and owned by Oliver and Sifton, respectively. It would have made more sense to place the advertisement in another Alberta district newspaper instead of a Manitoba one.

The poster also didn't include any description of the land. Any potential bidder not living in the area would have to make a trip to inspect the quarter-sections. Nor was it clear whether an applicant could apply for more than one quarter-section, and those who tried bidding for several parcels faced considerable paperwork. If anyone wanted to submit tenders for all of the land, then fifty-six separate tenders, including the cash deposit, would have to be prepared.

Smart also used his position to secure privileged information in preparing bids for the Enoch land. When Ponton subdivided the Enoch land, he estimated the market worth of each quarter-section and then added these amounts together to come up with a value for the entire tract: $58,145, an average price of $6.50 per acre.[44]

This valuation was double the average price for farm land per acre in 1903 ($3.56).[45] It was also strictly confidential. But on October 27, Smart asked McLean for a copy of all of the surveyor's materials. The deputy minister received the documents the next day.[46]

Once Smart had the valuation and notes in hand, he set to work with Frank Pedley and William White to secure the Enoch land. They once again engaged Pedley's former law partner in Toronto, A.C. Bedford-Jones, to prepare tenders on their behalf. He, in turn, called on George Angus, a stenographer working in the same building, to sign each bid in his name.

Two large envelopes were prepared: one containing separate bids for all the quarter-sections in township 52, range 25; the other for quarter-sections in township 52, range 26. The package was sent to Ottawa on December 1, 1902.[47]

Smart, Pedley, and White didn't realize there was another party in the field equally determined to acquire the Enoch land. Richard Secord and John A. McDougall, owners of a downtown Edmonton retail and wholesale store (McDougall & Secord Ltd.), also submitted tenders for all fifty-six Enoch quarter-sections. As speculators in real estate and Métis scrip, it was only natural that they would be interested in the Enoch reserve and the profits to be realized by acquiring the entire fourteen-square-mile parcel. They had even tried to circumvent the sale by making an offer to Sifton in early June 1902 to buy all of the surrendered tract.

Months later, when tender bids were due, Secord and McDougall had a stroke of good fortune. Ponton was in Edmonton, having just arrived from Lesser Slave Lake, and apparently shared with them his knowledge about the character and value of the land throughout the surrendered block.

Three days after the tender deadline closed, W.A. Orr of the Lands and Timber Branch prepared a list that matched the highest bid against each quarter-section. Even though Smart, Pedley, and White had access to Ponton's valuation, the George Angus tenders submitted on their behalf were generally low ($2.47 per acre) and largely unsuccessful.

The trio of government conspirators had seriously underestimated the value of the land near Edmonton and may have been overconfident, given their past success acquiring the Moose Mountain lands for only $1.23 per acre. This time, they secured only one parcel. That was the same amount of land successfully bid on by Ellen Carruthers, the wife of Edmonton agency clerk Henry A. Carruthers.[48]

McDougall & Secord Ltd. scooped up thirty-eight quarter-sections — about 68 percent of the Enoch land. Their average bid ($6.39 per acre) was only eleven cents less than Ponton's valuation ($6.50).[49] The Edmonton businessmen stood to make a handsome windfall by beating Smart and his friends at their game. As for the trio, they may have lost out, but they were fortunate not to be caught trying the same scam again.

Smart's association with Indian Affairs came to an end late that November — just before the Enoch tenders were submitted. The timing had nothing to do with the deputy minister's speculation in First Nations lands. Rather, the strain of his heavy workload was taking its toll after five years on the job.

Since 1897, Smart had been regularly away from Ottawa, spending months each year travelling to the northern United States, Great

Britain, and continental Europe, attending to immigration and settlement issues. When he returned to the capital, Smart had to deal with Interior and Indian Affairs issues that had been held over in his absence for his review. Additionally, he was at the call of a demanding minister who was also overworked and overwrought.

Smart had been in London in August 1902 when Sifton ordered his deputy to head immediately to Dawson City to salvage Liberal fortunes and restore confidence in the Laurier government by cleaning up an administrative mess in the territory. This political operation mostly involved shaking up the Yukon civil service by getting rid of several incompetent patronage appointees.

Smart hated the two-month assignment and complained in a long, self-pitying tirade to Sifton. "I need perhaps not again express my regret," he whined, "that I have been held up here as I was sure that I was clear of the Territory." He then added for extra sympathy, "a rest will not do me any harm after perhaps the worst experience I have ever had in my official capacity."[50] Smart returned to Ottawa on October 14 and was done as deputy minister of Indian Affairs five weeks later. He was probably relieved to have only Interior matters on his plate.

Secretary McLean wanted the position. He was the one called upon to serve as acting deputy minister during Smart's many absences — so often that Sifton never bothered with official paperwork. "I . . . know the work better than any outsider can ever know it," McLean said in his appeal to the minister.[51]

After the Liberals' first term in office, though, Sifton had a better handle on where the problem areas persisted and who could be depended upon to best serve his needs. Smart may have been his old Brandon colleague, but he had his shortcomings. What Sifton needed in Indian Affairs was a known fixer — and that's why he turned to his superintendent of immigration.

Frank Pedley had recently demonstrated his considerable talents when Smart bungled what should have been a straightforward promotional opportunity. Smart, along with W.T.R. Preston, the inspector of emigration for Europe, wanted to do something "distinctly Canadian" for King Edward VII's coronation in London on August 9, 1902.

The pair settled on a grand ceremonial arch with a central dome and two side turrets, adorned with sheaves of Canadian grains, and the words "Canada Britain's Granary." It was to be erected in the Whitehall district, not far from Westminster.

Getting the ceremonial arch in place became something of a nightmare. They had to obtain sheaves of wheat, rye, and oats from western Canada and then attach them to several hundred battens that were shipped by boxcar to port. Once in London, as the wooden arch was being assembled, the battens fastened, and the framework wired for light, it was found that the structure was too large and impeded local traffic. Three weeks before the coronation, the sheaves had become "quite dilapidated" and a frantic call went out to an experimental farm in Ottawa to send replacement decorations.

Pedley assumed command of the project — his supervisory hand is everywhere in the file — and managed to get everything resolved in time for the coronation. That included securing $33,000 (over $750,000 in 2021 dollars) in government funding to cover all the invoices received by November 1902. But there was one coronation headache that Pedley couldn't control. According to an Irish journalist, local birds were becoming quite obese feeding at the arch.[52]

Canada erected a grand ceremonial arch in London in honour of King Edward VII's 1902 coronation. Frank Pedley had to step in when the project floundered.
(Library and Archives Canada)

Pedley's new challenge was to manage the Indian Affairs department to Sifton's liking and keep the proverbial chickens — his private
speculating in Indian lands — from coming home to roost. He didn't
lack in confidence. Pedley had learned a great deal during his past five
years in government service, in particular how it was best to opt for the
direct approach.

That included asking Sifton for the maximum salary ($4,000) in his
new position as deputy minister. When the Privy Council objected to the
sizeable raise, one that put Pedley at the top of the pay bracket, Sifton
provided a glowing recommendation that highlighted the skills and acumen of the young man. The question, though, was how Pedley would use
those skills and acumen at Indian Affairs — and to whose benefit.

Notes

1. *Library and Archives Canada* (*LAC*), RG10, v. 3732, f. 26,623, R.S. Lake
   Rideau Club note, n.d.
2. Ibid., C. Sifton to R.S. Lake, April 29, 1899.
3. *Edmonton Bulletin*, January 17, 1881.
4. For an explanation of the route change, see B. Waiser, "A Willing
   Scapegoat: John Macoun and the Route of the CPR," *Prairie Forum*, v.
   10, n. 1, spring 1985, pp. 65–81.
5. J.B.D. Larmour, "Edgar Dewdney, Commissioner of Indian Affairs
   and Lieutenant Governor of the North-West Territories, 1879–1888,"
   unpublished M.A. thesis, University of Saskatchewan, 1969, p. 74.
6. The presence of the Qu'Appelle Valley reserves might also have
   been a contributing factor in the decision to make Regina the
   capital of the North-West Territories. Battleford, at the junction of
   the North Saskatchewan and Battle Rivers, had served as the seat
   of the territorial government since 1876. When the Canadian Pacific
   Railway (CPR) remade the map of the North-West in 1881, a new
   capital had to be found. A strong candidate was Fort Qu'Appelle,

a Hudson's Bay Company (HBC) post and North-West Mounted Police (NWMP) divisional headquarters on the river of the same name in southeastern Assiniboia. The Nakoda, Cree, and Saulteaux had also signed Treaty Four there in 1874. But Edgar Dewdney, who doubled as lieutenant governor for the territories, chose a site about a hundred miles farther west, on the open, treeless prairie, where the main line crossed Pile of Bones (Wascana) Creek. When the first CPR train arrived in August 1883, the community was christened Regina in honour of the Queen. Dewdney is said to have selected Pile of Bones because he owned a section of land next to the original townsite. It's noteworthy, though, that Regina was well away from the Touchwood Hills, File Hills, Fishing Lakes, and Crooked Lakes reserves. Had the capital been placed at Fort Qu'Appelle, there might have been an attempt to relocate some of the neighbouring reserves.

7. Of the total number of homestead applications between 1872 and 1930 (the start and end of the program), only 8.8 percent of the entries had been recorded by 1885 and only 20 percent by 1900. K.H. Norrie, "The National Policy and the Rate of Prairie Settlement" in R.D. Francis and H. Palmer, eds., *The Prairie West* (Edmonton: University of Alberta Press, 1992), pp. 245–6; J.H. Archer, *Saskatchewan: A History* (Saskatoon: Western Producer Prairie Books, 1980), p. 83.

8. A. McPherson, *The Battlefords: A History* (Saskatoon: Modern Press, 1967), pp. 127, 151, 156–7.

9. P. Voisey, "The Urbanization of the Canadian Prairies," *Histoire Sociale/ Social History*, n. 15, May 1975, p. 83.

10. Quoted in W.L. Morton, *Manitoba: A History* (Toronto: University of Toronto Press, 1967), p. 293.

11. House of Commons, *Debates,* July 11, 1908, pp. 12730–1.

12. *LAC,* RG10, v. 3732, f. 26,623, petition, March 1902.

13. *LAC,* RG10, v. 3732, f. 26,623, A.P. Collier to J.D. McLean, March 31, 1902.

14. Ibid., D. Laird to J.D. McLean, May 6, 1902.

15. *Edmonton Bulletin,* September 26, 1908.

16. L. Goyette and C.J. Roemmich, *Edmonton: In Our Own Words* (Edmonton: University of Alberta Press, 2004), p. 173.

17. Quoted in P. Berton, *The Promised Land* (Toronto: Anchor Canada, 2002), p. 207.

18. R.M. Hess, "A Social History of Cycling in Edmonton, 1890–1897," unpublished M.A. thesis, University of Alberta, 1991.

19. *Edmonton Bulletin*, July 14, 1930.

20. Quoted in L.H. Thomas, *The Struggle for Responsible Government in the North-West Territories, 1870–97* (Toronto: University of Toronto Press, 1956), p. 127.

21. *LAC*, Clifford Sifton papers [reel C407], Ottawa letterbooks (August 20 to September 15, 1897), C. Sifton to J.G. Rutherford, August 23, 1897.

22. *Edmonton Bulletin*, September 30, 1882.

23. Ibid., January 17, 1881.

24. *LAC*, RG10, v. 7542, f. 29110-6, F. Oliver to C. Sifton, February 14, 1898.

25. Ibid., F. Oliver to C. Sifton, March 5, 1898.

26. Ibid., W.A. Orr to J.D. McLean, March 22, 1898, marginal comment by McLean.

27. *LAC*, RG10, v. 1124, Deputy Superintendent General's Letterbooks, J.D. McLean to J.A. Smart, March 8, 1901.

28. *LAC*, RG10, v. 7542, f. 29110-6, F. Oliver to James Smart, April 12, 1899.

29. Quoted in D.J. Hall, *Clifford Sifton, v.1: The Young Napoleon, 1861–1900* (Vancouver: University of British Columbia Press, 1981), p. 282.

30. *Sessional Papers*, n. 27, 1902, "Annual Report of the Department of Indian Affairs for 1901," p. J-123 (Enoch Band Capital Account).

31. *Edmonton Bulletin*, October 28, 1901.

32. *LAC*, RG10, v. 7543, f. 29120-1, J.A.J. McKenna to C. Sifton, February 8, 1902.

33. *LAC*, RG10, v. 4001, f. 209109, J.A.J. McKenna to C. Sifton, January 3, 1902.

34. *LAC*, Sifton papers [reel C540], General Correspondence, J.A.J. Mckenna to C. Sifton, April 10, 1902.

35. Surveyor Thomas Fawcett, while conducting a topographical survey of the region in 1892, was forever being slowed by "a series of boggy marshes . . . separated by narrow ridges covered with brûlé or timber . . . intermixed with thick scrub." See Canada, *Sessional Papers*, n. 13, 1893, "Annual Report of the Department of the Interior for 1892," p. 59. It was

not until well into the twentieth century that the land would be cleared; apart from the predominance of sloughs, the landscape looks completely different today.

36. See B. Waiser, *In Search of Almighty Voice: Resistance and Reconciliation* (Markham: Fifth House Publishers, 2020).

37. *LAC*, RG10, v. 3562, f. 82, pt. 9, C.S. Lowrie to T.O. Davis, January 30, 1902.

38. Ibid., J.D. McLean to D. Laird, March 6, 1902.

39. That same day, at Laird's urging, the James Smith and Cumberland bands signed an amalgamation agreement.

40. *Edmonton Bulletin*, July 11, 1902.

41. *LAC*, RG10, v. 7542, f. 29110-6, J.A. Smart to J.D. McLean, April 21, 1902.

42. Ibid., J. Gibbons to J.D. McLean, March 10, 1902.

43. Ibid., A.W. Ponton to J.D. McLean, July 19, 1902.

44. Ibid.

45. Frank Oliver provided this figure during the House of Commons discussion of the Ferguson report. *Debates*, April 14, 1915, p. 2550.

46. *LAC*, RG10, v. 7542, f. 29110-6, J.A. Smart to J.D. McLean, October 27, 1902.

47. Ibid., envelopes containing tenders for Stony Plain, G. Angus, December 1, 1902.

48. P. Martin-McGuire, *First Nations Land Surrenders on the Prairies, 1896–1911* (Ottawa: Indian Claims Commission, 1998), p. 475.

49. *LAC*, RG10, v. 7542, f. 29110-6, "Schedule of Tenders received for Stony Plain Lands," W.A. Orr to F. Pedley, December 6, 1902.

50. *LAC*, Sifton papers [C528], General Correspondence, J.A. Smart to C. Sifton, September 15, 1902.

51. Ibid., [C579], General Correspondence J.D. McLean to C. Sifton, February 25, 1902.

52. The coronation arch saga is found in *LAC*, RG76, v. 258, f. 198190.

⊷ *Six* ⊶

LITTLE PATCHES KNOWN AS RESERVES

aria Allison was an unlikely speculator in western lands. In June 1904 the Ottawa widow, who worked as an after-hours cleaning lady for $5 a month, bought three quarter-sections (480 acres) of land in the North-West Territories. It's quite likely Allison couldn't locate her newly acquired land on a map, let alone decipher the survey coordinates. She couldn't even spell acre correctly. Even more perplexing was how Allison managed to secure the land for the ridiculously low price of $1.50 per acre when it had been valued at more than twice that. Either she was uncannily shrewd or she benefited from someone's guiding hand.

That someone was Herbert N. Awrey, a clerk in the Indian Affairs department where Allison served as nighttime janitor. Awrey knew that the Michel band, northwest of Edmonton, had recently surrendered 7,800 acres of their reserve, and he secretly arranged for Allison to bid for some of the land when it came up for sale by tender. He cut and pasted the surveyor's description of three quarter-sections on a sheet of paper and then instructed Allison what she should offer per acre. She also scrawled "tender for Indian lands" across the top of the page and signed her name, along with her address and the date, at the bottom. The tender document was then placed in an Indian Affairs envelope, conveniently supplied by Awrey, and hand-delivered just hours before the noon submission deadline.

For several years thereafter, Awrey quietly paid the instalments for the purchased land until Allison formally turned over two of the three quarter-sections to him. She kept one quarter-section as her reward.[1]

◄◄‹‹··››►►

Maria Allison was one of many buyers of surrendered reserve lands during Frank Pedley's eleven-year tenure as deputy minister of Indian Affairs. In fact, his appointment to the position in the Wilfrid Laurier Liberal government in November 1902 marked a watershed in the securing of reserve surrenders in the prairie west. It was a time when land speculation and corruption trickled down through the department to clerks, reserve officials, even janitorial staff.

Under Pedley's predecessor James Smart, Indian Affairs had pursued surrenders whenever there was an opportunity, but government action was rarely hurried and often took many months. If necessary, the department was also prepared to back off — albeit at times only temporarily — whenever there was band resistance. Pedley, though, thrived on getting things done and invariably chose action over delay in responding to whatever came across his desk. At the same time, his decisiveness was tempered by the political need to limit, if not prevent, criticism of the Laurier government and its policies. Pedley the fixer would ensure that reserve surrenders and subsequent land sales weren't bungled and proceeded as expeditiously as possible.

Pedley consequently had a relatively free hand in running Indian Affairs. His boss, Clifford Sifton, was beginning to tire of his double duties as Interior and Indian Affairs minister and looked to Pedley to carry some of the load. He was someone Sifton could trust, someone who had his confidence and could be relied upon. That was terribly important to Sifton at this stage in his federal political career. The minister was a workaholic, but it came at the price of exhaustion, insomnia, and frayed nerves. He was also increasingly deaf. Sifton regularly sought treatment in Europe and the United States and was often absent from Ottawa for several weeks, if only to get some much-needed rest.

The minister also needed someone to handle the Indian Affairs side of his portfolio because he was coming under criticism for his Interior policies, especially in the Yukon. When the Laurier government introduced hydraulic mining leases in the Klondike goldfields, the Conservative Opposition accused Sifton of seeking to benefit his business friends by giving the companies and their backers exclusive access to the gold-bearing creeks.[2] These kinds of attacks on the minister's integrity meant that Indian Affairs would have been largely neglected if Pedley hadn't been at the helm on his behalf.

Pedley's parachuting into Indian Affairs in November 1902 probably didn't sit well with J.D. McLean, the department secretary who had wanted the position as deputy minister for himself.[3] But just as Smart and McLean had reached an understanding about work arrangements in 1897, so too did Pedley and McLean. McLean remained the "nuts and bolts" guy, the one with the department corporate memory, while Pedley was the decision-maker who looked to McLean to run the office and bring matters forward that required attention.

What McLean likely came to appreciate was that the new deputy minister took his job seriously and kept himself informed about department matters. Unlike Smart, Pedley was there at his desk, attending to his Indian Affairs duties and not distracted by Interior business or some other side scheme. It would be a mistake, though, to assume that First Nations finally had a government champion who was devoted to their interests. Pedley came from the Interior side of government operations, and as the former superintendent of immigration, he placed western settlement before treaty rights and obligations.

If there was a chance that a band would give up some or all of its reserve land, then the new deputy minister was more than willing to take it on behalf of the Crown.

Pedley's position on reserve surrenders found support in public, government, and political circles. Ever since the Liberals assumed power in 1896, there had been the occasional query whether reserve

There was money to be made in the great western settlement boom — and that included speculating in surrendered First Nations lands. (Glenbow Archives)

land could be taken away from prairie First Nations. But in the early twentieth century, these requests became a chorus.

Settlers that petitioned Clifford Sifton now refused to give up. The residents of the Broadview district, for example, once again called for the opening of the Crooked Lakes reserves in 1902. When they were informed that it might happen "in the near future," their representative refused to be fobbed off and asked for a "definite reply" as to when.[4]

Some of Sifton's Liberal friends also made recommendations. John Gillanders Turriff, the commissioner of dominion lands in the Department of the Interior and the leading Liberal organizer for the prairies, called for the surrender of the Swan Lake reserve in Manitoba. George Bulyea, the commissioner of agriculture in the North-West Territories government and future lieutenant governor of Alberta, wanted the Pasqua and Muscowpetung reserves opened to settlement.[5] It's not known whether they had personal interest in the land.

Conservative Opposition leader Robert Borden also raised the matter of reserve surrenders on the floor of the House of Commons

Liberal George Bulyea (bottom left), named lieutenant governor of the new province of Alberta in 1905, also pushed for reserve surrenders. (Library and Archives Canada)

in October 1903 when he claimed that First Nations weren't using the land set aside for them. "It is better to do something with it," he exhorted Prime Minister Laurier, "exchange it, sell it, dispose of it, but do not let it be ruined." When Laurier reminded him that the government was bound by legislation, Borden shot back "in the meantime the land is useless." The prime minister agreed that the situation was frustrating. "They [First Nations] are always averse," he confessed, "to surrendering anything they have."[6]

One politician who made a parliamentary career out of calling for reserve surrenders — in this case, the Roseau River reserve — was Alphonse-Alfred-Clément La Rivière. A former provincial cabinet minister and journalist,[7] the Conservative member for Provencher had first targeted the Treaty One Anishinaabe band and its rich agricultural lands when he entered the Commons in 1889. He never let up for the next decade and a half. At one point in February 1901, La Rivière pointedly asked

Clifford Sifton whether the band would "soon be moved to some more convenient and profitable place."[8] Sifton's one-sentence response was equally brusque: nothing could be done without band consent.

The Roseau River band's determination to hold on to its reserve soon ran up against local Liberal forces that wouldn't take no for an answer. George Walton, an Emerson merchant and auctioneer, headed a Liberal delegation that met with Sifton during a visit to Winnipeg in the fall of 1902. They wanted the reserve opened to local settlers so that they could expand their farming operations in step with the booming wheat economy. It's not known what was said, but the Dominion City *Echo* later reported that Sifton had been persuaded to reverse his stand.[9] Instructions were issued in January 1903 to take an immediate reserve surrender.

Inspector Samuel Reid Marlatt of the Manitoba superintendency handled the surrender meeting. Indian commissioner David Laird and his assistant J.A.J. McKenna, based in Winnipeg, would later complain that they had been excluded from the negotiations.

Marlatt, though, had a ready familiarity with the Roseau River band because he had been pushing a possible reserve surrender for several years now. He also owed his position to Sifton. The Portage la Prairie civic politician and merchant had been appointed to the Indian Affairs outside service in 1897 because of his Liberal credentials. Marlatt was someone who could be entrusted to carry out Ottawa's directive — if he didn't want to jeopardize his patronage job. Just to make sure that Marlatt didn't back down in the face of continuing band intransigence, George Walton privately met with him beforehand to reinforce the importance of his assignment.[10]

In late March 1903, Marlatt informed the Indian Affairs department that he had successfully negotiated the surrender of twelve square miles from the eastern side of the Roseau River reserve — about 57 percent of its entire area. "The surrender was obtained not by the desire of the Indians," Marlatt admitted, "but by the strong wish of the Department." He then added, as if to justify the agreement that had been struck, "it was with great difficulty secured . . . they are fully posted as to the value of their land."[11]

These remarks didn't tell the whole story. Marlatt had met with the eligible male members of the band on January 20, but left without an agreement. He went back at the end of the month and managed to get twelve men to sign the surrender agreement. But he never recorded how many male band members participated in this second meeting. Nor did he fully document his verbal promises in the surrender agreement.

These inducements included 10 percent of the land sale proceeds and any interest (5 percent) collected on land sale instalment payments. The band also received an immediate $500 signing bonus. Indian Affairs would later suggest that Marlatt had made statements that went against department practice, while the Roseau River band threatened to take back the surrendered land over the government's failure to distribute the annual interest payments.[12]

With one eye on the forthcoming Manitoba provincial election, expected later that year, Pedley moved to sell the former Roseau River reserve land as quickly as possible. He initially leaned towards marketing the 7,680 acres by private tender.[13] But the Roseau River reserve had been coveted by settlers for more than a decade, and the surrendered portion would fetch premium prices in a heavily settled district.

About 300 people turned up for the auction at Dominion City on May 15, 1903. The bidding was feverish, with two-thirds of the land acquired by local buyers, including the band farm instructor John C. Ginn. The average price was $13.50 per acre.[14]

Astonishingly, La Rivière wasn't satisfied. He was back on his feet in the House of Commons in July 1904, seeking the surrender of the rest of the Roseau River reserve. It was time, La Rivière admonished the minister, for the government to introduce "a policy whereby all these little patches of land known as reserves may be thrown open."[15]

The partial surrender of the Roseau River reserve coincided with that of the Michel reserve immediately northwest of Edmonton. On January 19, 1903, several members of the Michel band, including the Chief and headman, signed a statement that they were prepared to surrender seven square miles of mostly timbered land in exchange for agricultural implements and livestock.

Indian agent James Gibbons endorsed the request. Not only were they "all good workers" in need of machinery and other farming assistance, but the surrender would still leave the band with a thirty-three-square-mile reserve. The Canadian Northern Railway (CNoR), Gibbons added, had been surveyed to run only a few miles south of the reserve and its arrival in the district "would make the land valuable."[16]

It was a curious proposal, in that a surrender was rarely initiated by a band unless pushed in that direction. Sifton had once warned, "It is possible for persons to get Indians to sign almost any kind of statements . . . we are unable therefore to rely to any extent upon written statements that come in signed by Indians."[17] It's also puzzling why the Michel people would even contemplate a surrender. Since entering Treaty Six in 1878, the Iroquois-Cree band had successfully worked the land to the point where, in Gibbons's words, "they are self-supporting, getting no help from the Department."[18] The second generation of reserve farmers deserved to be supported instead of being required to give up land to get the assistance they needed to improve their operations.

The Michel surrender request arrived in Ottawa at the same time that Indian Affairs was absorbed with the anticipated Roseau River surrender. Pedley wondered about the need for farming equipment and turned to Indian commissioner Laird for guidance. Laird recommended that the matter be temporarily put on hold. He wasn't opposed to a surrender. He even believed that the Michel band could give up more land, that it had more than it needed. But he wanted to wait until after the rail line near the reserve had been laid before taking the surrender. He also maintained that Indian Affairs, and not the band, should determine what agricultural assistance was actually needed.[19]

Nothing was done about a possible Michel surrender until after the disposition of the Roseau River lands in mid-May 1903. A few weeks after the auction sale, the Michel band sent another request to Ottawa, this time a letter dictated to Gibbons, along with a list of nineteen male members who supported a surrender. "We ask you

Chief Michel Callihoo (third from left) and members of his family.
(Musée Héritage Museum)

to let us sell part of our reserve," they appealed. "It is the only way
we see for the young people to make a living . . . they have not the
money to buy what they need if they have not the help from the
Department."[20]

W.A. Orr of the Lands and Timber Branch forwarded this "very
urgent" matter to Pedley in early July, together with his recommendation that a surrender be taken but for a larger reserve area.[21] The
deputy minister concurred, and before the end of the week, the surrender documents were mailed to Gibbons. Laird was never informed
or aware that a surrender had been taken until after the fact.

Gibbons took the surrender on July 20, 1903. Only eight male
members of the band signed the agreement — even though the letter
to Indian Affairs a month earlier listed nineteen men who were prepared to give up reserve land for implements and livestock. The amount
of land surrendered had also almost doubled in area from the seven
square miles (4,480 acres) initially proposed by the band to more than
twelve square miles (7,800 acres).

Gibbons also continued his past practice of keeping a poor record
of the proceedings. He never documented how many band members
participated or what was discussed during the meeting. That might

have seemed unnecessary to the agent because the band had called for the surrender. Ottawa would decide, moreover, what the Michel men received for selling their land. The surrender document gave Indian Affairs the authority to determine how much from the sale of the Michel lands was to be spent on farming assistance, and what kind of assistance.[22]

The Michel partial surrender was made official by government order on September 12, 1903 — a mere six weeks after Pedley had authorized the action. The surveying of the land into quarter-sections was also to proceed, at the deputy minister's urging, "without any delay."[23] Pedley wanted to market the land that autumn. But because the survey field notes, including land valuation, weren't submitted to Ottawa until after Christmas, the sale had to be postponed until the spring of 1904. The Michel band had to wait too. It wanted to be ready for spring field work, but a request to get an advance from the pending land sale to purchase draft horses was turned down.

Indian Affairs planned to sell the Michel land by private tender. The method had proven most successful over the past few years in disposing of thousands of acres of surrendered reserve land. It also lent itself to manipulation by Pedley and his civil servant friends who had scooped up land in the past.

When the tenders were opened on June 1, 1904, bids were received for just twelve quarter-sections — about 23 percent of the Michel land for sale. Only a few local people and some speculators from Ontario, including cleaning lady Maria Allison, submitted bids. What they were offering was well below $4.39 per acre, the average rate for western lands at the time.[24]

Pedley didn't submit a single bid. He might have been stretched financially because of past purchases and couldn't raise the funds this time. Or he might have lost his nerve, not wanting to tempt fate again and possibly be found out. Whatever the reason, he passed on the opportunity and may have regretted it. Pedley could also have cancelled the sale, citing the few tenders and poor returns, and held the surrendered land back for another day. Instead he recommended that the highest bids be accepted.[25]

This decision underscored how the deputy minister was more interested in disposing of First Nations' land than looking out for their best interests. The Michel band was disappointed with the result. The limited proceeds from the sale wouldn't help the men with their agricultural needs and suggested that the band would have been better off selling reserve timber. It's little wonder they joined with other Edmonton district bands in calling for the removal of Gibbons.[26]

Around the same time that the Michel band gave up twelve square miles of reserve land, the Canadian Northern Railway figured into another surrender. In May 1903, survey crews started to locate the new transcontinental railway across the southwest corner of the Cote reserve, along the Assiniboine River and immediately west of the present-day Saskatchewan-Manitoba border. Indian Affairs, though, had never granted permission to run the right-of-way through the reserve, let alone approved construction.

Pedley immediately ordered the CNoR to cease operations within reserve boundaries until it submitted a plan and $250 deposit. An agreement was subsequently reached in July that provided the railway company with a four-mile roadbed through the reserve (about forty-five acres) for $8 an acre.[27] The Treaty Four Cree-Saulteaux band could probably have demanded a higher price because the railroad would have been reluctant to relocate its main line. Instead, the department acted on the advice of Indian agent Henry A. Carruthers. Carruthers had a checkered career in the Indian Affairs outside service, was known to be lazy, and may not have put much effort into determining a competitive price for the right-of-way.[28]

In September 1903, the CNoR asked to buy more Cote land. This time, the company wanted nearly 575 acres for a townsite and station. The southwest corner of the reserve was deemed ideal for the placement of a railway divisional point. Laird challenged the need for so much land and warned that such a large parcel couldn't simply be sold as if it were just a piece of real estate, but required a formal surrender.[29] To this end, his assistant McKenna served as a mediator between the

Cote band and the CNoR solicitors, trying to bring the two parties to an agreement over how much reserve land would be made available to the railroad.

That didn't seem likely at the beginning of negotiations. Chief Joseph Cote, according to McKenna, was "not anxious" to give up any part of the reserve for a townsite. He too questioned the size of the request — almost one square mile — and said he might sell only what was "absolutely requisite" to the needs of the railway.[30] But it would cost the CNoR dearly. The Chief wanted $25 per acre for the station grounds and other railway facilities, and $100 per acre for the townsite. The CNoR countered in December with a greatly reduced request: 55.76 acres for the townsite (at $25 per acre) and 30.06 acres for the station grounds (at no cost). Land for stations was normally freely provided because of the local economic spinoffs from the coming of the railway and townsite development.

Sifton wasn't privy to these negotiations, but when he learned about the CNoR request, he ruled in January 1904 that no town could be established within three miles of any First Nations reserve. This edict irked agent Carruthers, who viewed any reserve land sale as a way to provide the Cote band with farming implements and livestock. McKenna was also displeased with Sifton's decision and prepared a report for the minister on what a townsite would mean for the reserve, while continuing to negotiate with the company.

In March, the CNoR revised its offer again. It proposed to purchase 272 acres at $10 an acre, as well as split with the band any proceeds over $5,000 that it derived from town lot sales. This offer, considered final, was endorsed by the Indian Affairs department and its officials in the field.[31] But McKenna still had to win over Sifton. In his report, dated April 13, 1904, the assistant commissioner argued that the band couldn't stand in the way of progress and should embrace the townsite. "The West," McKenna reasoned, "cannot attain its proper development without the passage of railways through Indian reserves."[32] Sifton agreed.

The CNoR immediately began work at the new siding, named Kamsack after a Saulteaux man (kâ-mišâk, "that which is big") who once lived in the Fort Pelly district in the mid-nineteenth century.

The Cote band surrendered land to the Canadian Northern Railway for the Kamsack townsite, a divisional point along the main line. (prairie-towns.com)

Kamsack was already the name of a post office to the southeast, and the railway simply appropriated it for the new station and townsite.[33] In choosing the name, the CNoR might have been acknowledging the Indigenous role in the founding of Kamsack. But the partial surrender had still not been approved when construction gangs moved onto the reserve that spring to build the train station, elevator, and hardware and other stores.

On May 20, 1904, Pedley confirmed the terms of the deal with the railway, adding at the Chief's insistence that the sale proceeds could be spent at the band's discretion. None of these particulars, though, were written into the surrender document forwarded to Carruthers.[34] Instead, Indian Affairs included the standard clause that the government would hold the funds in trust for the Cote band and decide if, when, and how they were to be expended.

The surrender was taken by Carruthers on June 21. There were fourteen signatories, including Chief Cote. Little is known about the meeting because of the agent's failure to record even basic information, such as how many male band members participated. The surrender of 272 acres of Cote land was confirmed by order-in-council in late September 1904.

That same month, Parliament was dissolved and Prime Minister Laurier called a general election for the first week of November. Sifton was once again tasked with organizing and directing the party campaign in western Canada. John Wesley Dafoe, editor of the Sifton-owned Manitoba *Free Press*, predicted a resounding Liberal victory: "There was hardly a cloud in the sky."[35] Sifton, though, had his hands full in Manitoba, where he was expected to do better than the 1900 federal contest when the Liberals won four seats to the Conservatives' three. Arrayed against him was the Conservative tag-team of Premier Rodmond Roblin and his henchman Robert Rogers and their political organization.

The other potential wild card in the coming federal campaign was Sifton's health. Overworked and stressed out, he spoke to Laurier about retiring in late 1903, but the Liberal leader "emphatically refused . . . he would not hear of it."[36] The demands of the job, though, continued to weigh heavily on Sifton's mind and undermine his health. He complained of the "burden of carrying the affairs of the West" to a Liberal colleague in February 1904, "[to] say nothing of the enormous mass of departmental work and political details . . . forced upon me at every turn . . . No one should be charged with this duty."[37]

These comments were certainly self-pitying, but even his private secretary, A.P. Collier, seemed to have had enough of the workload and resigned.[38] Sifton fled south for a brief late-winter vacation and returned seemingly refreshed and ready to do battle whenever the writ was dropped. He had carefully chosen lieutenants with particular responsibilities across the West, while he largely supervised operations from Ottawa. His new private secretary, former Ottawa journalist James Bernard Harkin, endured a baptism of fire. "It should be done immediately," Sifton demanded at one point during the election. "In fact, everything should be done immediately."[39]

The Laurier Liberals were returned to office with a smashing victory (138 seats to the Tories' 75), including capturing 52 percent of the popular vote. The returns in Manitoba, where the Liberals secured seven of the ten seats, were particularly gratifying to Sifton. The Conservatives, on the other hand, cried foul. R.E.A. Leech, a member of Sifton's constituency staff, had earlier confessed to Harkin, "We may have to take a hurried trip after the elections are over."[40] Robert Rogers looked for an opportunity to get even one day.[41]

Because of Sifton's heavy involvement in the 1904 election campaign, any Interior and Indian Affairs business that fall was largely restricted to housekeeping matters. Senior department officials who held patronage positions were expected to help their boss and the Liberal party win re-election. It was how the political game was played, leaving Pedley and others little time for actual government work.

In December, Sifton also had to deal with a major administrative shake-up. Once the election was over, the minister's long-time Brandon associate James Smart announced his intention to step down as deputy minister of the Interior at the end of the year. Even though Smart had given up his other deputy minister duties at Indian Affairs, the two departments remained linked, albeit with Interior having the upper hand. Interior, for example, was forever pressing Indian Affairs to make reserve land available for white settlement.

Sifton consequently had to find a replacement who would ensure that his two areas of responsibility ran smoothly and in lockstep, especially with the first session of the new Parliament about to open the first week of January. He reached inside the Interior department to promote William Wallace Cory, then assistant commissioner of dominion lands. Another Ontario-born Manitoba Liberal and lawyer by training, Cory had joined Sifton's Ottawa team in 1901 after serving as his constituency organizer in the 1900 general election. He would serve as deputy minister for a quarter century, including more than ten years as commissioner of the Northwest Territories.

It's debatable whether Smart's departure represented much of a loss to Sifton — or whether, as Interior deputy minister, he had done much work for the government over the past two years. Smart had always been something of a gadfly, mixing personal gain with public business and never thinking twice about it. He probably was tired of the demands that came with the position, especially after eight years. He might also have been worried that his government-fronted money-making schemes would be found out. Not only had he been illegally speculating in First Nations lands, but along with William Preston, Canada's commissioner of emigration for Europe, he was skimming off immigrant bonuses that were supposedly earned by the North Atlantic Trading Company through its secret, exclusive contract with the Interior department.

Smart might simply have concluded that there were more lucrative opportunities outside government service. He had certainly prepared the way before he stepped down. In 1903, he established the James A. Smart Company in Montreal.[42] It specialized in passenger bookings, immigrant recruitment, and western real estate, including First Nations land sales. Smart and Will White, inspector of United States immigration agencies, had also enlisted Sifton's assistance in 1903 to help cut a deal with the Canadian Pacific Railway to buy 10,000 acres of railway land at $4 per acre. These lands were to be sold to settlers who couldn't find homesteads or who wanted larger operations.[43]

Dealing with Smart's departure temporarily diverted Sifton's attention from a much more important government file. In the late 1890s, Frederick Haultain, the leader of the North-West Territories government, started calling for western provincehood. Faced with thousands of immigrants pouring into the prairie district in the late 1890s, his administration simply didn't have enough federal funding to meet the ever-growing service and infrastructure demands. "We are confronted with impossible conditions," Haultain informed Sifton.[44]

Haultain wanted one large western province, to be called "Buffalo," created between Manitoba and British Columbia. But in February 1905, Prime Minister Laurier countered with two autonomy bills. There was to be not one but two provinces, Saskatchewan and Alberta, oriented north–south and roughly equal in size. Regina and Edmonton were named as temporary capitals, the final decision resting with the new provincial governments. The legislation also gave the federal government continued control over western lands and resources.

Territorial premier Frederick Haultain and the Laurier government tangled over the size and number of new western provinces. Clifford Sifton resigned over the prime minister's handling of the matter. (Provincial Archives of Saskatchewan)

Even more controversial were the draft educational clauses, which seemed to call for the restoration of separate school practices from 1875. Members of the House on both the government and Opposition benches reacted angrily to this seemingly blatant attempt to turn back the clock on educational matters when the largely Protestant population of the territories had been moving towards secular education and public schools. Laurier eventually backed down and allowed a redrafting of the clauses to bring them in line with current practice in the territories.[45]

Sifton, a great believer in national schools, left the cabinet as a matter of principle. Absent from Parliament when the autonomy bills were tabled, he hurried back to Ottawa, and following an unsatisfactory meeting with the prime minister over the educational clauses, submitted his resignation on February 28, 1905.

There were probably other reasons, though, why Sifton decided to step down. Sifton was never comfortable with Laurier's style or how he treated his ministers. He wanted to be considered for other cabinet portfolios, wanted new challenges, but had been pigeonholed. Sifton once described the prime minister as "a masterful man set on having his own way."[46] There were also rumours of an affair with a married Ottawa woman — the subject of a tell-all exposé in the Calgary *Eye-Opener*. It's been suggested that Sifton resigned before the tryst became public and thereby spared the government any embarrassment.[47] Or maybe he had just lost interest in his cabinet duties because of his poor health.

As Liberal backbencher Walter Scott explained Sifton's decision, "I am pretty sure that it has been for some time his wish to get free."[48]

Sifton's two cabinet posts were left vacant for two weeks. No one served in an acting capacity until Laurier himself temporarily assumed responsibility for both Interior and Indian Affairs on March 13. The prime minister had to deal immediately with two possible reserve surrenders.

In December 1904, Indian agent Thomas W. Aspdin had informed Ottawa that the Carry the Kettle band of the Nakoda agency wanted to surrender nine square miles of reserve land. It was a surprising request, especially coming from the band.

The Carry the Kettle reserve, located southeast of Indian Head on the Canadian Pacific Railway main line, was made up of Cypress Hills refugees. Entering Treaty Four at Fort Walsh in 1877, the Man Who Took the Coat and Long Lodge bands wanted reserves in their traditional territory in and around the hills. But they were forced to vacate the region in 1882 and moved to a new home east of Regina, where they were amalgamated with the Carry the Kettle band.

After a few years of struggle and failure, the Nakoda made steady progress at farming and were able to meet most of their flour, beef, and vegetable production needs by the start of the twentieth century. Annual reports for the band mentioned implements being used in the fields, a large cattle herd being grazed, and hay being sold to the local market. It was puzzling, then, why the band wanted to give up some of its reserve in 1904.

Three years earlier, when western Liberal MP James Douglas forwarded a complaint from a Montmartre constituent that Carry the Kettle lands should "serve the interest of white men before Indians,"[49] Smart had Indian Affairs investigate whether a partial surrender was possible. Aspdin, an original member of the North-West Mounted Police, reported back to the department in February 1901 that the band was "categorically opposed to surrendering any of their land."[50] The Indian agent was firmly against it too, especially the loss of any pasture. "It would in my opinion be suicidal to part with any of this land," Aspdin cautioned.[51]

Indian Affairs never questioned why the Carry the Kettle band was now prepared to give up some of its reserve or why Aspdin had reversed his position, given his strenuous opposition to the idea only a few years earlier. Moving on the surrender was temporarily set aside, though, because of Smart's resignation, the dust-up over the autonomy bills, and then Sifton's resignation. It wasn't until Laurier became acting minister of the two departments that Inspector William Morris Graham was sent to meet with the band on March 30, 1905.

Graham, despite his Conservative leanings, was something of a golden boy in Indian Affairs circles. Hired as a clerk in 1885, Graham

Indian Affairs inspector William Graham (far left) and his wife with Indian Affairs accountant Duncan Campbell Scott (far right) and his wife. Both men played a role in reserve surrenders. (Glenbow Archives)

had risen to Indian agent in 1897, was placed in charge of the Qu'Appelle agency in 1901, and then appointed head of the southern Saskatchewan inspectorate in 1904. He was continuously lauded, especially by Sifton in the House of Commons, for his "particular ability in leading the Indians to become self-supporting."[52]

What this reputation meant in practice was reducing or withholding rations to forcibly get First Nations to bend to his will. Graham's promotion of reserve agriculture was counterbalanced by his belief that First Nations didn't have initiative and that reserves only prospered because of his presence and his heavy-handed methods.[53]

Saskatchewan First Nations thoroughly disliked the severe Graham. They mockingly called him "Pegleg Bill" because of the wooden leg that replaced the lower limb he had lost in a childhood accident. Graham would have considered the nickname contemptible, and all the more reason to be dismissive of First Nations and their interests. He would play a prominent role in reserve surrenders in the coming years. He would later try to use his family connections to secure the deputy minister position.[54]

Graham's visit with the Carry the Kettle band was intended to pave the way for the surrender of 5,760 acres (nine square miles) from the southern reserve boundary. From his account, there is no indication that alternatives to a surrender were contemplated. Graham's sole purpose was to establish the surrender terms.

The band needed cash to pay off the existing debt on its threshing outfit, trade up for a newer machine and cover the difference from the land sale proceeds, and pay back the department for fencing the reserve pasture. Graham communicated these conditions to the department, along with his emphatic endorsement of the surrender.[55] He seemed oblivious to the contradiction staring him in the face — the band had to forfeit some its land for agricultural improvements to work the land.

The other surrender that Laurier personally handled involved the "Stony band." They were actually three Nakoda bands, collectively dismissed by the department as troublesome and unprogressive.

In August 1878, Chief Mosquito signed an adhesion to Treaty Six at Battleford, then capital of the North-West Territories. The following year, a thirty-six-square-mile reserve (#109) was set aside for the band in the Eagle Hills west of Battleford. In 1884, two other Nakoda bands were settled in the area. Lean Man entered Treaty Four at Fort Walsh in September 1877, while Grizzly Bear's Head was recognized as a leader of his own band during the payment of Treaty Four annuities in 1880. Both bands were moved north from the Cypress Hills in 1882 and granted an undivided block of land (roughly thirty-six square miles) next to the Mosquito people.

During the 1885 North-West Rebellion, the Nakoda were drawn into events in and around Fort Battleford, including the battle of Cut Knife Hill. Indian Affairs declared the three bands disloyal and denied them effective leadership. What further sullied their reputation was their resistance to sending their children away to school. The three bands also struggled at farming, in part because their reserve lands were better suited to traditional activities like hunting and gathering. Over time, they raised stock, in addition to providing hay and firewood to the settler market.

As in the case of the pending Carry the Kettle surrender, and the 1904 Michel partial surrender, the idea to release part of the Nakoda reserves apparently originated with the bands. On February 6, 1905, Battleford Indian agent Joseph P.G. Day, a Liberal appointee, advised Indian commissioner Laird that the Stony Indians wanted to "dispose of . . . twenty-two and a half sections (14,400 acres) of land" from the combined Lean Man and Grizzly Bear's Head reserve (23,168 acres). "These Indians are to all intents and purposes one Band," Day explained, "and that as a band they are decreasing rapidly." He added that "they would like to have the chance of realizing in this life some benefit from their land."[56]

McKenna seized the offer. The surrendered land, he advised Ottawa, would fetch a good price at auction. Pedley sent the matter to Laurier for his approval on March 23. He told the prime minister "the land is lying idle and there are a large number of old people."[57] Laurier initialled his approval in the margin, and the surrender documents were sent to Laird in the first week of April.

Before either the Carry the Kettle or Lean Man/Grizzly Bear's Head surrenders could be formally executed, the Governor General swore in a new Interior and Indian Affairs minister on April 8. It was Frank Oliver. His appointment to the dual posts was a head-scratcher because of his withering criticism of the Laurier government's settlement, immigration, and Indian Affairs policies. He not only ridiculed Sifton's pandering to First Nations, but constantly carped about his open-door immigration policy and how it was populating the West with "scum." He once declared that a Ukrainian was "only a generation removed from a debased and brutalized serf" and deeply resented "the millstone of this Slav population hung around our necks."[58]

It didn't make sense, then, why the prime minister chose Oliver over someone like the affable Walter Scott, the owner of the Regina *Leader* and Liberal MP for Assiniboia West since 1900. It could be that Laurier was tired of Oliver's backbench criticisms and believed that the government and the party would be better off if the Edmonton Liberal had to sponsor and defend western policies. It could be that Laurier was rewarding Oliver for his support of the autonomy bills and wanted to strengthen his hold on the new province of Alberta, especially when Conservative Calgary would be upset not being named capital. Or it could be that Laurier wanted to get back at Sifton by replacing him with his rival.[59] Whatever the prime minister's motive — and he never said why — Oliver had the energy and drive that the two positions demanded.

Oliver's assumption of the Indian Affairs portfolio was expected to bring about a significant departure from how the department had been run. His acid opinion of First Nations was well known, matched only by his ceaseless calls for the opening of prairie reserves to white settlement.

Sifton hadn't acted much differently, despite his public policy stand on surrenders. "Under the arrangement [treaties] we have made with them," Sifton once responded to an Opposition question about reserves, "we will not disturb them in the occupation of the land . . . except upon their own consent being given in a specified form . . . when we think it will not interfere with the livelihood of the Indians."[60]

Pedley offered similar assurances in an optimistic talk on "Canada and Redman" before the Canadian Club in March 1905. "The right to that [reserve] land was absolutely safeguarded," he affirmed at his sanctimonious best, "and not one foot could be sold except by an order from the Governor in Council even if the consent of the Indians had been given."[61] Yet over the previous eight years, during Sifton's tenure as minister, not one foot but rather thousands of acres of reserve land had been surrendered and sold under circumstances that went against the best interests of First Nations by any measure.

If anyone ever questioned this yawning gap between principle and practice, senior Indian Affairs officials were ready with a scripted response. "We have to proceed in a diplomatic way and get the Indians to surrender their lands when they are willing to do so," Sifton reminded his House of Commons colleagues. "The officers of the department, having constant dealings with the Indians, know how far it is safe to go in each particular case."[62]

Pedley used similar phrasing in his Canadian Club speech, adding extra emphasis so that there was no mistaking his intent: "The outside officers of the department, being in constant touch with the Indians . . . policy was largely determined *through them*."[63]

Pedley knew it wasn't true. Indian agents may have brought forward surrender requests, but they were only responding to department encouragement and outside pressure to make reserve land available. The Ottawa office also generally determined the timing, amount, and terms of any surrender and subsequent land sale arrangements. None of these decisions put First Nations' well-being and interests first. It would take a decade for the House of Commons to learn how Pedley and other patronage appointees personally benefited from reserve surrenders.

As for Ottawa cleaning lady Maria Allison, her clandestine purchases of former Michel land remained a secret for more than half a century.[64]

Notes

1. Tyler and Wright Research Consultants Limited, "The Alienation of Indian Reserve Lands During the Administration of Sir Wilfrid Laurier, 1896–1911: Michel Reserve #132," unpublished report, 1978, pp. 135–40.

2. M. Zaslow, *The Opening of the Canadian North* (Toronto: McClelland and Stewart, 1971), pp. 114–15.

3. *Library and Archives Canada (LAC)*, C. Sifton papers, v. 128, J.D. McLean to C. Sifton, February 25, 1902.

4. House of Commons, *Debates*, July 18, 1904, p. 6951.

5. P. Martin-McGuire, *First Nations Land Surrenders on the Prairies, 1896–1911* (Ottawa: Indian Claims Commission, 1998), pp. 94, 100.

6. *Debates*, October 12, 1903, p. 13782.

7. La Rivière was also an investor in the Canadian Colonization Company, one of the first syndicates to come together in the early 1880s to capitalize on western settlement.

8. *Debates*, February 12, 1901, p. 82.

9. Dominion City *Echo*, February 19, 1903.

10. Ibid., January 24, 1903.

11. *LAC*, RG10, v.3730, f. 26306-1, R.S. Marlatt to D. Laird, June 19, 1903.

12. Martin-McGuire, *First Nations Land Surrenders*, pp. 258–9, 450–1.

13. Ibid., p. 107.

14. Ibid., pp. 344–5.

15. *Debates*, July 18, 1904, p. 6952.

16. *LAC*, RG10, v. 6667, f. 110A-4-1, pt. 1, J. Gibbons to J.D. McLean, January 30, 1903.

17. Quoted in D.J. Hall, "Clifford Sifton and Canadian Indian Administration, 1896–1905," *Prairie Forum*, v.2, n.2, 1977, p. 136.

18. *LAC*, RG10, v. 6667, f. 110A-4-1, pt. 1, J. Gibbons to J.D. McLean, January 30, 1903.

19. Tyler and Wright, "Michel Reserve #132," p. 127.

20. *LAC*, RG10, v. 6667, f. 110A-4-1, pt. 1, Chief Michel Callihoo et al. to Indian Affairs, June 8, 1903.

21. Ibid., W.A. Orr to F. Pedley, July 2, 1903.

22. Tyler and Wright, "Michel Reserve #132," pp. 129–30.

23. *LAC*, RG10, v. 6667, f. 110A-4-1, pt. 1, F. Pedley to R.W. Lendrum, September 28, 1903.

24. See average price per acre for western lands for the years 1900–1911 in *Debates*, April 14, 1915, p. 2551.

25. Tyler and Wright, "Michel Reserve #132," pp. 134–6.

26. Martin-McGuire, *First Nations Land Surrenders*, pp. 348–9.

27. Ibid., p. 184.

28. Ibid., p. 475.

29. *LAC*, RG10, v. 3560, f. 82, pt. 8, D. Laird to Munson & Allan, September 16, 1903.

30. Ibid., J.A.J. McKenna to Munson & Allan, October 29, 1903; v. 7668, f. 22117-2, J.A.J. McKenna to J.D. McLean, November 4, 1903.

31. Martin-McGuire, *First Nations Land Surrenders*, pp. 261–2.

32. *LAC*, RG10, v. 3560, f. 82, pt. 8, J.A.J. McKenna to J.D. McLean, April 13, 1904.

33. B. Barry, *Geographical Names of Saskatchewan* (Regina: Centax Books, 2005), p. 213. Barry does not mention in the Kamsack entry that the land for the station and townsite was purchased from the Cote band.

34. Martin-McGuire, *First Nations Land Surrenders*, pp. 262–3.

35. Quoted in J.M. Beck, *Pendulum of Power: Canada's Federal Elections* (Scarborough: Prentice Hall, 1968), p. 97.

36. Quoted in D.J. Hall, *Clifford Sifton, v.2: A Lonely Eminence, 1901–1929* (Vancouver: University of British Columbia Press, 1985), p. 158.

37. Quoted in ibid., pp. 157–8.

38. Collier opened an emigrant service in Winnipeg — offering farm land, passenger booking, and mail order — and tried to use his government connections to get on the patronage list. *LAC*, Sifton papers [reel C579], General Correspondence, A.P. Collier to C. Sifton, January 4, 1905.

39. Quoted in E.J. Hart, *J.B. Harkin: Father of Canada's National Parks* (Edmonton: University of Alberta Press, 2010), p. 14.

40. Quoted in W.L.R. Clark, "Politics in Brandon City, 1899–1949," unpublished Ph.D. thesis, University of Alberta, 1976, p. 63.

41. William L. Morton, *Manitoba: A History* (Toronto: University of Toronto Press, 1957), p. 294. The *Winnipeg Free Press* reported on

October 30, 1905, that Leech was to be "arraigned on the charge of irregularities during the late Dominion election."

42. Smart's spouse, Eliza Frances, was a company director.
43. Martin-McGuire, *First Nations Land Surrenders*, pp. 61, 102.
44. Quoted in D. Owram, ed., *The Formation of Alberta: A Documentary History* (Calgary: Historical Society of Alberta, 1979), p. 115.
45. D.J. Hall, "A Divergence of Principle: Clifford Sifton, Sir Wilfrid Laurier, and the North-West Autonomy Bills, 1905," *Laurentian University Review*, v. 7, n. 1, November 1974, pp. 11–19.
46. Quoted in Hall, *Sifton, v. 2*, p. 198.
47. P. Berton, *The Promised Land: Settling the West, 1896–1914* (Toronto: McClelland and Stewart, 1984), pp. 194–204.
48. Quoted in Hall, *Sifton, v. 2*, p. 185.
49. Quoted in D.J. McMahon, "The Surrender of Land at Carry-The-Kettle Band," unpublished report for FSIN, 1985, p. 2.
50. Ibid., p. 3.
51. Ibid., p. 3.
52. Quoted in B. Titley, *The Indian Commissioners: Agents of the State and Indian Policy in Canada's Prairie West, 1873–1932* (Edmonton: University of Alberta Press, 2009), p. 181.
53. Ibid., p. 185.
54. Ibid., pp. 184–5.
55. Quoted in McMahon, "The Surrender of Land at Carry-The-Kettle Band," p. 4.
56. *LAC*, RG10, v. 4013, f. 271245, J.P.G. Day to D. Laird, February 6, 1905.
57. Ibid., F. Pedley to W. Laurier, March 23, 1905.
58. Quoted in Berton, *The Promised Land*, pp. 57–8.
59. The relationship between Sifton and Oliver was frosty. In August 1900, just before the federal election, Sifton asked his brother, Arthur, to speak to Oliver: "Ask him [Oliver] to be sensible for the next three months even if he has to be otherwise afterwards." In D.J. Hall, *Clifford Sifton, v.1: The Young Napoleon, 1861–1900* (Vancouver: University of British Columbia Press, 1981), p. 296.
60. *Debates*, July 18, 1904, pp. 6952–3.
61. Toronto *Globe*, March 28, 1905.

62. *Debates*, July 18, 1904, p. 6953.

63. Toronto *Globe*, March 28, 1905. The newspaper report published the last two words of Pedley's sentence in italics.

64. Maria Allison's land purchases were first discussed in Tyler and Wright, "Michel Reserve #132."

Seven

THE INDIAN GOT WHAT WAS OWING TO HIM

ndian agent Henry A. Carruthers was puzzled. In early September
1905, Methodist missionary John McDougall of Calgary had turned
up, without warning, at Kamsack in east-central Saskatchewan and
talked to the Cote band about surrendering a portion of its reserve.
McDougall told the agent that he would be back the following month
"to try and induce them to do so."[1]

Carruthers knew nothing about Reverend McDougall's mission
— or whether he even had department authority to negotiate with
the Cote band — and asked Ottawa what he was doing there. Indian
Affairs confirmed that the sixty-three-year-old McDougall had
recently been appointed a special negotiator for the department. It
was his job to visit First Nations bands identified by Indian Affairs
and get them to agree to a partial release of their reserves; once he had
worked out the draft terms, formal surrender meetings would be held.

McDougall was one of several agents who actively pursued prairie
reserve surrenders on behalf of the Wilfrid Laurier Liberal government. These senior officials in the Indian Affairs outside service keenly
engaged in an unofficial competition to see who could secure surrenders, especially in the face of determined band resistance.

Their negotiation methods, no matter how questionable, didn't
matter to Frank Oliver, as long as reserve land, particularly along new
railway lines, was opened to settlement. Much more land might have

been taken if not for the fact, as Oliver complained, that "it was not possible for the government to enforce a surrender."[2]

⋖⟵⇥⟶⋗

No sooner had Oliver assumed the Interior and Indian Affairs portfolios in April 1905 than he moved to distance himself from his predecessor Clifford Sifton's shadow. A keen proponent of British recruitment, he sponsored amendments to the Immigration Act in 1906 and again in 1910 that made entry to Canada dependent on racial origin, while giving the government greater flexibility to deport so-called undesirables. There was to be a clear pecking order, with British at the top.

Oliver was also an avowed champion of settlers' rights. In 1908, he bowed to the demand for more homesteads by amending the Dominion Lands Act to allow for the settlement of the open range country in southern Saskatchewan and Alberta, over the protest of ranchers. Thousands of settlers poured into the dry mixed-prairie district and broke land better suited for grazing. Oliver also directed Interior officials

Frank Oliver, speaking in Vegreville, Alberta, in 1908, pursued reserve surrenders with a singleness of purpose. (Provincial Archives of Alberta)

to investigate starting a second settlement frontier north of the North Saskatchewan River.

These policy changes were to be expected after Oliver's past comments from the Liberal backbenches. His handling of Indian Affairs represented a departure from Sifton's tenure — if only because he was more forthright, more damning, about the failure of prairie First Nations to become successful farmers. Oliver believed that reserves were too large and that the land was being wasted as settlement boomed across the West and the prairie provinces were running out of homesteads. He consequently began to promote surrenders as a department priority, moving land from the Indian Affairs side of the ledger to the Interior side wherever and whenever possible.

Oliver's attitude towards prairie reserves — and that of many of his fellow parliamentarians on both sides of the House — was grounded in the belief that Canada had dealt honourably with these First Nations, but there was nothing wrong in trying to get around its treaty obligations.

Three decades earlier, in October 1877, Oliver had been present at the signing of Treaty Seven at Blackfoot Crossing as correspondent for the Toronto *Globe*. In his account, parts of which were reproduced by treaty commissioner Alexander Morris in his *Treaties of Canada* (1880), Oliver contrasted the peacefulness and sanctity of treaty-making in Canada with the volatile situation south of the border in Montana, where negotiating an agreement with the Blackfoot was improbable. He acknowledged, almost as a point of pride, that Canada's First Nations "have rights which we are morally bound to respect."[3]

Respecting those rights, though, had its limits. On May 25, 1905, just weeks into his new cabinet duties, Oliver was called upon in the House of Commons to explain Indian Affairs spending estimates for the coming budget year. During questioning, Oliver was repeatedly caught flat-footed, unable to recall details or pilloried for past practices. One Opposition member growled "the minister's explanation is hardly in accordance with the facts," while another quipped that "it would surprise a great many housewives to learn [what] the Indians . . . were supplied."

Oliver was on firmer ground in speaking about his duty to First Nations. "There is one condition that is not changed," he said about becoming minister, "[which is] that the Indians are ... the wards of the government." At the same time, he reported that Indian Affairs was doing all it could to encourage bands to agree to surrenders: "Efforts are being made to induce the Indians to part with portions of their reserves which they do not need."

He was silent, though, about how the excess land was to be determined, preferring to assure the House that bands could count on "the government acting as their trustees." No one raised any objections or reminded the government of its treaty relationships. The members were only interested in hearing about what land the First Nations were willing to sell and what it would take to get them to give up some of their reserves. It was deemed necessary to the greater interest of promoting settlement.[4]

By the time Oliver defended the Indian Affairs budget in the House, two surrenders had already been executed on his watch: Carry the Kettle and the "Stony band of Indians." Even though the groundwork for the partial release of these two reserves had been carried out while Prime Minister Laurier was serving as the acting department minister, the fact that they took place during Oliver's first few weeks on the job served notice that surrenders would become a hallmark of his tenure.

On April 26, 1905, the Carry the Kettle band agreed to surrender 5,760 acres (nine square miles) from the southern portion of its reserve. Indian agent Thomas Aspdin had hired an interpreter for the event and arranged for one of the band members to summon people to the meeting. Beyond that, Aspdin didn't report much — except that "a most decided majority" approved the surrender.[5] There was no record of how many eligible male band members attended the meeting or how many voted yes.

The surrender document contained the terms that inspector William Graham had worked out with the band at an earlier meeting.

But some band members, those who did not farm or raise cattle, now wanted to be compensated in cash once the lands had been sold. Graham overruled the request, and the surrender was confirmed by government order on May 23. It had taken less than a month.

The Indian commissioner's office wasn't happy with how the surrender had come about. For several months, both David Laird and his assistant James McKenna had been complaining that department headquarters communicated directly with officials in the western agencies instead of going through the Winnipeg office. The fact that they knew nothing about the Carry the Kettle surrender until after it had happened was further proof — and a source of growing animosity between McKenna, who was once Sifton's private secretary, and Graham, who often acted as a power unto himself.

Deputy Minister Frank Pedley, whose administrative style was to exercise a direct hand from Ottawa, did nothing to smooth things over between the men. Given Oliver's stand on surrenders, Pedley wasn't going to put Graham on a leash. He even told Laird, in response to his continued griping about being bypassed, that if his officials in the field didn't keep his office informed of their activities, then that was his fault.[6]

The other surrender, taken May 19, 1905 by Indian agent Joseph P.G. Day, was even more haphazard, if not plain sloppy. A whopping 23,168 acres (22.5 sections) was forfeited by the combined Grizzly Bear's Head/Lean Man reserve, even though men from the neighbouring Mosquito reserve participated in the vote.

The account of the surrender meeting was also suspect. Not only was there no official record of how many were present and how people voted, there was no documentation about how the meeting was handled. To complicate matters, none of the bands had Chiefs at the time — one of the long-term consequences of the 1885 North-West Rebellion. Agent Day also failed to properly execute the surrender documents — not once, but twice. These problems only delayed the inevitable, and the Indian Affairs takeover of half the Grizzly Bear's Head/Lean Man reserve was approved later that year.[7]

Frank Oliver lost little time in pushing other surrenders at the request of the Canadian Northern Railway. Through the summer of 1905, the railway continued to extend its lines westward across the northern prairies: from Kamsack to Edmonton, the new Alberta capital, and from Melfort to Prince Albert, the gateway to northern Saskatchewan. An amazing 546 miles of track were laid that construction season, which bested the Canadian Pacific Railway record from 1882.[8]

The CNoR was a powerful determinant of the urban landscape. The main line bypassed Saskatoon, the "wonder city," running further north through Warman. As it neared Battleford, it crossed the North Saskatchewan River several miles upstream where the valley wasn't as steep and wide. This unexpected blow was bad enough for the former territorial capital, but what made things worse was the establishment of a second rival townsite and divisional point — North Battleford — on the opposite, north side of the river. Battleford, or "old town" as it came to be called, greatly resented the "theft of its name."[9] It lost much more, though, as it soon found itself eclipsed by the upstart community.

In the new province of Saskatchewan, the CNoR had already secured part of the Cote reserve for Kamsack and a right-of-way across Fishing Lake, a Saulteaux reserve, near Wadena. Now, in July 1905, it wanted the southern portion of Cote and a northern section from Fishing Lake opened for sale and settlement. Even though the CNoR never gave a reason for the request, it probably wanted to generate traffic by bringing in settlers' supplies and shipping out grain. It's also interesting that the railway appealed directly to Oliver, probably knowing that the minister and Edmonton MP eagerly anticipated the arrival of the main line in his home community later that summer.

Oliver turned to Pedley for an assessment of whether surrenders were feasible. Even though Pedley was a Sifton appointee, Oliver had come to rely on him. The correspondence between the two Franks suggests that the pair worked well together.

James J. Campbell, a department clerk, prepared separate memos for Pedley "as to the advisability of encouraging or permitting the Indians to make the necessary surrender." It was curious wording since neither band was seeking to give up part of its reserves. Nor did Indian Affairs consult either band.

Campbell was lukewarm about a possible Cote surrender. He suggested that it was "imperative" to ensure that the band had "the necessary . . . cultivable lands" and that it would be "advisable" to consult with someone "more exactly informed as to the existing facts and conditions."[10] In a handwritten note at the bottom of the Cote memo, Campbell added that the band would get more for its land if it waited until Kamsack and the surrounding area had more settlers.

The Fishing Lake memo, by contrast, endorsed a surrender as "the best policy, in the interests of all concerned." Campbell noted that the Yellow Quill band had three reserves in the area — the one at Fishing Lake and others at Nut Lake and Kinistino — and that the band had largely subsisted by trapping, hunting, and gathering since entering treaty in 1876. Given their traditional lifestyle, Campbell suggested that the Fishing Lake reserve could be swapped for another, more isolated parcel of land. Failing that, he recommended that a surrender of the northern half of the reserve "could be easily obtained as the Indians have apparently . . . [an] aversion to contact with white men."[11] Reading between the lines, it was more likely that Indian Affairs and the Laurier government had an aversion to the Fishing Lake reserve occupying good farm land in a district undergoing rapid settlement with the coming of the railway.[12]

Campbell's memos made no difference to Oliver, who had already decided to engage Reverend John McDougall to do "special work" for the department in securing surrenders.[13] Their friendship probably dated back to 1877 when they met at the Treaty Seven negotiations. Both men would come to be widely known throughout the region — if only by reputation — by the late nineteenth century.

Oliver likely admired McDougall's decision to join the Alberta Field Force during the 1885 North-West Rebellion to help put down the imagined First Nations threat in the region.[14] The Liberal MP had also attended temperance meetings at the McDougall Methodist

The bearded Methodist missionary John McDougall with his family. McDougall helped negotiate reserve surrenders for Frank Oliver. (Glenbow Archives)

church in Edmonton (named in honour of John's father, George).[15] It didn't make sense, though, why McDougall decided to work with Oliver in initiating reserve surrenders unless he too had given up on First Nations becoming successful farmers.

Thirty years earlier, the missionary had actively participated in treaty negotiations at Fort Pitt in 1876 and then Blackfoot Crossing in 1877, encouraging the Cree and Blackfoot to settle down, take up reserves, and embrace farming. Now, his special work for Indian Affairs sought to undo what he had advocated on behalf of the Crown — that reserves, according to his account of the negotiations, were to be "inviolate."[16]

Oliver had good reason to place his confidence in McDougall. He was fluent in several Indigenous languages, having learned them from an early age at missions run by his father. He had also lived the better part of his life in western Canada, engaged in what was called "Indian service" for the Methodist Missionary Society.

When not preaching, McDougall doubled as a teacher and interpreter. In 1863, the McDougalls established the Victoria mission at

Pakan on the North Saskatchewan River, about fifty miles east of Fort Edmonton. Ten years later, the pair extended the reach of their proselytizing work into Nakoda territory and opened Morleyville on the Bow River in present-day southern Alberta. In 1875, the Canadian government engaged father and son to travel throughout the Saskatchewan country, preparing the Cree for treaty meetings the following summer.

It was only John, though, who attended the Fort Pitt negotiations. The elder McDougall had perished in January 1876 when he got lost hunting bison; his frozen body was found gnawed upon by wolves. It was said that George's fate was retribution for taking the "flying rock" (papamihaw asiniy or manitou stone), a meteorite revered by Indigenous people for its spiritual powers. The elder McDougall had considered the stone an impediment to his conversion work and stole it away from its resting place on a hill near the Battle River.[17]

John was no less controversial, if only because he drew on this treaty experience and his renowned speaking ability to try to influence bands to give up their lands.

McDougall's appointment letter, prepared by Pedley at the end of August 1905, called on the reverend "to be good enough to take up negotiations with the Indians" at Cote and Fishing Lake for the partial surrenders of their reserves. A copy of the Indian Act accompanied his official instructions. Pedley wanted to ensure that McDougall understood the surrender provisions, especially how only 10 percent of land sale proceeds "can be paid to the members of the band." The remainder had to be placed in the band's capital account, administered by Indian Affairs.

Pedley also asked the missionary to confirm the amount and location of the land to be released so that this information could be included in the surrender documents. McDougall was to be paid $10 per day plus his expenses.[18] It was a bargain. The average price per acre in 1905 was $5.07. McDougall was negotiating for thousands of acres, potentially worth tens of thousands of dollars.

McDougall may have made initial contact with the Saulteaux at Fishing Lake in the early autumn of 1905, but he never followed up on the initiative.[19] Instead, he directed his energies to working out a draft

*Chief Joseph Cote was asked
repeatedly to surrender portions
of the band's reserve.
(Library and Archives Canada)*

surrender agreement with the Cote band over two days of meetings in early October.

Chief Joseph Cote was a shrewd negotiator — as he had been in 1904 when the Canadian Northern wanted reserve land for the Kamsack station and townsite. The band was prepared to exchange 6,000 reserve acres for land to the west between the Assiniboine and Whitesand Rivers. It was also willing to release another 12,000 acres, provided that the land sold at a minimum $10 per acre. Ten percent of the sale proceeds were to be distributed to the band in two payments — within one month and six months of the surrender.[20]

McDougall communicated these conditions to Oliver, warning that the Cote band adamantly refused to accept anything less for its land.[21] But in the surrender documents, prepared by William Andrew Orr of Indian Affairs' Lands and Timber Branch, nothing would be paid until after the land sale, not the surrender vote.

McDougall cautioned Oliver that the revision was a deal-breaker — the surrender was in jeopardy if the band's terms weren't met. Pedley, the department fixer, intervened and drafted an order-in-council to provide an immediate cash settlement if the surrender was approved. An $8,000 cheque was mailed to David Laird shortly thereafter.

On December 14, 1905, with Laird and McDougall in attendance, agent Carruthers formally took the surrender of 18,937 acres: 6,676 in exchange for the Pelly haylands and 12,261 for sale. Only ten men signed the surrender document. None of the Indian Affairs officials bothered to record how many band members attended the meeting. The Indian commissioner only reported that there was a "good representation."[22]

If that was the case, then why was the first cash payment delayed until the next day when seventy-three people returned from hunting? In the January 12, 1906, government order confirming the surrender, moreover, there was no mention of the exchange for nearby haylands. The timing of the second band payment had also been quietly changed, at Pedley's doing, until after the land sale.[23]

There was a second surrender taken that December, which was from the Alexander reserve (#134), northwest of Edmonton just beyond St. Albert. The Cree band had entered Treaty Six in 1877, but its reserve wasn't surveyed until 1889. In August 1904, John A. Markle, inspector of Indian agencies in Alberta, had written Laird about the band's desire to give up 11,700 acres, mostly pasture, in exchange for a fence, draft animals, a planer, and a shingle mill.[24]

It's not clear who initiated the request because the band was leaderless. (Chief Alexander had been deposed in May 1903.) Laird put the matter on hold for the time being, but Markle raised the partial surrender again in October 1905. His persistence was probably attributable to Oliver's takeover of the Indian Affairs portfolio and the minister's well-known desire to rid the Edmonton area of reserves. Markle also had an interesting view on surrenders. He maintained that if a band's population had declined from the time of reserve survey — in effect, "holding more land [than] they are entitled to" — then the federal government should be able to take away land without consent.[25]

In this second pitch to Laird's office, Markle confidently proclaimed that the Alexander surrender would meet no resistance.[26] It was either a declaration of confidence in his negotiating abilities or an indication that there might be an agreement with the former Chief over possible reinstatement if he lent his support. McKenna forwarded the surrender proposal and terms to Indian Affairs secretary McLean, along with the recommendation that something might be included for the old, sick, and infirm.

At the surrender meeting held at the end of the year, seven band members, including the deposed Chief, approved the release of 9,518 acres. It was a smaller amount of land than first proposed, but it still represented more than a third of the reserve (26,240 acres).

Markle kept no record of the December 29 meeting. He did, however, append a handwritten list to the formal surrender terms, indicating that he had promised other agricultural items, such as work teams, harnesses, wagons, mowers, rakes, and plows, as part of the deal. These additional benefits were made without department authority — and probably exceeded the 10 percent available to the band from the sale proceeds. Indian Affairs wasn't happy, but nonetheless reinstated Chief Alexander, even though that wasn't part of the formal agreement either.[27]

No sooner had the reserve surrenders been formally approved by the Laurier government than Indian Affairs had the lands prepared for sale. During the summer of 1905, dominion lands surveyor James Keachie McLean measured the Carry the Kettle lands into quarter-sections before moving on to the Grizzly Bear's Head/Lean Man surrender. Prairie bands had waited for years after treaty just to get their reserve boundaries surveyed and confirmed by order-in-council, but now the more exacting and time-consuming subdivision, valuation, and description were being completed on the surrendered land in a matter of months.

The last marketing of reserve land by tender — the Michel reserve in June 1904 — was a dismal failure, and the department henceforth decided to sell surrendered acres by public auction. Indian Affairs also wanted to ensure that as much of the land as possible was sold, and consequently ignored the 1888 Regulations for the Disposal of Surrendered Indian Lands, which placed a limit on how much land could be bought by a single purchaser. These regulations could only be set aside by order-in-council — a legislative requirement that was regularly neglected.

The Carry the Kettle sale was held February 14, 1906, at Sintaluta, Saskatchewan, on the CPR main line. Surveyor McLean had valued the nine square miles at an average price of $6.20 per acre, but assured Pedley that the land was probably worth more based on nearby farm values.[28] Sale notices were placed in a few local and regional newspapers in January and generated some initial interest, including a query from Sifton's former deputy minister James Smart.[29]

Only a handful of buyers, though, turned out for the auction. There was no great stampede for the land, no feverish bidding over quarter-sections. Maybe it was the cold. The temperature in nearby Regina was minus-thirty-nine degrees Fahrenheit. All but two of the thirty-six quarter-sections were sold that day, but at prices that roughly matched McLean's valuation. It would seem that the few buyers had agreed not to compete with one another.

William Graham, who had engineered the Carry the Kettle surrender the previous spring, was struck by how the auction sale had been monopolized by people from outside the province. There was only one successful local buyer for only one quarter-section.[30] The other six purchasers were all good Liberals, the majority with Brandon or Winnipeg connections.[31] These and other purchasers were expected to pay for the land in instalments, but some were delinquent in meeting the deadlines, in a few cases by several years.

Oliver, before becoming a cabinet minister, had regularly decried land speculation and profiteering. But he apparently wasn't bothered that a handful of men had snatched up 5,440 acres of Carry the Kettle land. That they happened to be Liberals also seemed inconsequential. It was a perfectly legitimate business transaction from Oliver's perspective.

As he later said in response to another purchase of reserve land, the buyers never "got an acre . . . for less than full value . . . the Indian got what was owing to him."[32]

Frank Oliver said much the same thing when news of the Laurier government's controversial contract with the North Atlantic Trading Company became public a few months later. Asked about the immigrant recruitment scheme in the House of Commons on April 26, 1906, the minister mused, "What does it matter . . . as long as we get good value for our money."[33] But the NATC did matter to the Conservative Opposition, which believed that the secretive deal was little more than a scam, funnelling taxpayer money into Liberal pockets for questionable services. Prime Minister Laurier deftly sidestepped any responsibility — and stonewalled the Conservative leader Robert Borden — by shuffling the matter off to the House of Commons select standing committee on agriculture and colonization and the select standing committee on public accounts.

The dual committee hearings were frustrated by the antics of Smart and William Preston, Canada's inspector of emigration for Europe. Both men suffered profound memory lapses when not hiding behind the confidentiality provisions of the contract.

Smart did admit that the company's corporate headquarters were a small Amsterdam office, but the door was locked the only time he visited. A combative Preston, on the other hand, only wanted to talk about all the good the company did in diverting tens of thousands of agricultural immigrants to Canada. It was learned, though, that Preston's son-in-law had arranged to incorporate the company on the isle of Guernsey, where it was beyond the reach of British law.[34]

The Laurier government closed ranks. The two standing committees, dominated by Liberals, failed to submit final reports about their investigations. The Liberal majority in the House also easily defeated a Conservative motion to cancel the NATC government contract — even though Oliver later quietly did so, if only to save the government from any more embarrassment.

After ten years in office, rumours of secret deals and political kickbacks dogged the Laurier government. (Library and Archives Canada)

There was a certain irony to Oliver's position. As Interior minister, not only did he have to defend a government contract that wasn't his doing, but he also had to defend Sifton for entering into the agreement. His promotion to the front government benches, though, probably made him even more partisan. What he called, with a straight face, "good value" was actually a boondoggle where the NATC was paid on the basis of a simple head count at Canadian ports.

Nor would Smart or Preston be held to account, no matter how disreputable their behaviour. The former deputy minister had been out of government service for almost a year and a half, while Preston was sent to the other side of the world as trade minister to Japan, China, and Korea.[35]

The Conservative Opposition may have lost that round, but they still continued to throw punches, hoping they might land a crippling body-blow to the Liberal government. They did their best to try to goad Sifton, now a Liberal backbencher, into the ring, believing that the NATC was only one of many lucrative deals during his tenure as government minister and that he personally had benefited.

By May 31, 1906, the normally stoic Sifton had tired of Conservative jabbing and rose from his seat to give a spirited and defiant account of his stewardship of the Interior department. He boasted how the Liberals had populated the west with hundreds of thousands of people — with assistance from large colonization companies. He also hailed large grazing leases as the most responsible use of the dry, short-grass prairie district. And he provided a damning comparison between the Liberal immigration and settlement record and the woeful Conservative one.[36]

The Opposition didn't lay a glove on Sifton. But as his biographer noted about the match, "The real thrust of their [Conservative] argument, so often obscured, was that while the West had prospered, so too had Sifton's friends to an undue extent, and at the expense of others."[37] That should also have applied to Sifton's past handling of Indian Affairs. It didn't seem to matter, though, because it was never raised.

While the Interior department was under scrutiny in the House of Commons, Indian Affairs continued to press ahead with the sale and surrender of First Nations lands. On June 13, 1906, the first of several public auctions was held in Battleford for the Grizzly Bear's Head/ Lean Man lands. Two months earlier, Indian Affairs had received an unsolicited offer from M.J. Kane of the Kane Land Company of Battleford and Winnipeg to purchase all of the surrendered parcel for $7 per acre, but nothing came of it.

There was also some internal department debate over whether to return to tender sales. Instead, information about the upcoming auction was placed in newspapers and mailed to interested individuals. Sidney S. Simpson was hired to serve as auctioneer. He had worked in the Battleford area for both the Indian Affairs and Interior departments as a farm instructor, an immigration clerk, and a dominion lands office agent.

This background may not have qualified Simpson as an auctioneer, but it did for more patronage work, especially given his Brandon Liberal background. One week before the Battleford auction, Simpson's name was added to the Battleford real estate firm of Champagne, Speers, and Simpson. His father-in-law was Robert S. Speers.[38]

The turnout for the auction was sparse, and it was delayed until the next day. Even then, only fifty-nine of ninety quarter-section lots were sold. The average price was only $4.01 per acre — $2 less than the average price across the prairies.[39] Over the next few years, three attempts were made to sell the remaining land, with similar results.

The limited attendance at the first auction was raised by Conservative R.S. Lake in the House of Commons as an example of Indian Affairs bungling. "We should do the best we can with them [surrendered lands] for the Indians," he said. Lake claimed that auctioneer Simpson had been scrambling around the Battleford district, putting up sale notices only two hours before the scheduled start. "Few people knew of the sale," he told Oliver. "The attendance was small [and] the prices realized not high."

Lake blamed patronage for the poor auction results, insisting that advertisements for future land sales not be restricted to Liberal newspapers. Oliver dodged the issue, saying only that it was Indian Affairs' "desire to give every reasonable publicity."[40] At no point during the brief exchange did anyone suggest that the settler demand for First Nations lands was perhaps exaggerated or that bands shouldn't be expected to surrender part of their reserves.

Speculation also figured in the first Grizzly Bear's Head/Lean Man auction. Unlike the recent Carry the Kettle land sale, though, local people took part in the bidding. The major buyer was Edward H. White, a player in the local real estate market. His father was William White, inspector of United States immigration agencies, and a co-conspirator in the fraudulent acquisition of the two Moose Mountain Nakoda reserves in 1902. Father and son had formed the White Land Company, probably to give some legitimacy to their land dealings.

Robert Speers also bought a good chunk of land. That he was related to the auctioneer through marriage might have been a factor in his favour. There were also several smaller purchases, including partial lots. Sidney Simpson and apparently his wife, Margaret, secured land, as did Indian agent Day and his wife, M.J. Day.

Many consigned their purchases to Wilbur Van Horn Bennett, a Canadian immigration agent in Omaha, Nebraska, for sale to American buyers. He had performed a similar service in the past and was ready to reprise his role. Given this connection, he might have been contacted before the auction sale about handling the Grizzly Bear's Head/Lean Man lands. It might also explain why both White and the Champagne, Speers, and Simpson firm offered to buy any unsold land at a discount price per acre.[41]

Indian Affairs actively pursued several other reserve surrenders in the spring of 1906. Four years earlier, George Bulyea, the commissioner of agriculture in the North-West Territories government and representative for the South Qu'Appelle constituency, had contacted Sifton about a possible surrender from the Muscowpetung and Pasqua reserves for homesteading purposes.[42] They were two of three Treaty Four bands, the third being Piapot, whose contiguous reserves hugged the south side of the Qu'Appelle River immediately northeast of Regina. Collectively, they were known as the Fishing (Qu'Appelle) Lakes reserves and part of the Qu'Appelle agency that fell under the direction of Inspector Graham at the time.

Despite some initial setbacks, the Muscowpetung and Pasqua bands had thrived at agriculture. In 1893, they had complained to the House of Commons that the Indian Affairs machinery ban, one of several restrictions under Hayter Reed's peasant farming policy, was reducing their productivity. Their petition asked that they be allowed to purchase a binder machine for cutting grain instead of trying to harvest their crops with hand cradles before the first frost.[43]

By 1902, Graham was touting the progress being made on the reserves in his agency, noting that rationing had been greatly reduced because of the growing ability of bands to support themselves. The Indian agent may have been burnishing his star, but one newspaper picked up on Graham's department reports and called the First Nations of the Qu'Appelle agency "the most prosperous in the Dominion."[44]

This success story, though, made no difference to local settlers, who wrote Ottawa calling for the opening of the three reserves along the Qu'Appelle River. It was happening elsewhere throughout the territories. Why not there?

A second new transcontinental railway, the Grand Trunk Pacific (GTP), had also started building west from Winnipeg in 1905, and it was expected that a branch line would run from Melville, on the main line, southwest to Regina. There was a good chance the branch line would pass through a corner of the Pasqua reserve, or at least close to it. The coming of the GTP intensified the demand for surrenders. White settlers wanted to be located as close as possible to a rail line — and an elevator — for the handling and marketing of their grain.

Graham pursued surrenders from only two of the three Qu'Appelle reserves. He expected stiff resistance from the Muscowpetung and Pasqua bands, based on his past probing of the surrender question, but was convinced that he could find the terms "on which I think the Indians could be induced to surrender."[45] He chose not to approach the Piapot band, probably because its elderly Chief, also named Piapot and the most respected Plains Cree leader at the time, staunchly defended his treaty rights. In his reminiscences, Graham described him as "a very obstinate man."[46]

Piapot had once tangled with Indian commissioner A.E. Forget in 1895, when he was arrested and imprisoned in Regina for hosting an illegal Sun Dance ceremony on his reserve. When Forget attempted to extract a promise from the Chief before his release that he would no longer perform the ceremony, Piapot replied through a translator, "Very well, I will agree not to pray to my God in my way, if you will promise not to pray to your God . . . in your way."[47] Piapot's continued defiance of government policies led to his 1902 removal as Chief for "bad behaviour." But even with this opening, Graham knew that the Chief still commanded considerable influence with his followers and a surrender was unlikely.

Graham outlined his strategy for taking surrenders at Pasqua and Muscowpetung in a memorandum to Oliver on December 20, 1905. It all hinged on the offer of cash — which would become a key feature of his negotiation style.

The Pasqua band, Graham maintained, had too much land for its population. It could easily afford to give up 15,900 acres. He even calculated that, based on its 1905 population, the band would still have more land after the surrender than it qualified for at the time of treaty some thirty years earlier. Graham planned to suggest a minimum sale price of $8 per acre — even though he reported that farms bordering the reserve were worth $25 to $30 per acre. The band would receive an estimated $12,720, 10 percent of the projected sale proceeds, in two instalments: the first payment on the day of the surrender, the second after the land sale.

Graham planned to deal with Muscowpetung in the same way, using different figures — the band would be expected to release 17,600 acres at a minimum sale price of $7 per acre. In effect, the inspector was using the proceeds from sales of reserve lands as an inducement to get the bands to give up part of their reserves. There was a perverse logic behind the scheme, but that was just fine with Oliver. In mid-January 1906, the Indian Affairs minister arranged for an order-in-council to supply the cash advance.[48]

Pedley decided to give Graham greater latitude in securing the surrenders. The surrender documents contained two different surrender descriptions for each reserve: 16,077 and 21,200 acres from Pasqua, and 18,000 and 25,000 acres from Muscowpetung. Graham met with the Pasqua band on February 28, 1906, but couldn't reach an agreement for either acreage amount. He was also rebuffed at Muscowpetung on March 15.

That should have been the end of it. Graham, however, returned to Pasqua on June 5 to take another run at a surrender — even though he may not have had the authority to do so. The band was leaderless at the time. Chief Pasqua, a signatory to Treaty Four at Fort Qu'Appelle in 1874, had died from tuberculosis in 1889 and, at the insistence of Indian Affairs, wouldn't be replaced until 1911. Graham came away with an agreement, but it isn't clear how it was achieved, including whether proper procedure was observed.

The Pasqua band gave up 16,077 acres of its best farm land — approximately 42 percent of the reserve. Even then, Indian Affairs was displeased and admonished Graham for not taking more.[49] Indian commissioner Laird was once again blindsided by the news, only learning afterwards about Graham's activities.[50]

The June 1906 surrender of Alberta's Michel reserve also required two meetings. In the fall of 1905, the settlers of Villeneuve, Alberta, petitioned the Laurier government for the removal of a strip of land along the eastern edge of the Michel reserve for a roadway. Oliver wanted to accede to the request, but when Indian agent Gibbons raised the matter with the band, he found that "they are unanimously opposed to it."[51]

The sticking point was how little the Michel band had benefited from the previous surrender of twelve square miles in July 1903. Much of the land remained unsold and off the market. On November 23, 1905, Oliver wired Pedley from Edmonton, wanting to know the "price of [the] balance" of the surrendered Michel land.[52] Pedley replied that same day by return telegraph that the average price was $3.84 per acre. Four days later, an Edmonton firm offered to buy all the unsold Michel land for an identical $3.84 per acre.

Indian Affairs gladly accepted the proposal. It's not known who was behind the offer — the firm may have been acting on behalf of another party — but the timing was suspect. That the land was apparently sold might have convinced the department that another Michel partial surrender was viable. It wasn't until July 1906 that the firm announced that it wouldn't be proceeding with the purchase.[53]

The second surrender was taken on by inspector Markle as if it were a bit in his teeth. He used a mixture of familiarity and bluster to try to make the band agreeable to another surrender. At one point in January 1906, he told Chief Michel Callihoo that he was only acting as a friend in the negotiations. "It makes no difference to me whether the land is surrendered or not," a disingenuous Markle wrote. "I did what I thought would be in your best interests, not my own interests."[54]

By mid-May 1906, Gibbons had made a breakthrough. It appeared that the band was willing to surrender more of its reserve, provided that the land was sold for no less than $10 per acre and that the proceeds from the sale of both surrendered sections would be used to purchase individual farming outfits and agricultural implements. Markle encouraged the department to proceed with a surrender as quickly as possible. The necessary documents, specifying the taking of another 2,400 acres, were hurriedly drawn up and dispatched to Edmonton.

Gibbons held a formal surrender meeting at Michel's reserve on June 2, 1906. The majority of those in attendance refused. In fact, the band used the opportunity to complain about returns from the first surrender and wanted "to know how much of the surrendered part has been sold and how much was realized from the sale."[55]

Markle rejected the meeting results, despite his earlier claims about being on the side of the band, and stormed off with Gibbons in tow. When he returned a few weeks later, the Michel men approved the surrender. They only agreed, though, because Markle had promised considerably more than the 10 percent from land sale proceeds that was permitted under the Indian Act.

In justifying his actions, Markle explained that he had been forced to add to the list of equipment and animals — or there would have been no surrender. That amount now came to "about $5,000 . . . required to meet their wishes, or about 20% of the value of the land recently surrendered."[56] Supplying the band with these items, Markle sheepishly suggested, was better than simply giving them cash. He also knew that it was better than facing the possible wrath of Oliver for failing to get the surrender.

Markle rivalled Graham in his blind determination to secure reserve surrenders. It was missionary John McDougall, though, who served as Oliver's troubleshooter for particularly difficult negotiations. He was like an arbiter, called upon to hammer out a deal between First Nations bands and Canada over how much land would be given up — not whether it would be given up. And he was backed by the authority of the Indian Affairs minister.

In March 1906, secretary McLean asked McDougall to take a surrender at the Hobbema (Peace Hills) agency. These were a collection of Treaty Six Cree reserves south of Edmonton, near Wetaskiwin. It was a tough assignment. The bands were unlikely to want to give up land because they were doing so well as agriculturalists. On-reserve activity accounted for 72 percent of the Hobbema economy.[57] Chief Ermineskin also stood between the department and a surrender. In January 1904, assistant Indian commissioner McKenna had candidly admitted, "I am convinced that the Indians will not during the lifetime of Chief Ermineskin entertain such a proposition."[58]

The matter had been brewing since 1902. The Calgary and Edmonton Railway (purchased by CPR in July 1903) and local settlers wanted a townsite with elevator facilities along the rail line that ran through the Hobbema reserves. The best place was on Ermineskin land. Oliver, as the Edmonton MP for the area, was wholly behind the request. But Chief Ermineskin refused to consider any surrender, no matter how small, and gave the same answer every time some Indian Affairs official broached the subject.

The department should have expected this reaction. When the reserve was surveyed in 1885, the Chief was keenly involved in the location of the boundaries, mindful of their significance at the time and into the future.[59]

In the fall of 1905, Laird recommended that a straight cash offer — $25 per acre — might convince Ermineskin to turn over land for a railway siding. The Chief still said no. Markle countered with a different approach. He reasoned that if the nearby Samson band agreed to a surrender, then Ermineskin and Bobtail (also known as Montana or Muddy Bull) might be won over and give up land too, especially if Samson were seen to benefit from the sale proceeds. He rationalized these surrenders — above and beyond what was needed by the CPR — on the grounds that the Hobbema reserves had more land than needed. Both Samson and Ermineskin were sixty square miles, twice the size of Bobtail.

McDougall was called upon to execute the plan. He had the advantage of being known to the bands, having lived for a time at Hobbema. He also sensed that the Samson band was interested in a possible surrender and could use that as a wedge to splinter band opposition.[60]

McDougall had limited success. Samson would surrender some of its reserve, but as the missionary told Pedley in late May 1906, the other Hobbema bands "made some violent speeches against the surrender of any parts of their reserves and then left the council."[61]

Oliver was miffed too, but for different reasons. The land that the Samson band was willing to forfeit was nowhere near the rail line but on the outskirts of the reserve. That would never do. The surrender was also contingent on several conditions, including the band exercising greater control over its own affairs and being allowed to leave the reserve without a permit. The Samson people also didn't want to be asked about another possible surrender in the future.[62] "It does not appear to me,"

Frank Oliver was expected to shake things up when he was appointed to the Laurier cabinet in the spring of 1905. (Provincial Archives of Ontario)

Oliver freely told McDougall, "that the best interests either of the Indians or of the Government are to be served by the surrender." Oliver saw no point in proceeding. "I regret that the Indians have taken the view [that] they have," he grudgingly conceded, "but they are masters in what they have to sell as we are masters in what we wish to buy."[63]

The Indian Affairs minister wasn't prepared to let it happen again, though. He was going to fix it so First Nations bands would want to sell their reserve lands. To do that, he would break through the maximum for what could be legally paid to bands after the surrender and sale. Oliver was going to hike it from 10 percent of the proceeds to a lofty 50 percent. The expectation was that many bands, sitting on valuable farm land, would find it too tempting. It all boiled down to a matter of cash.

Notes

1. *Library and Archives Canada* (*LAC*), RG10, v. 4020, f. 280,470-2, H.A. Carruthers to J.D. McLean, September 11, 1905.

2. House of Commons, *Debates*, May 25, 1905, p. 6552.

3. Quoted in S. Krasowski, *No Surrender: The Land Remains Indigenous* (Regina: University of Regina Press, 2019), p. 261. The Oliver account of the Treaty Seven meeting ("The Blackfeet Treaty") appeared in the *Globe* on October 30, 1877.

4. *Debates*, May 25, 1905, pp. 6547–8, 6550, 6552.

5. *LAC*, RG10, v. 4001, f. 208,590-1, T.W. Aspdin to J.D. McLean, May 15, 1905.

6. P. Martin-McGuire, *First Nations Land Surrenders on the Prairies, 1896–1911* (Ottawa: Indian Claims Commission, 1998), pp. 117, 267.

7. K.J. Tyler, "Interim Report: The History of the Mosquito, Grizzly Bear's Head, and Lean Man Bands, 1878–1920," n.d., pp. 18–20; Martin-McGuire, *First Nations Land Surrenders*, pp. 189, 265–6.

8. T.D. Regehr, *The Canadian Northern Railway: Pioneer Road of the Northern Prairies, 1895–1918* (Toronto: Macmillan, 1976), pp. 168–9.

9. A. McPherson, *The Battlefords: A History* (Saskatoon: Modern Press, 1967), p. 149.

10. *LAC*, RG10, v. 4020, f. 280,470-2, J.J. Campbell to F. Pedley, Cote memorandum, July 19, 1905.

11. Ibid., J.J. Campbell to F. Pedley, Fishing Lake memorandum, July 20, 1905.

12. C.L. Nicholat, "Exploring a Shared History: Indian-White Relations between Fishing Lake First Nation and Wadena, 1882–2002," unpublished M.A. thesis, University of Saskatchewan, 2002, p. 30.

13. *LAC*, RG10, v. 4020, f. 280,470-2, F. Oliver to F. Pedley, July 3, 1905.

14. See B. Waiser, "Too Many Scared People: Alberta and the 1885 North-West Rebellion" in M. Payne et al, eds., *Alberta Formed Alberta Transformed, v. 1* (Edmonton: University of Alberta Press, 2006), pp. 271–300.

15. W.S. Waddell, "The Honourable Frank Oliver," unpublished M.A. thesis, University of Alberta, 1950, p. 275.

16. J. McDougall, *Opening the Great West: Experiences of a Missionary, 1875–76* (Calgary: Glenbow-Alberta Institute, 1970), p. 60.

17. L. Goyette and C.J. Roemmich, *Edmonton in Our Own Words* (Edmonton: University of Alberta Press, 2004), pp. 87–90.

18. *LAC*, RG10, v. 4020, f. 280,470-2, F. Pedley to J. McDougall, August 29, 1905.

19. Ibid., H.A. Carruthers to J.D. McLean, October 7, 1905.

20. Martin-McGuire, *First Nations Land Surrenders*, p. 264.

21. *LAC*, RG10, v. 4020, f. 280,470-2, J. McDougall to F. Oliver, October 11, 1905.

22. Ibid., D. Laird to F. Pedley, December 26, 1905.

23. Martin-McGuire, *First Nations Land Surrenders*, p. 265.

24. *LAC*, RG10, v. 6666, f. 110A-3-1, J.A. Markle to D. Laird, August 12, 1904.

25. *LAC*, RG10, v. 4012, f. 266,600, J.A. Markle to J.D. McLean, January 25, 1906.

26. *LAC*, RG10, v. 6666, f. 110A-3-1, J.A. Markle to D. Laird, October 12, 1905.

27. Martin-McGuire, *First Nations Land Surrenders*, pp. xxxvii, 268–9, 359.

28. *LAC*, RG10, v. 4001, f. 208,590-1, J.K. McLean to F. Pedley, September 11, 1905.

29. Ibid., J.A. Smart to J.D. McLean, January 12, 1906.

30. Ibid., W.D. Graham to J.D. McLean, February 20, 1906.

31. Peter Mitchell was a Brandon hardware merchant who had once worked for James Smart's hardware business. Then, there were the Mathesons. Dr. John Sutherland Matheson was a Brandon physician. His brother, R.M. Matheson, was a Brandon solicitor with connections to both Smart and Clifford Sifton. Another brother was William A. Matheson, a Winnipeg grain merchant. This third Matheson bought land at the Sintaluta auction for George Hastings, a Liberal friend also in the Winnipeg grain business. The other non-resident buyer was Samuel Clarke, a long-serving Liberal member (1898–1926) of the Ontario legislature for Northumberland West. He was likely tipped off about the sale through his friendship with Frank Pedley's father-in-law. D.J. McMahon, "The Surrender of Land at Carry-The-Kettle Band," unpublished report for FSIN, 1985, pp. 7–8; Martin-McGuire, *First Nations Land Surrenders*, pp. 357, 458, 465, 476, 482, 487, 491.

32. *Debates*, April 14, 1915, pp. 2549–50.

33. Ibid., April 26, 1906, pp. 2092, 2103.

34. J. Petryshyn, "Canadian Immigration and the North Atlantic Trading Company 1899–1906: A Controversy Revisited," *Journal of Canadian Studies*, v. 32, n. 3, 1997, pp. 67–71.

35. Ibid.

36. D.J. Hall, *Clifford Sifton, v. 2: A Lonely Eminence, 1901–1929* (Vancouver: University of British Columbia Press, 1985), pp. 184–8.

37. Ibid., p. 188.

38. Martin-McGuire, *First Nations Land Surrenders*, pp. 353–4.

39. Tyler, "Interim Report: The History of the Mosquito, Grizzly Bear's Head, and Lean Man Bands, 1878–1920," p. 22; *Debates*, April 14, 1915, p. 2550.

40. *Debates*, July 11, 1908, pp. 12729–34.

41. Martin-McGuire, *First Nations Land Surrenders*, pp. 354–5, 463.

42. *LAC*, RG10, v. 3994, f. 195126-1, G.H.V. Bulyea to C. Sifton, January 13, 1902.

43. S. Carter, *Lost Harvests: Prairie Indian Reserve Farmers and Government Policy* (Montreal: McGill-Queen's University Press, 1990), pp. 225–6.

44. Martin-McGuire, *First Nations Land Surrenders*, p. 219.

45. *LAC*, RG10, v. 3994, f. 195,126, pt. 2, W.M. Graham to F. Oliver, December 20, 1905.

46. W.M. Graham, *Treaty Days: Reflections of an Indian Commissioner* (Calgary: Glenbow-Alberta Institute, 1991), p. 87.

47. Quoted in W.P. Stewart, *My Name is Piapot* (Maple Creek, Saskatchewan: Butterfly Books, 1981), p. 109.

48. *LAC*, RG10, v. 3994, f. 195,126, pt. 2, W.M. Graham to F. Oliver, December 20, 1905; F. Oliver to Governor General in Council, January 18, 1906.

49. Martin-McGuire, *First Nations Land Surrenders*, pp. 294–5.

50. *LAC*, RG10, v. 3994, f. 195,126, pt. 2, J.D. McLean to D. Laird, March 9, 1906.

51. Ibid., J. Gibbons to J.D. McLean, November 4, 1905.

52. *LAC*, RG10, v. 6667, f. 110A-4-1, pt. 1, F. Oliver to F. Pedley, November 23, 1905.

53. Tyler and Wright Research Consultants Limited, "The Alienation of Indian Reserve Lands During the Administration of Sir Wilfrid Laurier, 1896–1911: Michel Reserve #132," unpublished report, 1978, p. 152.

54. Quoted in ibid., p. 159.

55. *LAC*, RG10, v. 6667, f. 110A-4-1, pt. 2, J. Gibbons to J.D. McLean, June 4, 1906.

56. Ibid., J.A. Markle to J.D. McLean, June 26, 1906.

57. D.J. Hall, *From Treaties to Reserves: The Federal Government and Native Peoples in Territorial Alberta, 1870–1905* (Montreal and Kingston: McGill-Queen's University Press, 2015), p. 168.

58. *LAC*, RG10, v. 774, f. 32-10-138, J.A.J. McKenna memorandum, January 14, 1904.

59. R. Irwin, "No Means No: Ermineskin's Resistance to Land Surrender, 1902–1921," *The Canadian Journal of Native Studies*, v. 23, n. 1, 2003, pp. 167–8, 173.

60. Ibid., pp. 173–4.

61. *LAC*, RG10, v. 4012, f. 266,600, G. McDougall to F. Pedley, May 25, 1906.

62. D. Lupul, "The Bobtail Land Surrender," *Alberta History*, v. 6, n. 1, winter 1978, p. 34.

63. *LAC*, RG10, v. 4012, f. 266,600, F. Oliver to G. McDougall, June 26, 1906.

⊹ *Eight* ⊹

MEN WITH SPECIAL QUALIFICATIONS

A ll the letter-writers wanted the same thing. "Would you please send me descriptions of the Indian lands you propose selling in the West," asked H.M. Kelvie of Toronto, Ontario. "Give price, terms, quality of land." Mrs. Annie Keighley, also of Toronto, begged to submit an application, while Alf Ellis of Wetaskiwin, Alberta, proposed to carry on his own negotiations with the Chief of a local band. M.M. Smith of Mankato, Minnesota, requested a map of the available reserve land before he struck north to inspect it. "Is the number of acres to each person limited?" he wondered. "Is there any railroad near it?"

These letters, from across Canada and the American West, are just a sampling from a bulging Indian Affairs correspondence file dating from about 1905. People saw the opening of prairie reserves as their chance to take part in the great western land rush and wrote to the department seeking details.

All inquiries were usually answered with a form letter, in most instances signed by department secretary J.D. McLean, with the assurance that their name would be placed on the notification list for future land sales.[1] It was well understood at the time that Frank Oliver was on a personal crusade to secure more reserve surrenders. To do so, though, Oliver, department officials, and Indian Affairs representatives in the field had to override the interests of treaty bands to get their land.

A little more than a year after he was named Interior and Indian Affairs minister, Oliver brought an Indian Act amendment before the House of Commons. Speaking to the bill on second reading on June 15, 1906, Oliver noted that the legislation "contains only one section and has only one object . . . to change the amount of the immediate and direct payment that may be made to Indians upon the surrender of their lands." He then explained how band members received only 10 percent of land sale proceeds and that this amount offered "very little inducement to them to deal for their lands." In fact, he slyly declared that the department faced "very considerable difficulty in securing their assent to any surrender."

That was a shame, according to Oliver, because of "the large areas of land held by Indians . . . these reserves [not] being of any value to the Indians and being a detriment to the settlers and to the prosperity and progress of the surrounding country." The solution, he concluded, was to raise the immediate payment to as high as 50 percent.

Most of the questioning of the bill's purpose came from the Conservative Opposition benches. The governing Liberals expressed their support through their silence. Sam Hughes, a militia officer from Lindsay, Ontario, pointedly asked the minister if he was going to acquire underutilized reserve lands. Oliver eagerly assured the House "that is the policy of the department," before embarking on a detailed accounting, prepared in advance, of "surplus" acres held by bands in the three prairie provinces. Because the First Nations population had declined over the past three decades, he reported, bands occupied reserves "in excess of the amount contemplated by treaty."

Oliver would have known, though, that the band's reserve area was based on the population at the time of survey. The Treaty Seven agreement, one he had personally witnessed in 1877, used the formula of one square mile for a family of five. The minister was being disingenuous by suggesting that reserve size should reflect the band's current numbers. Yet he insisted that "the present condition, when [western] land is in demand . . . demands attention."

Ontario Conservative MP Richard Blain then asked, seemingly in disbelief, "How did the Indians become possessors of such a large quantity of land in excess of what they are entitled to?" Oliver, who should have known better, claimed "at that time land was of very little consideration and that it was very desirable to get the treaty made with the Indians . . . a great deal was taken for granted." What consequently happened, according to Oliver, was that bands probably received "too much" land — a "disparity between the people and the land" that had become "that much greater" because of population decline since treaty.

What made things worse from Oliver's perspective was that reserves were considered "the absolute sacred right of the Indians." If Indian Affairs were going to successfully pursue land surrenders, it needed the amendment in place to give department representatives greater influence during negotiations.

Only one voice objected to Oliver's bill — that of Conservative David Henderson. He called for "fair treatment of the Indians," especially since they had already lost their lands and the bison. He wanted them to be left alone on their reserves and free from interference.

Hughes attacked his colleague's stand, proclaiming that it would be best to break up reserves and distribute the land among the white population. "Not one acre in a thousand is utilized by them," Hughes barked. "Anyone who knows the Indians of the Northwest knows that the Indian on the reserve is no use."

Fellow Conservative Richard S. Lake readily concurred, but offered a more noble reason for taking surrenders: "So long as they [First Nations] are isolated on large reserves, only a small portion of which they bring into cultivation, the more difficulty will be experienced in bringing them into accord with civilized life."

Lake, the representative for Qu'Appelle, was the only western MP to wade into the discussion. He certainly shared Oliver's belief that the amendment was both necessary and urgent. Since January 1899, he had been calling on the Laurier government to open the Crooked Lakes reserves in the face of determined band resistance. His motives, though, had been anything but noble. The three bands, Lake argued, were sitting on excess land that should rightfully be cultivated by the white settler population. That these reserves were a treaty right was irrelevant in his view.

Opposition leader Robert Borden wrapped up the House of Commons's second reading of the bill by raising a "difficulty." He wanted to know how the proposed 50 percent from land sale proceeds was to be distributed. If the money was simply handed over to individual band members, Borden cautioned, it could be "squandered." Oliver replied that First Nations were never given cash "to expend in any way they please." Instead, the proceeds were used for "principal requirements," such as equipment, work animals, or buildings, but only after consulting with the band and securing its agreement.

This statement was misleading. In the past, it was Indian Affairs that largely determined what was purchased, regardless of what was decided upon at the surrender meeting, because of the wording of the agreement. Many bands subsequently complained that the government had not honoured surrender provisions, or they had to wait several months, if not years, to see some of the benefits.

What was also divulged during Oliver's brief exchange with Borden was his intention to use funds from reserve land sales to pay for Indian Affairs expenses that had not been covered by the annual parliamentary appropriation. Oliver admitted that his department had tried to "do the best we can with the funds at our disposal . . . to improve the condition of the Indians in the west." The available budget could only go so far, though.

Money from reserve surrenders presented an alternative funding source. "We think it is only reasonable," Oliver said, "that some of these vast values which [reserves] hold should be turned to account . . . using the money to the best advantage of the Indians." That best advantage, for example, could be a school building or other reserve capital projects.[2] It was a devious solution to a decades-old complaint — namely, paying for Canada's treaty commitments — and it struck a chord with both parties in the House that day. The amendment was later passed and became law on July 13, 1906.

Secretary McLean followed up the passage of the legislation with a directive to Indian commissioner David Laird about preparing his spending estimates for the next fiscal year. "Those bands which have surrendered lands and consequently have funds at their credit sufficient to supply their needs," McLean instructed, "should not be provided for in the Estimates beyond the provision called for [in] the Treaty stipulations." To ensure that there was no mistaking his meaning, he added, "Indians . . . should not any longer be a charge upon the country."[3]

The first surrender taken immediately after the Indian Act amendment had nothing to do with settlers demanding access to reserve lands in their district, but much more to do with the routing of the Canadian Northern Railway. In July 1905, in anticipation of extending its Prince Albert line northeastward, CNoR contacted Indian Affairs about securing a right-of-way and station grounds at The Pas on the Saskatchewan River, just east of the Manitoba-Saskatchewan boundary. The Pas band (known today as the Opaskwayak Cree Nation), a signatory to Treaty Five, occupied several small reserves in the area. The one at The Pas Mission (#21A) straddled the river.

The most suitable location was on the south side of the river, where the band was expected to turn over about seventy-five acres. Indian Affairs inspector S.R. Marlatt was convinced that the site would "become an important place in the district" if the Laurier government tendered a line to Hudson Bay.[4]

Shipping grain from a deep-sea port directly to European markets had been a dream of prairie farmers since the 1880s. It held the promise of breaking the monopoly of the Great Lakes–St. Lawrence route. Now with the Canadian Northern building northward to The Pas, that dream seemed one step closer to reality. Local settlers even began asking about turning the reserve into town lots in anticipation of the expected boom.

At Marlatt's urging, The Pas band consequently surrendered 500 acres at a meeting on August 21, 1906. It was seven times the original Canadian Northern request. The irony was that Canadian Northern had no intention of building its network beyond The Pas because of the prohibitive construction costs. The company was more interested in strengthening its strategic position by ensuring that any future road to the bay had to use its Canadian Northern lines south of The Pas.[5] It was not until 1929 that the Hudson Bay railway was completed.

Action was also taken at the Crooked Lakes reserves. Acknowledging past failures to secure surrenders, Oliver vowed in March 1906 that "we hope at some favourable time and at an early date to make another attempt." These encouraging words earned praise from both sides of the House, prompting Oliver to add, almost as an exclamation point, "The interests of the people must come first, and if it becomes a question between the Indians and the whites, the interests of the whites will have to be provided for."[6] This line had been a constant refrain in Oliver's verbal arsenal against First Nations reserves.[7] The difference, though, was that Oliver was now a minister of the Crown and could do something about it.

Even though Indian commissioner Laird had advised the department in 1904 that any surrender attempt at the Crooked Lakes reserves shouldn't be pushed "too hastily," it "requires very careful handling."[8] Oliver asked Inspector William Graham to pursue the matter. After visiting the bands, Graham reported in mid-June 1906 that "these Indians would consent to sell," but only if the surrenders were handled discreetly and the bands were presented with a package deal. He also asked for a "little latitude" to meet "any small request" that might come from the bands at the meetings.

Graham clearly had a plan to overcome the "several futile attempts . . . to get this surrender."[9] His mission was probably aided by the new Indian agent for the bands — Matthew Millar, a Moosomin merchant, and of course a Liberal.[10]

At Oliver's behest, the department worked up the surrender documents with input from Graham, especially about the acreage figures. The inspector was adamant that he had to have the money for the first payment on hand the day of the meeting.[11] That amount was based on the estimated price per acre multiplied by the amount of surrendered land.

Authority to take the surrenders was given in early October, but Graham deliberately delayed meeting with the three bands until January 1907. He knew that the winter months, and the sickness and hunger that often accompanied the cold, would sap band opposition. He also expected less opposition because of the recent death of Chief Kahkewistahaw, who had once upbraided Laird at an earlier surrender meeting.

Graham's first round of meetings failed. At Cowessess on January 21, and then Ochapowace and Kahkewistahaw over the following two days, the majority of male band members in attendance said no in each instance. Undeterred, Graham returned to Kahkewistahaw on January 28 and held a second, successful vote. He also secured a narrow yes vote at Cowessess the next day. Only the Ochapowace band turned him away at a second meeting on February 9.

This reversal in only a week was probably attributable to Graham's promise of immediate cash, which was placed on a table for all to see during the negotiations. Once he secured the surrender at Kahkewistahaw, he began paying $94 to every person, a process lasting several hours into the night. At Cowessess, it was $66 per person over several days. Graham's actions put the lie to Oliver's public statements that money was never put in the hands of those being asked to surrender land.

Another sad feature of the two Crooked Lakes surrenders was the amount of valuable farm land that the bands forfeited. Kahkewistahaw lost 33,281 acres, roughly 70 percent of its reserve (46,816), and Cowessess 20,704 acres or 40 percent (49,920).[12] Almost three years earlier, assistant Indian commissioner James McKenna had advised Ottawa, "It would not be advisable from an Indian standpoint, to dispose of the land."[13]

Graham, on the other hand, expected the department to be "pleased with what has been done." In a self-congratulatory report, he noted that white communities along the Canadian Pacific Railway main line were "delighted with the prospect of having this country thrown on the market . . . this land lying idle has been a great drawback."[14]

Graham next volunteered to fix a problem that had arisen with the partial Cote surrender in December 1905. The land sales from that surrender had attracted little interest because of the generally poor quality of the land, and Indian Affairs consequently balked at making the required second band payment. Graham's solution was to return the unsold land to reserve status and take a new surrender — this time from the south of the reserve. Even though he said he was acting "in the interests of the Indians, the Department and the Public at large," the proposed surrender would not only create a buffer zone between the band and Kamsack, but force reserve farmers to give up their cultivated fields.[15]

Graham knew that any new surrender had to be financially attractive because of the department's failure to honour promises in the 1905 agreement. He proposed to distribute 20 percent of the estimated sale proceeds as a cash inducement. On June 20, 1907, at what Graham described as a "very representative meeting,"[16] the Cote band agreed to surrender 10,740 acres. Two hundred and thirty-three members each received $87 in cash. The prospect of instant money proved seductive to those who had incurred debt in anticipation of the 1905 surrender's second payout. What influence the Chief might have had remains unclear; he'd been deposed by Indian Affairs six weeks earlier.[17]

Graham also served as a troubleshooter that summer for the stalled Fishing Lake surrender. In August 1905, at Oliver's request, Indian Affairs had hired Reverend John McDougall as a special department negotiator to work out a tentative deal for some of the Fishing Lake reserve at the request of the Canadian Northern Railway. But the Methodist missionary made little headway. Not meeting with the Saulteaux band until the summer of 1906, he found that its leaders didn't want to contemplate a possible surrender if the other two Yellow Quill Saulteaux bands, at Kinistino and Nut Lake, shared in the land sale proceeds.

That's when Graham waded into the matter. The cocksure inspector insisted that he could have secured a surrender if given the authority and means to do so.[18]

It wasn't until March 1907 that Graham was given his marching orders — he was to get the three bands to sign a formal separation agreement from one another and then secure the Fishing Lake surrender. Graham left a somewhat convoluted account of his visit to the region in the summer of 1907, with his wife and secretary, as part of his reminiscences prepared in the early 1930s. In places, the arduous month-long wagon trip, especially the muskeg and mosquitoes, gets more attention than his purpose in going there.[19]

Graham alluded to resistance in his memoir, but it is only in his 1907 report to the department that he admitted, "I was surprised to find that they [Fishing Lake band] were not at all anxious to sell." Even though the three bands willingly signed the separation agreement, the Fishing Lake men turned Graham down on August 7 when he asked them to surrender 13,170 acres. "I had given up any hope of getting the surrender," he told secretary McLean. But "just before

In August 1907, Indian Affairs inspector William Graham made a special trip by wagon to Fishing Lake First Nation to secure a surrender agreement. (Glenbow Archives)

The Graham camp, under the Union Jack flag, at Fishing Lake. (Glenbow Archives)

At the Fishing Lake meeting, Inspector Graham secured the surrender of two-thirds of the reserve. (Glenbow Archives)

starting for home" two days later, band members asked for another meeting and agreed to the surrender.[20]

Little more is known, except that those who opposed the surrender had apparently left to go hunting before the second vote. Graham also used cash — $100 per person — to cement the deal. He had no sooner distributed the money, though, than he asked for some of it back to pay for rations and reserve farming equipment.[21]

It's also not clear why Graham believed the surrender of two-thirds of the Fishing Lake reserve was to the band's "advantage."[22] It was certainly to his. Less than a year later, Oliver rewarded Graham with a sizeable pay raise for "so satisfactorily further[ing] the wishes of the Department in connection with land matters."[23]

While Graham, with the Fishing Lake agreement in hand, was making his way home to his headquarters in Balcarres, Saskatchewan, another surrender was playing out in Manitoba. It's considered one of the most egregious in Canadian history.[24]

The 1907 surrender of St. Peter's reserve was advanced as a solution to a long-standing problem dating back to the 1870s. The Peguis band, a Saulteaux group, had entered Treaty One in 1871. It was another three years, though, before St. Peter's reserve was set aside in the Selkirk area, along the Red River between Lower Fort Garry (Hudson's Bay Company headquarters) and Lake Winnipeg. Some of the Peguis band members occupied individual river lots, and these holdings were included within the 1874 reserve boundaries. This anomaly was wrapped in another layer of complexity when these lots were sold over time to outsiders.

Peguis leaders repeatedly complained about non-band members occupying reserve lands, but the issue remained unresolved by the time the Laurier Liberals assumed power in 1896. T.G. Rothwell, a law clerk in the Department of the Interior, took a fresh look at the file and recommended in 1900 that the Peguis band simply be asked to surrender St. Peter's (48,000 acres) in favour of taking a reserve elsewhere. Such a move would avoid trying to sort out the competing land claims, but it came at the expense of the band and its interests.

The problem continued to fester until the spring of 1906, when Peguis leaders petitioned Samuel Jackson, the Liberal MP for Selkirk and former Indian Affairs official for the Lake Winnipeg inspectorate, to evict non-band members from the reserve. Jackson raised the matter with Deputy Minister Frank Pedley, who discovered that the Rothwell report had never been forwarded to Indian Affairs. It now found new life, especially because its key recommendation — the surrender of St. Peter's reserve — dovetailed nicely with Oliver's agenda.

In November 1906, Oliver decided to revisit the Peguis situation by means of a one-person commission, headed by Hector Howell, chief justice of the Manitoba Court of Appeal and a Liberal. Howell was supposed to sort out the land claims mess, and if necessary "to consider the advisability and necessity of obtaining from the members of the band a surrender."[25] The commissioner wouldn't disappoint Oliver. Howell later admitted, "I made up my mind that for the good of the Indian tribe beyond any question they ought to get off that reserve."[26]

Others thought likewise, but not because it was in the best interests of the band. Local settlers coveted St. Peter's reserve and the rich lands along the river. So too did investors and speculators who wanted to cash in on Selkirk's rising fortunes during the settlement boom. Many had good Liberal connections. So too did the men who had been appointed to represent the various parties at the commission hearings. Orange H. Clark, the Winnipeg lawyer for the Peguis band, was Sifton's cousin.

The Howell Commission hearings opened in February 1907 in tandem with informal meetings with band representatives to secure a surrender. The Peguis people repeatedly rejected attempts at a surrender agreement — at least half a dozen over six months — before Oliver dispatched Pedley, the fixer, to Selkirk. The deputy minister conferred first with the Chief and councillors before calling a surrender meeting at the old reserve schoolhouse on September 23. The surrender proposal met stiff resistance even though Pedley promised every band member $90 from the sale of half the reserve lands.

The formal vote was deliberately held over until the next day. That afternoon, after a speech in favour of the surrender by the Chief, the vote was held outside and members were asked to separate into two groups, for and against. The surrender carried 107 to 98. In summing up his success as if it was just part of a day's work, Pedley told Oliver that the surrender "will afford an opportunity long looked for of having the land available for farming and other purposes . . . passing into the hands of whites."[27] Howell was much more elated in his December 1907 report, taking credit for getting Canada "readily and cheaply out of a nasty tangle."[28]

The Conservative Opposition would later ask damning questions in the House of Commons about whether the Peguis surrender meeting had been valid and whether bribery and intimidation had been involved. These and other apparent irregularities provided a glimpse into how Indian Affairs conducted its surrender business — and business it was — but the Laurier government refused to reopen the matter, let alone admit to any wrongdoing.[29] That didn't dissuade the Conservatives from continuing to probe corruption in Liberal ranks.

These "scandal sessions," as they become known, were more than a matter of scoring political points against a government that had been in power for a decade and was perhaps vulnerable on an issue here, a policy there. The Conservatives continued to hear alarming stories about shady deals, patronage kickbacks, and personal gain in the Liberal bureaucracy.

One of the Opposition's prime targets remained Clifford Sifton, even though he had resigned as head of the Interior and Indian Affairs departments three years earlier. On February 6, 1908, the Conservatives forced Sifton to respond to damning revelations about his past handling of timber berths. The former minister had apparently used senior officials to get around procedures and practices, including rigging tenders, to favour his brother-in-law T.A. Burrows. During a two-year period, for example, Burrows secured all nine timber limits he bid upon; his successful bids were uncannily just slightly more than all others.[30]

An embattled Sifton withstood the attack as best he could, but at the conclusion of his remarks, Conservative W.J. Roche couldn't resist taking a swipe at former minister. "Had he been as conscientious in the discharge of his public duties . . . as he has been in his own interests," Roche sarcastically pointed out, "would it not have paid us to have had him as Finance Minister?"

Attempts to secure a formal investigation, though, were repeatedly stymied by the "blockers' brigade," a trio of Liberal backbenchers whose unofficial House duties included shielding Prime Minister Laurier and his ministers.[31] There may have been cause for the rumours of Liberal insider corruption, but without an official inquiry, they remained only rumours.[32]

The Conservative smearing of the Laurier government carried over into the October 1908 general election. The governing Liberals, running on what they had accomplished and the need to let Laurier finish the job, faced a steady Tory barrage of open-ended accusations of fraud and graft. When the prime minister publicly bemoaned the muckraking tactics, suggesting that the Conservatives had nothing else to offer, they responded with, "But who made the muck?"[33]

This "most unpleasant"[34] campaign wasn't enough to topple the Liberals, not even deny them another majority win, even though the popular vote was close. It did have an impact, though, in western Canada, often considered "the Gibraltar of Liberalism."[35]

The Liberals romped in Saskatchewan, but they barely won a majority of the Alberta seats, and the Manitoba returns were just bleak. Once considered the personal stronghold of Sifton, the province swung decisively Conservative (eight of ten seats), thanks in large part to the active involvement of the Roblin government and its attack dog Robert Rogers. Sifton, hounded about his "sudden new wealth,"[36] narrowly retained his Brandon seat. His brother-in-law Burrows suffered an ignominious defeat in his Dauphin riding.[37] A Montreal newspaper, in assessing the results, complained that "the Liberals have not even got the scare they should have had."[38]

The Conservative attack on the integrity of the Laurier government didn't bring about a pause in Oliver's single-minded pursuit of reserve surrenders. Nor did the Opposition want it stopped. Indeed, surrenders were one of the few things that the two warring parties agreed upon.

In the spring of 1906, William Staples, a Manitoba Conservative MP, asked Oliver whether he'd received a petition from the citizens of Swan River calling for the opening of the nearby reserve. "It is situated," Staples reported, "in one of the best wheat growing districts of Manitoba." Oliver didn't know whether his department had received the request, but he pledged to "make every effort to secure a surrender of such portion of the reserve as we can get."

When Staples offered to put together a second petition, the minister said, "No, I think not: we find that any agitation amongst their white neighbours in such a case arouses their antagonism." Staples then asked when the surrender would happen. "We have a good many orders on hand and not very many men with special qualifications for negotiating with Indians," Oliver replied, "but we appreciate fully the desirability of securing a release of that reserve."[39]

Reverend McDougall, Oliver's special agent, visited the Swan Lake reserve in September 1907 to sort out a possible surrender arrangement — only to "[come] up against resentment and suspicion."[40] The Yellow Quill people, a Treaty One band, had been repeatedly pestered since 1899 about giving up its Manitoba lands. The band was also unhappy with its reserve assignment. It never received all of its entitled land in the Swan Lake district, southwest of Portage la Prairie, but was instead assigned an additional parcel of 2,400 acres at Tramping Lake, southwest of Battleford, Saskatchewan. If any land was going to be surrendered, then the band was willing to give up the Tramping Lake reserve that it had never occupied.

McDougall floated several possible options — all turned down — before enlisting the help of the band's farm instructor in reaching a surrender proposal. Indian Affairs inspector S.S. Swinford convened a meeting on January 21, 1908, and accepted on behalf of the Crown 2,880 acres at Swan Lake and all of the Tramping Lake reserve.[41] The band received an immediate $100 per head.

It was only then that Swinford learned about the missionary's methods. "After the payments were over," the inspector related to

Secretary McLean, "the Chief remarked that Rev. John McDougall had informed them that all their old [privileges] of holding sun dances etc were going to be returned to them." Swinford disabused him of the notion. Whatever had been said or promised, he told the Chief, the department had "no intention" of lifting its prohibition.[42]

Two years later, when Staples asked Oliver in the House about taking the rest of the reserve, the minister "did not think it would be wise or successful" because Indian Affairs first had "to clean up the arrangement that had been made."[43] That was an understatement. The band leadership had appealed directly to the Governor General about being misled: "He [McDougall] made a lot of nice promises on behalf of the government . . . and we believed everything he said was true."[44]

The Swan Lake surrender was just one example of how Oliver's "men with special qualifications" had become quite brazen, almost reckless, in prying reserve land away from prairie bands. Any complaints about the process were largely dismissed or simply ignored. That happened in May 1908 when the Enoch Cree, living immediately west of Edmonton, were effectively forced to make a second reserve surrender — once again at the urging of Oliver.

In November 1907, Oliver had asked Pedley whether there was any "possibility" of taking a surrender at Stony Plain (Enoch reserve).[45] The minister may have used the word "possibility," but Pedley knew that his boss was dead set on removing any and all reserves from the Edmonton district. He consequently replied that he would "have the matter taken up," even though he had been warned that the band "would be very much opposed."[46]

Inspector John Markle also knew that the Enoch people "did not want . . . to talk about such matters," but asked the department in late December for two blank surrender forms in the hope that Oliver's request might be "settled on the spot."[47] Several months later, on May 14, 1908, Markle reported that he had overcome "considerable objection" and succeeded in getting the release of 6,300 acres from the east side of the reserve by a vote of fourteen to twelve.[48] The men of the band were to receive work horses and farming equipment rather than the cash payout common to other surrenders. In addition, as Markle happily noted, land sale proceeds (estimated at $16 per acre, a total of over $100,000) would relieve Indian Affairs of future band expenses.

Within days of the vote, Father Christophe Tissier, a local Oblate missionary, penned a blistering letter to Oliver accusing Markle of "not act[ing] as an honest man" in dealing with the Indians. According to what band members had told the priest, the inspector had engaged in "unfair means" and "harsh dealing" to secure the surrender of the reserve's best farm land.[49]

Markle fought back in a hard-hitting, five-page response that dismissed Tissier's complaints as "false," while intimating that he had been duped by the band in "a case of the goats leading the shepherd." The inspector also conceded that there might be difficulties "when untying any of the strings made under solemn treaty," but that the priest's views should be discounted because he "opposed the surrender of any land . . . on any terms or conditions."

Perhaps most galling was Markle's insistence that an apology wasn't necessary.[50] The department accepted Markle's version of events and moved immediately to have the surrender formalized.

Two religious men were also involved in the surrender of the Moosomin and Thunderchild reserves in August 1908. But unlike Tissier, they actively used their influence on behalf of Indian Affairs. The contiguous Treaty Six Cree reserves (over 10,000 acres) were situated immediately northwest of Battleford between the North Saskatchewan and Battle Rivers. Therein lay the problem. Moosomin and Thunderchild, and their fine agricultural lands, were "in the line of [a] march of settlers," protested Joseph Benjamin Prince, the member for Battleford in the North-West Territories legislative assembly and a future Liberal senator, in 1902.[51]

Prince wanted the Laurier government to open the reserves to white settlement, but his call for their surrender didn't gain any traction until the Canadian Northern Railway arrived in the district in

Members of the Thunderchild band were forced to relocate to poor agricultural land following the surrender of their reserve. (Provincial Archives of Saskatchewan)

1905 and crossed the reserves. Indian Affairs asked the two bands to give up their entire reserves and use the sale proceeds to purchase land elsewhere. It didn't matter that the Cree had lived there for two decades and enjoyed sustained farming success.

Discussions with the bands went nowhere in August 1907, and in frustration, Indian agent George Day endorsed Thunderchild's request that he go to Ottawa to meet personally with department officials.[52] That idea was flatly rejected, but the pressure to act only intensified. George Ewan McCraney, the new Liberal MP for Saskatoon, called on Pedley to do something about "the removal of the Indians,"[53] while Reverend Jervois Arthur Newnham, the Anglican bishop for Saskatchewan, claimed "the present Reserves constitute a great waste of land."[54] Oliver even took the unusual step of visiting the bands during a trip west to Edmonton that fall.

The following spring, Father Henricus Delmas, a local Oblate priest, reported to Oliver that he had convinced the Thunderchild band to consider a possible surrender in exchange for a new reserve south of the Battle River. He wanted some of the vacated reserve for a colony of Catholic settlers from Quebec. Delmas was assisted in his efforts by Reverend D.D. McDonald, an Anglican priest who was based in Battleford and ministered to the local reserves.[55]

Delmas's letter prompted Indian Affairs to create new surrender agreements for Thunderchild and Moosomin in 1908. But when agent Day received the documents in mid-June, he said that surrenders were unlikely unless each band received an immediate cash distribution of $15,000, and even then, their answer still might be no.[56]

Indian Affairs agreed to provide the money. The department also called on Indian commissioner David Laird to assist with the surrender meeting. His involvement was surprising. Laird was never a big proponent of surrenders, and his office had routinely been bypassed by Ottawa in dealing with these matters. He had once lived at Battleford, though, during his first term as Indian commissioner in the late 1870s, and likely visited the Moosomin and Thunderchild reserves and known the bands' leaders at one time.

The Thunderchild negotiations opened the afternoon of August 26, 1908, in a small schoolhouse on the reserve.[57] Laird was accompanied by Delmas and McDonald, there to wear down any resistance and win over the wavering. A small mounted police escort guarded the money. After the terms were read aloud and translated, band members complained about getting only six months of rations to help with resettlement. Laird granted two years' support. After more discussion, he then called for a vote and found the surrender was overwhelmingly opposed.

Laird adjourned the meeting until the next morning. During the second day of discussions, men were asked to line up on one side of the room if they supported the surrender, the opposite side if they opposed. The proposal still failed to pass.

On the third day, Laird removed $15,000 in small denominations from a suitcase and piled the cash on top of a table that he had placed in the middle of the room. This time, when the vote was called, the commissioner "would point a finger at the money, at the voter, put his face into the face of the band member and demand, 'How do you vote?"⁵⁸ The result was a tie: fifteen-fifteen. Laird looked to Chief Thunderchild to cast the deciding vote. The Chief had abstained up to then, but after receiving Laird's assurance that the terms would be honoured, he moved to the surrender side.

Once the documents were signed, Laird began paying $120 to each of 107 band members. The Thunderchild people now had to make a new home. Indian Affairs placed the new reserve not south, but some distance to the north, around Brightsand Lake, on marginal land.

Laird left that same day for Moosomin and put forward the same terms at an afternoon meeting. The band had no interest in any surrender offer and resoundingly sent Laird away without any hope of reaching an agreement. As he told the department, "it seemed useless to prolong the negotiations."⁵⁹

Indian agent Day bore the brunt of Indian Affairs' displeasure. Pedley wanted both surrenders executed at the same time and censured the agent for disobeying orders.⁶⁰ Laird also paid a price, albeit indirectly. In early January 1909, just months after Laird had failed to deliver Moosomin, Oliver moved to shutter the Winnipeg Indian Affairs office and do away with the positions of commissioner and assistant commissioner. The minister said the office no longer served any useful purpose. Laird returned to Ottawa as a "department advisor," but did little more than hold down a government patronage position until his death in 1914.

This department pressure to secure surrenders was publicly disavowed by Oliver in the House of Commons in response to an Opposition question about handling another difficult surrender case. "In negotiating with them [bands], it is not good policy to keep continually urging them to make a surrender," he said on July 11, 1908. "It is better to make a liberal offer, and if it is not accepted, cease all efforts for the time."⁶¹

Agent Day, though, was not willing to "cease all efforts" after his department reprimand and redoubled his efforts to secure a surrender at Moosomin. He was confident that the band would be willing to deal after seeing how the Thunderchild people had benefited from their agreement. He was once again aided by Father Delmas and Reverend McDonald, as the pair had done at Thunderchild.

By January 1909, the Moosomin band indicated it was ready to consider a surrender. It's not known what prompted the change in attitude — there was no recognized Chief at the time — but there was nothing imprecise about the proposed terms. The band wanted, among other things, $5,000 more than had been paid at Thunderchild, and a new reserve at Jackfish Lake.

Indian Affairs, with Day serving as mediator, haggled over the band's surrender conditions, but eventually a meeting was convened on May 7, 1909. It appears that Day decided to strike and secure the surrender as soon as he received $20,000 in cash. He also leaned on acting band leader Josie Moosomin, telling him that his department confirmation as Chief depended on a successful vote. Day said little about the meeting beyond reporting that Moosomin gave up its entire reserve.[62] In exchange, the band got a parcel of land that one senior Indian Affairs official dismissed as "hilly, stony, in the frost belt, and practically useless as a farming operation."[63]

Inspector Graham also had unfinished business that he wanted to tidy up. Still unhappy with his failure to secure a surrender at Muscowpetung in the Qu'Appelle Lakes region in March 1906, Graham had nagged the band about the matter whenever he visited the reserve. It was also discussed with Oliver during the minister's visit to Indian Head in October 1907.

By late 1908, Graham was ready to try again for the "best half" of the reserve, employing his standard negotiation ploy — payment upon surrender (in this case, $10,000) and another payment in the same amount a year later. The meeting with the Muscowpetung band was held on January 4, 1909 — a bitterly cold day — and lasted the afternoon. Graham provided no formal account of what had transpired, only informing Pedley in a private note that the negotiations had been difficult. Perhaps that's why only ten men, a minority of the eligible band members, signed the document. That was good enough for Graham, and with another 17,600 surrendered acres in his breast pocket, he began paying $120 to each band member into the late evening.[64]

Graham then left to investigate the possibility of taking a surrender at The Key, a Saulteaux reserve along the Assiniboine River in east-central Saskatchewan, just inside the border with Manitoba and north of the new Canadian Northern town of Kamsack. As in several other surrender cases, the initiative came from a Member of Parliament — in this case, from Dr. Edward L. Cash, the Liberal representative for Mackenzie, Saskatchewan.

Cash practised medicine in Yorkton and once served as medical officer to the reserves in the Pelly agency. He would have interacted with the bands and local Indian Affairs officials. In the spring of 1908, Cash contacted the department about a possible surrender at The Key. Pedley responded that the reserve wasn't under consideration for any such action.

Then, in the summer of 1908, it was learned that The Key band wanted to sell part of its reserve (thirteen sections from the east and west sides) for farming outfits and equipment. "They feel they have too much land and not enough horses and implements to work satis-factorily," Indian agent W.G. Blewett explained to Graham. "I think it would be a good thing [if they] sell part of their Reserve . . . instead of getting government assistance."[65] Blewett could also have added that The Key people likely heard about other bands getting money for their land — they wanted a first payment of $80 per band member.

On January 18, 1909, Graham visited The Key and convinced the band to increase the amount of land to be surrendered — from 8,320 acres to 10,880. He didn't think it would "bring a high price," but added that "there is a time coming when the Land would sell."[66] Graham also worked out a tentative deal with a delegation from the nearby Keeseekoose reserve. They came to him that same day with an offer — the sale of 6,000 acres. Once again, Graham pushed for a larger amount and got them to agree to an 8,000-acre surrender.

Indian Affairs approved the inspector's surrender packages — except for increasing The Key amount to 11,500 acres (almost 50 percent of the reserve) — and authorized him to proceed in February. Graham, though, didn't return to the Pelly agency until May, a delay that may have been intentional because the two bands, according to agent Blewett, became "very anxious." The Keeseekoose band approved the surrender on May 15 and received an immediate cash advance on the land sale proceeds of $85 per person. The Key meeting followed three days later with the same result, but with a higher initial payment of $100 because more land was being surrendered.

Graham told Pedley that the vote in both cases was unanimous, adding little more about the proceedings.[67] He seemed to believe that record-keeping wasn't his job, especially when he bent the rules in the Indian Act to get his way. He also behaved as if the bands had no choice but to agree to a surrender, regardless of their treaty rights and the sanctity of their reserve holdings.

While Graham was meeting with the Muscowpetung band in early January 1909, Reverend McDougall was attending to an outstanding surrender in Alberta's Hobbema agency. Almost three years earlier, Oliver had turned down a surrender agreement with the Samson reserve because he did not like the band's terms, especially what land it was willing to give up.

McDougall had negotiated that draft agreement, and he was able to reach a new tentative deal with the band in late 1908. This time, Samson was prepared to surrender 9,380 acres — representing all of the reserve west of the Calgary and Edmonton Railway main line — for the maximum 50 percent of land sale proceeds (10 percent, $20 per person, to be distributed as first payment).

Inspector Markle would normally have been authorized to call a meeting to take the surrender, but the task fell to McDougall for the first time. The Methodist missionary had only handled pre-surrender negotiations up to then. Oliver, though, had great trust in McDougall's abilities, and that trust was rewarded with a signed agreement in January 1909.[68]

There was also a second purpose to McDougall's trip to Hobbema — namely the surrender of the Bobtail reserve, immediately south and contiguous to Samson. In 1877, the Bobtail Cree had signed an adhesion to Treaty Six and taken up a reserve (surveyed in 1885) at Hobbema.

Most of the band members left treaty in 1886 to secure Métis scrip, only to petition Indian Affairs to be readmitted the following year. Those who resumed their treaty status settled on the Ermineskin and Samson reserves.

The original Bobtail reserve had sat empty until it was occupied by a group of refugee Montana Cree who had left Canada after the 1885 North-West Rebellion and been deported by the United States in 1896. The Montana Cree were understood not to have ownership of the reserve, but that was a moot question when Markle proposed that the band amalgamate with other Hobbema bands so that the reserve could be taken.

McDougall pursued the matter with the Montana band, but they wanted to keep their own home, especially after their ten years in exile. He left them with a warning that the reserve "really belonged to the Government" and that it was not really necessary to seek a surrender.[69]

A showdown over the reserve was avoided when the department discovered that some original Bobtail members who had never left treaty were living with the Samson and Ermineskin bands. McDougall was sent back to Hobbema in early June 1909 to negotiate with four men. They agreed to give up the Bobtail reserve, a total of 20,160 acres. But not all the land was turned over to the Crown. Some of the former reserve was retained by the Montana Cree; another parcel was added to Samson. The remainder, 9,819 acres, would be put up for sale.

The former Bobtail members were officially accepted into the Samson and Ermineskin bands in exchange for a share of the payments. McDougall had delivered. But it wasn't a complete success. He had predicted that the surrenders "will have a good effect . . . on the adjacent Bands,"[70] but the Ermineskin band never wavered in its determination to turn down any and all surrender appeals.[71]

Even without the Ermineskin surrender, Indian Affairs, acting on behalf of the Crown, had amassed a whopping amount of reserve land over twelve years of Liberal rule. By March 1909, 725,517 acres from

THE GREAT BLOOD-CURDLING WILD WEST SHOW

Hon. Frank Oliver dispossessing the Indians of St. Peter's Reserve of their lands.
(With Laurier & Co.'s Circus to Tour Western Canada)

Frank Oliver was portrayed as a desperado for his handling of the St. Peter's (Peguis) reserve surrender. (Public Archives of Ontario)

bands across the country had been sold.[72] That was equal to half the size of Prince Edward Island.

Oliver seemed to savour announcing these statistics during his regular updates to Parliament. The Conservatives, though, smelled another Liberal boondoggle. For several years, the Opposition had complained about how Indian Affairs was handling auction sales. It wanted wider advertising, not just in Liberal newspapers, and for a longer period.

Then it was revealed in March 1908 how little the Laurier government was actually getting for the land — on average less than $2.50 per acre. This remarkably low return prompted Conservative Joseph Elijah Armstrong to accuse Oliver of "acting most unfairly towards the Indians of this country . . . lands [are] being squandered." The minister was unfazed and recited his standard response: "The Indians get the price and the country gets whatever development the land may be capable of."[73] Armstrong raised the matter again in the House in April 1910, this time slagging "the work of the Indian Department . . . carried on in a most careless, indifferent, and I might say, corrupt manner."

Liberal James Conmee dismissed the accusations as baseless, insisting that surrenders were "a business-like transaction, carried out in the interest of the public and the interest of the Indians themselves."[74] But Armstrong wasn't really concerned with the interests of prairie bands. Nor was he saying that reserve land shouldn't be surrendered. What bothered Armstrong was that it was mostly Liberals who were profiting handsomely from the surrender "business" and the sale of former reserve lands at bargain prices. The Conservatives resented being on the outside looking in.

Notes

1. Correspondence is found in *Library and Archives Canada* (*LAC*), RG10, v. 4007, f. 241, 354.
2. House of Commons, *Debates*, June 15, 1906, pp. 5422–34.
3. Quoted in P. Martin-McGuire, *First Nations Land Surrenders on the Prairies, 1896–1911* (Ottawa: Indian Claims Commission, 1998), p. 126.
4. Quoted in ibid., p. 198. See also Indian Claims Commission, "Opaskwayak Cree Nation Streets and Lane Inquiry," unpublished report, 2007, pp. 6–9.
5. T.D. Regehr, *The Canadian Northern Railway: Pioneer Road of the Northern Prairies, 1895–1918* (Toronto: Macmillan, 1976), pp. 174–6.
6. *Debates*, March 30, 1906, pp. 947–50.
7. *Edmonton Bulletin*, April 15, 1882.
8. *LAC*, RG10, v. 3732, f. 26623, D. Laird to J.D. McLean, March 19, 1904.
9. Ibid., W.M. Graham to F. Oliver, June 19, 1906.
10. Martin-McGuire, *First Nations Land Surrenders*, p. 276.

11. *LAC*, RG10, v. 3732, f. 26623, W.M. Graham to J.D. McLean, September 24, 1906.

12. Indian Claims Commission, "Inquiry into the 1907 Reserve Land Surrender Claim of the Kahkewistahaw First Nation," unpublished report, 1997, pp. 39–46.

13. *LAC*, RG10, v. 3732, f. 26623, J.A.J. McKenna to J.D. McLean, March 19, 1904.

14. Ibid., W.M. Graham to J.D. McLean, February 13, 1907.

15. *LAC*, RG10, v. 4011, f. 260, 260-2, W.M. Graham to J.D. McLean, April 22, 1907.

16. Ibid., W.M. Graham to J.D. McLean, July 4, 1907.

17. Martin-McGuire, *First Nations Land Surrenders*, pp. 132, 200, 273–4.

18. Indian Claims Commission, "Inquiry into the 1907 Surrender Claim of the Fishing Lake First Nation," unpublished report, 1997, pp. 6–9; Martin-McGuire, *First Nations Land Surrenders*, p. 281.

19. W.M. Graham, *Treaty Days: Reflections of an Indian Commissioner* (Calgary: Glenbow-Alberta Institute, 1991), pp. 62–78.

20. *LAC*, RG10, v. 6704, f. 121A-3-2, W.M. Graham to J.D. McLean, August 21, 1907.

21. Martin-McGuire, *First Nations Land Surrenders*, p. 284.

22. Graham, *Treaty Days*, p. 62.

23. *LAC*, RG10, v. 1127, f. 639, F. Oliver to Governor in Council, April 8, 1908.

24. The best source is Tyler, Wright, and Daniel Ltd., "The Illegal Surrender of St. Peter's Reserve," unpublished paper, TARR Center of Winnipeg, 1983.

25. Quoted in Indian Claims Commission, "Peguis First Nation Inquiry Treaty Land Entitlement Claim," unpublished paper, 2001, p. 23.

26. Quoted in P.P. Burrows, "'As She Shall Deem Just': Treaty One and the Ethnic Cleansing of the St. Peter's Reserve, 1871–1934," unpublished M.A. thesis, University of Manitoba, 2009, p. 97.

27. Quoted in Martin-McGuire, *First Nations Land Surrenders*, p. 289.

28. Quoted in R.C. Daniel, "A History of Native Claims Processes in Canada, 1867–1979," unpublished report for Indian and Northern Affairs, 1980, p. 35.

29. Manitoba sponsored a royal commission investigation, the St. Peter's Reserve Commission, in 1911.

30. D.J. Hall, *Clifford Sifton, v. 2: A Lonely Eminence, 1901–1929* (Vancouver: University of British Columbia Press, 1985), p. 189.

31. F.B. Carvell, E.M. Macdonald, and A.K. Maclean "sat on the lid when the Conservatives with definite charges asked for a fuller inquiry." *Edmonton Journal*, April 12, 1915.

32. *Debates*, February 6, 1908, p. 2615.

33. J.M. Beck, *Pendulum of Power: Canada's Federal Elections* (Scarborough: Prentice-Hall, 1968), p. 111.

34. Ibid., p. 107.

35. Ibid., p. 114.

36. Quoted in W.L.R. Clark, "Politics in Brandon City, 1899–1949," unpublished Ph.D. thesis, University of Alberta, 1976, p. 96.

37. The defeat gave Burrows time to concentrate on his expanding lumber business and personal wealth before he was tapped by another Liberal prime minister two decades later for a vice-regal position.

38. Quoted in Beck, *Pendulum of Power*, p. 117.

39. *Debates*, April 5, 1906, pp. 1246–7.

40. Quoted in Martin-McGuire, *First Nations Land Surrenders*, p. 290.

41. Ibid., pp. 290–1.

42. *LAC*, RG10, v. 3624, f. 5217-2, S.S. Swinford to J.D. McLean, January 28, 1908.

43. *Debates*, April 22, 1910, p. 7851.

44. Quoted in Martin-McGuire, *First Nations Land Surrenders*, p. 293.

45. *LAC*, RG10, v. 4037, f. 316,676-1, F. Oliver to F. Pedley, November 4, 1907.

46. Ibid., F. Pedley to F. Oliver, November 11, 1907.

47. Ibid., J.A. Markle to J.D. McLean, December 28, 1907.

48. Ibid., J.A. Markle to J.D. McLean, May 14, 1908.

49. Ibid., C. Tissier to F. Oliver, May 18, 1908.

50. Ibid., J.A. Markle to J.D. McLean, June 29, 1908.

51. Quoted in J. Funk, *Outside, the Women Cried* (Lincoln, Nebraska: iUniverse, 2007), p. 18.

52. Martin-McGuire, *First Nations Land Surrenders*, pp. 231, 308.

53. Quoted in Funk, *Outside, the Women Cried*, p. 29.

54. Quoted in ibid., p. 37.

55. Martin-McGuire, *First Nations Land Surrenders*, p. 230; Funk, *Outside, the Women Cried*, p. 31.

56. Martin-McGuire, *First Nations Land Surrenders*, p. 308.

57. The account of the surrender meeting is based on oral history collected for Funk, *Outside, the Women Cried*.

58. Quoted in ibid., p. 38.

59. Quoted in Indian Claims Commission, "Inquiry into the 1909 Reserve Land Surrender Claim of the Moosomin First Nation," unpublished report, 1997, p. 52.

60. Martin-McGuire, *First Nations Land Surrenders*, p. 310.

61. *Debates*, July 11, 1908, p. 12751.

62. Indian Claims Commission, "Inquiry into the 1909 Reserve Land Surrender Claim of the Moosomin First Nation," pp. 53–68.

63. Quoted in B. Titley, *The Indian Commissioners: Agents of the State and Indian Policy in Canada's Prairie West, 1873–1932* (Edmonton: University of Alberta Press, 2009), p. 159.

64. Martin-McGuire, *First Nations Land Surrenders*, pp. 147–8, 296–8.

65. *LAC*, RG10, v. 4039, f. 329,759, W.G. Blewett to W.H. Graham, July 24, 1908.

66. Ibid., W.H. Graham to F. Pedley, January 21, 1909.

67. Indian Claims Commission, "The Key First Nation Inquiry 1909 Surrender Claim," unpublished report, 2000, pp. 43–50.

68. D. Lupul, "The Bobtail Land Surrender," *Alberta History*, v. 6, n. 1, winter 1978, pp. 33–5. In November 1914, the Samson band complained to Indian Affairs: "Several years have come and passed since then and a large portion of the land we surrendered is still unsold and the monies for these lands have come to us very slowly." Quoted in Martin-McGuire, *First Nations Land Surrenders*, p. 403.

69. Quoted in Lupul, "The Bobtail Land Surrender," p. 35.

70. Ibid.

71. See R. Irwin, "No Means No: Ermineskin's Resistance to Land Surrender, 1902–1921," *Canadian Journal of Native Studies*, v. 23, n. 1, 2003, pp. 165–83.

72. *Debates*, December 1, 1909, p. 784.

73. Ibid., July 11, 1908, pp. 12749–50; see also March 9, 1908, p. 4586.

74. Ibid., April 22, 1910, pp. 7840–2.

⊷ *Nine* ⊶

FAVOURITISM

In November 1909, J.N. Bayne, Saskatchewan's deputy commissioner of municipal affairs, contacted the Indian Affairs department secretary for a list of all reserve lands sold since September 1, 1905.[1] It's not known why Bayne wanted the sales records, which included names and addresses, or what he did with the information. He might have been surprised to learn, though, who had bought surrendered land.

The list included Saskatchewan's lieutenant governor Amédée Forget, who acquired a section (640 acres) of Pasqua land in October 1906. Another purchaser was Justice John Henderson Lamont, a former Liberal Member of Parliament for Saskatchewan and the province's first attorney general. He picked up over four sections (four square miles) of Moosomin/Thunderchild land in November 1909. So too did Saskatchewan Crown prosecutor James Thomas Brown at the same sale.[2] None of these men intended to hang up their robes to start over as farmers. They were simply gambling on western lands, seeking to turn their purchases into a timely profit.

In fact, a large proportion of surrendered acres fell into the hands of individual or corporate speculators. That they were devout Liberals, or had connections in one way or another to the Wilfrid Laurier Liberal government, was no coincidence. Party affiliation, especially when that party was in power, gave them a front row at the trough.

Saskatchewan's first attorney general J.H. Lamont, a future Supreme Court of Canada justice, acquired land at the Moosomin/ Thunderchild sale at Battleford, Saskatchewan, in 1909. (Provincial Archives of Saskatchewan)

‹‹--››

By the time Bayne made his request, auctions for former reserve lands were dominated by speculators. That had not been the plan. In September 1888, the John A. Macdonald Conservative government had introduced surrendered lands regulations (P.C. 1787) that limited "any one purchaser" to no more than 640 acres of land (up to four quarter-sections or one square mile). There was a loophole, though. Indian Affairs could set aside the regulations in favour of sale by tender.[3]

James Smart, the deputy minister of Interior and Indian Affairs, had chosen this option in selling the surrendered Pheasant Rump and Ocean Man reserves in November 1901. By manipulating the tender process, Smart and his co-conspirators fraudulently secured most of the Moose Mountain land. They netted 45,000 acres — seventy times the allowable amount under the 1888 regulations. The trio also used the same rigged tender process to secure half of the former Chakastaypasin reserve, more than 8,500 acres, that same month. They were outfoxed at their own game, though, in December 1902 when Edmonton's McDougall & Secord Ltd. used insider information to successfully bid on thirty-eight quarter-sections (6,080 acres) surrendered from the Enoch reserve. Once again, the sales regulations had been set aside, making it possible for the Edmonton firm to garner the majority of the land.

Private tender sales in the early 1900s enabled Indian Affairs to dispose of thousands of acres of surrendered land to a handful of speculators. The sales also worked against the interests of bands who had forfeited all or part of their reserve. Smart and his pals had amassed almost seventy square miles of Moose Mountain land for only $1.23 per acre. This bargain price generated meagre sale proceeds for the two Nakoda bands.

Sale by tender, though, eventually backfired. The limited department advertising, together with the need to prepare separate tenders for each quarter-section, only worked if there was a buyer waiting in the wings, primed with confidential survey information. But when the Michel land was put on the sales block in June 1904, bids were received for less than 25 percent of the available quarter-sections. The amount being offered was also well below the upset price (minimum acceptable bid), even below the average rate per acre for prairie land in 1904. It would be the last time that Indian Affairs held a tender sale for surrendered land.

Auctions didn't clip the wings of speculators, especially while sales continued to be exempted from the surrendered lands regulations. At the Carry the Kettle auction in February 1906, for example, four men obtained all but one of the thirty-four quarter-sections. This story was repeated at the Grizzly Bear's Head/Lean Man auction at Battleford in June. At least the prices paid per quarter-section were higher, a reflection of the increasing value of farm land as white settlement flourished and more acres were brought into production.

The domination of auctions by a few buyers would be repeated again and again as more and more surrendered land came on the market.

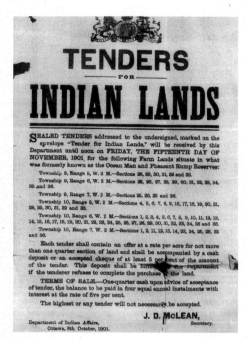

TENDERS

—— FOR ——

INDIAN LANDS

SEALED TENDERS addressed to the undersigned, marked on the envelope "Tender for Indian Lands," will be received by this Department until noon on FRIDAY, THE FIFTEENTH DAY OF NOVEMBER, 1901, for the following Farm Lands situate in what was formerly known as the Ocean Man and Pheasant Rump Reserves:

Township 9, Range 5, W. 2 M.—Sections 28, 29, 30, 31, 32 and 33.

Township 9, Range 6, W. 2 M.—Sections 25, 26, 27, 28, 29, 30, 31, 32, 33, 34, 35 and 36.

Township 9, Range 7, W. 2 M.—Sections 25, 26, 35 and 36.

Township 10, Range 5, W. 2 M.—Sections 4, 5, 6, 7, 8, 9, 16, 17, 18, 19, 20, 21, 28, 29, 30, 31, 32 and 33.

Township 10, Range 6, W. 2 M.—Sections 1, 2, 3, 4, 5, 6, 7, 8, 9, 10, 11, 12, 13, 14, 15, 16, 17, 18, 19, 20, 21, 22, 23, 24, 25, 26, 27, 28, 29, 30, 31, 32, 33, 34, 35 and 36.

Township 10, Range 7, W. 2 M.—Sections 1, 2, 11, 12, 13, 14, 23, 24, 25, 26, 35 and 36.

Each tender shall contain an offer at a rate per acre for not more than one quarter section of land and shall be accompanied by a cash deposit or an accepted cheque of at least 5 per cent of the amount of the tender. This deposit shall be forfeited to the Department if the tenderer refuses to complete the purchase of the land.

TERMS OF SALE.—One-quarter cash upon advice of acceptance of tender, the balance to be paid in four equal annual instalments with interest at the rate of five per cent.

The highest or any tender will not necessarily be accepted.

J. D. McLEAN,

Department of Indian Affairs,   Secretary.
Ottawa, 8th October, 1901.

The sales notice for the surrendered Ocean Man and Pheasant Rump reserves. A separate tender had to be submitted for every quarter-section parcel of land.

(Library and Archives Canada)

A new wrinkle, though, was the growing number of buyers from outside the region, particularly from Ontario. Ottawa's push to get bands to give up their reserves, especially after Frank Oliver took over as Indian Affairs minister, attracted speculators looking for new ways to make money in the booming Canadian economy. Western lands seemed to be a paying investment, especially if there were ways to snap up surrendered parcels in settled districts near rail lines. And Liberal connections enhanced buying opportunities. Many seemed to have information — even if it was just advance notice of the sales — that gave them a leg up over potential competitors.

At the Alexander sale in Edmonton on October 3, 1906, when 9,500 acres were auctioned, four men acquired two-thirds of the land: William Addison Wood, a Canadian Pacific Railway agent; Patrick Owen O'Dwyer, a developer; Charles Bacon, a gentleman; and Joseph Robert Miller, a Toronto commission agent. The only other buyer from Ontario was Frederick W. Grant, a lawyer from the small town of Midland on Georgian Bay, who had been provided survey information (plans and descriptions) about the Alexander lands by Indian Affairs. Even though Grant secured only three quarter-sections (480 acres) that day, he soon emerged as one of the most successful players in the field.[4]

Two weeks later, at Regina's city hall on October 17, 1906, twenty-four sections (15,360 acres) of surrendered Pasqua land were auctioned at an average price of $13.41 per acre, more than double the average price at the time. Not only was it prime agricultural land, but a Grand Trunk Pacific Railway branch line, from Melville to Regina, was to be routed through the district. Almost one-third was acquired by local settlers who knew the quality of the land and were willing to pay, in the words of the *Leader-Post*, "big money for wild prairie . . . freezing out local speculators."[5] The majority, though, still went to outsiders.[6] Fresh from the auction at Alexander, Miller went on a spending spree and picked up nearly ten sections of land, over 6,000 acres. Given the average price per acre, the Toronto commission agent would have paid roughly $15,000 in cash as a deposit on the land. His backers, though, had the money.[7]

Other buyers of Pasqua land included past and present employees of the Indian Affairs department.[8] The most noteworthy was Saskatchewan lieutenant governor Forget, who had once served as Indian commissioner. Even though Forget had once raised concerns about the department's surrender practices, he had no qualms in making a purchase at the Pasqua sale. Neither did his former secretary A.W.J. Bourget, who like his former boss was a member of Regina's exclusive Assiniboia Club. Maybe that's where they privately conferred about the upcoming sale. Horatio Nichol, a clerk for the Crooked Lakes reserves, also bought a half-section of land. Nichol would have had personal knowledge of the Pasqua land and likely shared that information with Miller, who was married to Nichol's sister.[9] Even Presbyterian minister R.B. Heron, principal of the Regina Indian Industrial Residential school, picked up a half-section of land. Heron once equated "the problem of the

Indian" to their race, much like "that of the negroes in the U.S., Hindoos of India, or native races of Africa."[10]

The other late 1906 auction sale — this time for Michel land — was held in Edmonton. It was initially set for mid-November, but Indian Affairs minister Frank Oliver delayed the event until December 5 to allow more time for advertising. He wanted to ensure that his constituents were informed of the coming sale, especially after another parcel of Michel land had failed to attract many buyers in June 1904. Any unsold land from the west side of the reserve would now be put on the market again, along with recently surrendered land on the east side.[11] Indian agent James Gibbons was worried, though, that there might be "a prejudice" against the west side lands and directed the auctioneer to alternate bidding between west and east quarter-sections instead of selling one block of land and then the other. A puffed-up Gibbons claimed that his scheme would "catch the giddy multitude."[12]

The Michel auction was scheduled for noon in the Edmonton dominion lands office. There was a large turnout, numbering around 300, and it had to be moved to the Empire Theatre.[13] Bidding was brisk, taking four hours to sell all of the Michel land (8,278 acres). The average price was $9.65 per acre: $8.47 for west side lands, $12.93 for east side. Oliver's *Edmonton Bulletin* heralded the sale as "an unqualified success from the standpoint of Poor Lo [First Nation]."[14] The Michel band, according to the newspaper report, could expect to receive nearly $80,000 for its surrendered lands. Yet only one-fifth of that sale total, close to $16,000, was due at the time of the auction. The band would never receive the full amount if buyers defaulted on any of the four instalment payments. That was a real possibility, given that the high prices probably reflected the boom mentality that gripped Edmonton. Interest in the land was largely based on the expectation that the Canadian Northern and Grand Trunk Pacific rail lines would be routed through or near the Michel reserve as the tracks left the city for the foothills.

Many speculators used their Liberal connections to secure First Nations land.
(Provincial Archives of Ontario)

Despite Oliver's attempt to give Edmonton area residents adequate notice of the Michel sale, only 25 per cent of the land went to local buyers. The remainder was sold in 3,000-acre parcels to two outside speculators: Christopher (Christian) Fahrni of Gladstone, Manitoba, and F.W. Grant of Midland, Ontario.

Fahrni had never purchased surrendered land before. Nor would he in the future. But the Swiss immigrant was a successful cattle breeder and horse trader. Fahrni would have known his way around auctions and buying and selling stock.[15] He also dabbled in real estate and used his time in Edmonton to invest in some city lots.[16] It still doesn't explain, though, what prompted Fahrni to travel two provinces away in early December 1906 to bid for land that he couldn't inspect because of the winter weather.

The answer was his business dealings and political friendship with fellow Liberal John Crawford, who had worked in the implement, grain, and lumber business in Neepawa, Manitoba.[17] Crawford was elected to Parliament in 1904 for Portage la Prairie. It's not unreasonable to assume that Crawford, as a member of the western Liberal caucus, was aware of the forthcoming Michel sale and informed Fahrni what the land might be worth once the railroad went through. Why else would the Manitoba farmer borrow the money for the down payment unless he thought it was a sure thing?[18] Fahrni walked away from the auction with receipts for almost five square miles of land (3,080 acres).

The second-place finish at the Michel auction went to Midland lawyer F.W. Grant, who secured 3,060 acres. Grant was a well-connected Liberal who shared a legal practice with his older brother George Davidson Grant after both men graduated from Toronto's Osgoode Hall. The younger Grant's specialty in marine law made him a natural partner for local entrepreneur James Playfair, founder of the Midland Navigation Company. Their association introduced Grant to a range of other Great Lakes business opportunities. At the height of his corporate power, Grant was president of the Canadian Dredge and Dock Company, the Hamilton Bridge Company, and the Midland Simcoe Elevator Company. He was also a director on numerous boards, including Montreal's landmark Mount Royal Hotel. By then, the early 1940s, his speculation in Michel land was a little-known footnote from his early Midland career.

Grant's interest in First Nations land had a modest beginning but soon expanded to match his ambition. In 1905, he privately bought, probably as holiday property, part of Baxter Island in Georgian Bay. The land, once part of a reserve, had been sold to Grant by Indian Affairs for the remarkably low price of $140. When William Humphrey Bennett, the Conservative MP for Simcoe East and coincidentally also a Midland lawyer, got wind of the sweet deal, he pointedly grilled Oliver in the House of Commons on May 25, 1905, about whether he was going to let the sale stand. Bennett lumped Grant in with "the rest of the army of grafters" seeking government favours. Oliver did his best to play dumb, talking without conceding much, eventually bringing both the prime minister and Opposition leader into the fray. The debate ended with the warning that Oliver was leaving himself "open to the charge of favouritism."[19]

Decades later, when some of the Midland law firm's old files were accessed, it was learned that the Grant brothers were part of a syndicate that relied on confidential survey information to buy surrendered land. The other members were James Playfair and his Midland business partner D.L. White, Midland department store owner W.E. Preston, and Midland lumber merchant Manley Chew. These speculators had a direct channel to Indian Affairs through Chew, the Liberal MP for Simcoe East. Indeed, many of the Indian Affairs documents in the Grant law office files were stamped with the words "Compliments of Manley Chew." There were sale notices, survey plans, and descriptions of the surrendered land, but most importantly, upset prices for each quarter-section parcel.[20] Someone in the department was secretly providing this restricted information. The most likely culprit was Orr's clerk J.P. O'Connor, who had specific responsibility for western land sales. His handwriting matches the pencilled notations in the margins of the land descriptions in Grant's possession.[21]

Grant was extremely pleased with the outcome of the Michel sale. No sooner had he returned to Midland, before Christmas 1906, than he wrote secretary McLean, telling him the auction "was a tremendous success . . . every person there seemed to think so." Grant was somewhat miffed, though, that he had to "pay such high prices . . . the good lands went like hot cakes."[22] He probably hadn't expected a bidding contest with Fahrni for the quarter-section lots. As one speculator told Prime Minister Laurier, he and his friends were after former reserve land "in or about possible town sites" along rail lines.[23]

Indian Affairs bent backwards to facilitate land speculation. Inspector William Graham once questioned the wisdom of holding an auction sale in late December. He was concerned that speculators or their representatives would have already left the region and miss the sale.[24] Graham also believed that better results could have been realized at the October 1906 Pasqua auction if the payment terms were relaxed. It was a peculiar conclusion, perhaps understandable if the Regina auction had been a failure — but it wasn't. The entire surrendered parcel

The Gladstone, Manitoba, home of Christopher Fahrni. He bought a large swath of surrendered Michel land in 1906 but could not meet the payments. (Library and Archives Canada)

had been sold at competitive prices. Still, Graham recommended to the department that the payment schedule be expanded to ten instalments (from the usual five) at 5 percent interest (down from six).[25]

This revision, effective December 1906, was justified on the grounds that it would lead to higher prices. Graham insisted that buyers would be encouraged to bid more for reserve land if a smaller down payment was required at the time of purchase.[26] But in effect it meant that speculators could bid on more land, not just make higher bids.

One of the first auctions under the new payment schedule was held at Kamsack, Saskatchewan, on June 24, 1908, for over 10,000 acres of Cote lands that had been surrendered a year earlier. The sales notification list was populated with Liberals — from current Members of Parliament to speculators who had bought land at auctions in the past. Anybody who asked for advance notice was put on the list, but it appears that Liberals knew to ask for this privilege. Prospective Liberal buyers either wrote directly to department secretary McLean for upcoming sale information or were simply added to the list at Deputy Minister Frank Pedley's instruction.[27]

Kamsack residents secured most of the Cote land at auction. They were either local merchants seeking to cash in on the land boom or farmers wanting to expand their holdings. The sales list also contained some interesting names. One was Presbyterian Reverend William McWhinney, principal of the Crowstand Indian Residential School on the Cote reserve, who bought 160 acres. Another was Herbert N. Awrey, the Ottawa clerk at Indian Affairs who bought three quarter-sections of Michel land in 1904 through the department cleaning lady. He successfully bid for only a quarter-section of Cote land but didn't hide his identity this time.

The more intriguing purchase was made by the partnership of Herman Finger and William McBrady. The Port Arthur, Ontario, pair acquired one and a half sections. They appear to have been part of a speculator network from northwestern Ontario, and more importantly, friends with James Conmee, the Liberal MP for Thunder Bay and Rainy River since 1904. Conmee probably alerted the men to the upcoming Kamsack sale. The former Cote lands represented a prime investment opportunity along the Canadian Northern main line through east-central Saskatchewan.

The Liberal MP might also have told Finger about the timber berths available in western Canada. Beginning in 1906, the same year he bought Cote land, Finger began acquiring the rights to timber stands in the Carrot River country, along the south side of the Saskatchewan River and straddling the present-day Saskatchewan-Manitoba border. He soon launched the Finger Lumber Company and built the first mill near the junction of the Carrot and Saskatchewan Rivers. In 1912, Finger became the first mayor of The Pas, another CNoR creation situated on former reserve land.

The other noteworthy feature of the Cote sale was the formation of the Kamsack Land Company Ltd. to take advantage of the upcoming auction and any others in the district. These local syndicates sprang to life to provide more purchasing punch and facilitate the transfer or consignment of land to other corporations or individuals, especially those with connections to the American market. The membership of the Kamsack company suggested there was no such thing as conflict of interest when it came to surrendered reserve land. One of the company directors was Dr. James Ira Wallace, the Kamsack justice of the peace who had certified the 1907 Cote surrender. Another was William George Blewett, the Pelly Indian agent who accompanied inspector Graham when he took the surrender. Dr. Edward L. Cash, the Liberal MP for Mackenzie and former medical officer for the Pelly agency, may not have been listed as a director, but it is suspected that he helped bring the group together and organize bidding.[28]

There was a similar sales pattern at the Crooked Lakes auction (Cowessess and Kahkewistahaw lands) at Broadview, Saskatchewan, in late November 1908. Only two-thirds of the land (199 of 322 parcels) was sold, a surprising result given the nearly two-decade demand to open up the reserves.[29] Neither the Cowessess nor Kahkewistahaw people were informed about the sale outcome. Indian Affairs rarely involved the bands once reserve lands had been surrendered. The department acted as if bands needn't worry — that it could be counted upon to do the right thing. More than a year after the auction, the Cowessess Chief had to ask "how much of their land was sold, how much money did the land sell for, how much is still unsold, [and] when do the Department intend to put the remaining land up for sale."[30] The most burning question, though, was when they would be paid again as agreed upon in the surrender arrangement.

Local settlers, many from Grenfell, picked up one or two quarter-sections at the Crooked Lakes auction. The sales statement also listed a number of Indian Affairs employees. Ottawa clerk Herbert Awrey continued to slowly add to his growing western real estate empire by purchasing another quarter-section. Local Indian agent Matthew Millar and interpreter Harry Cameron also bought land. Even Graham's long-time secretary, Alice Tye, who would help prepare his memoirs in

the 1930s, acquired two quarter-sections. Her brother Harry successfully bid on an adjoining quarter.[31] Even if she first secured permission,
the optics of Alice Tye buying surrendered land while her boss oversaw
the auction were not good.

It wasn't until January 24, 1910, though, that Pedley issued a notice
that "no Officer of this Department, or his Wife, or anyone dependent upon him shall directly, or indirectly, purchase any Indian land or
become proprietor of, or interested in, any such land, and every such
purchase or interest shall be void, the Sale cancelled, and the Officer
liable to dismissal."[32] Maybe there had been complaints. Maybe some
employees had failed to meet their instalment payments. Or maybe the
Conservative Opposition was going to make an issue of the practice.
Whatever the reason, Pedley's notice left no wiggle room. Nothing was
done, though, about employees who had already bought land up to the
time of the prohibition.

As with other Indian Affairs auctions, big-time speculators dominated the Crooked Lakes sales. Herman Finger and his Port Arthur
partner William McBrady raked in over six sections of land. William A.
Kenning, who ran a Winnipeg real estate investment firm, also secured
several sections, in co-operation with several family members. The largest purchaser was the Western Canada Colonization Company, which
had offices in Winnipeg and St. Paul, Minnesota. The company had
two representatives at the sale, C.H. McNider of Mason City, Iowa,
and Nicol Halsey of Chicago. While other buyers dabbled in quarter-
sections, the pair scooped up seventeen square miles, about a third of
the land sold at the auction.

Interestingly, one half-section that eluded them was bought by
A.J. Havey, the orchestra conductor at the Palace Hotel in Brandon,
Manitoba. Stephen Chapman Simms, assistant curator of ethnology
and later director of the Field Museum in Chicago, also acquired a
half-section. He had done field work in western Canada.[33]

Indian Affairs held five auctions for former reserve land in June 1909.
They were a mixed success. At Edmonton, all of the Enoch land that

had been surrendered the year before — except for the cemetery grounds — was sold at a large gathering in the Dominion Theatre. Inspector John Markle continued his habit of playing loose with department policies and regulations. When he found that several buyers refused to meet the upset price per acre for several parcels, "I lowered the upset price and closed out all of the land."[34] That these reduced land prices might have gone against the surrender conditions, and what had been promised the Enoch band, seemed less important to Markle than selling 5,073 acres. There was no such need to tinker with the upset prices at the Swan Lake auction (2,880 acres) at Portage la Prairie, Manitoba. Local settlers claimed most of the lots, bidding on average $17.70 per acre for land that had been coveted for two decades.[35]

Some of the June auctions attracted little interest. The Swan Lake band had also surrendered a parcel of 2,400 acres at Tramping Lake, southwest of Battleford, Saskatchewan. The band had never occupied this auxiliary reserve. But when the land was marketed, no lots were sold. It took another auction, almost a year later in Scott, Saskatchewan, to dispose of the quarter-section parcels at good prices. Speculators did much of the buying, in particular the Luse Land Company of St. Paul.[36]

Indian Affairs also tried to sell the unsold portion of the Grizzly Bear's Head/Lean Man reserve that had been surrendered in 1905. This third attempt failed to attract a single bid, largely because the best land went at the first sale, and it too would require another auction a year later to finally sell the remaining land.[37]

The other June 1909 auction, this time for Fishing Lake lands, was also a failure. Less than 10 percent of the land sold (eight of eighty-seven parcels). Graham blamed the high upset prices for the limited interest. A second auction, held at Wadena, Saskatchewan, on June 8, 1910, attracted only about twenty people, but one of them had a keen interest in the Fishing Lake lands and a sizeable bankroll. All but one quarter-section — over 12,000 acres — was purchased by Dunbar H. Hudson, proprietor of the Hudson Lumber Company of Winnipeg. The land was then flipped to two Chicago businessmen, George Hathaway and Myron McKinnon, who in turn formed the

Fishing Lake Farm and Land Company. The operation floundered. Facing overdue instalment payments, the company sold the land to the local Doukhobor community.[38]

The sale of Muscowpetung land at Balgonie, Saskatchewan, on October 27, 1909, was one of the most anticipated auctions that fall. Earlier that spring, after completing the subdivision of the surrendered land (17,600 acres) into quarter-sections, surveyor J.K. McLean had informed Pedley, "This should sell well . . . the farmers did state they are anxious to have an opportunity to purchase."[39] A new regulation, though, worked against small-time buyers. According to the auction advertisement, once a parcel had been declared sold, "the purchaser shall immediately deposit the sum of one hundred dollars with the Clerk of the sale. Otherwise the parcel will at once be put up for sale."[40]

This requirement was apparently designed to keep buyers from backing out of a sale when it came time to place the 10 percent down payment at the close of the auction. If they failed to have sufficient funds for the down payment, in cash or cheque, the deposit was forfeited and the land held back. Local settlers consequently had to be cautious, if not certain, about what they were buying before the auctioneer shouted "sold" and pointed in their direction.

Graham, assigned to oversee the auction, declared the sale "most successful." All of the land was sold — except for 352 acres — at an average price of $9.32 per acre.[41] The inspector must have been relieved after the dismal Fishing Lake auction a few months earlier. He seemed to have forgotten, though, that neighbouring Pasqua land was sold for $13.41 per acre three years earlier — and he had supervised that auction too. He had also claimed that the surrendered portion of the Muscowpetung reserve was "by far the best half."[42] Someone was getting a great deal.

About one-fifth of the land went to farmers. Government officials also placed successful bids. Simon James McLean, a political econo-mist and appointee to the federal Board of Railway Commissioners, happened to have official work in the area and bought a section of land. Saskatchewan district court judge Reginald Rimmer, a former law clerk for Indian Affairs in Ottawa, made the trip from Regina and purchased a quarter-section. These acquisitions were dwarfed by the eleven square miles (44 lots) secured by the Western Canada Colonization Company. It was the same St. Paul firm that had scored big at the Crooked Lakes sale in November 1908. The WCCC sold its Muscowpetung land to the Wallis Company of Dubuque, Iowa, which planned to rent the land.[43]

The Battleford town council and board of trade wanted to avoid a similar outcome when the Moosomin and Thunderchild lands were sold a week later on November 3, 1909. Two weeks before the sale, W.W. Smith, secretary to the board of trade, asked Pedley to postpone the auction, preferably until the following spring. Smith maintained that if the sale were "fixed for a more opportune time . . . a very large part of these lands will be purchased by farmers and so brought under cultivation at an early date." He also warned Pedley that "the greater part . . . will go to speculators" if the auction were held as scheduled, "and you know, the easy terms offered make possible the withholding of this land from settlement for an indefinite time."[44]

Secretary McLean pooh-poohed any delay, arguing that farmers would be flush with cash after the fall harvest and that it was "in the best interests of the Indians" to proceed.[45] Battleford Indian agent George Day, who had been involved in the Thunderchild and Moosomin surrenders, took charge of the sale. A Liberal patronage appointee, Day would later lose his job for partisan activities in the 1911 general election. Thomas Lecky served as auctioneer. He worked for the Battleford real estate firm of Champagne, Speers, and Simpson that had bought land at other Indian Affairs sales. It too had deep Liberal connections.[46]

The auction confirmed W.W. Smith's fears. In the hours before the start of the auction, a clandestine meeting was convened at Battleford's Windsor Hotel. A record of the gathering was found in Grant's law firm papers. The attendees included Grant associate W.J. Atkins of

Dunville, Ontario, who bought land individually or sometimes partnered with W.E. Preston from Midland; Winnipeg real estate agent W.A. Kenning, who fronted a family of speculators; Sidney Seymour Simpson of Battleford's Champagne, Speers, and Simpson and the Liberal MLA for Battleford in Saskatchewan's legislative assembly; and Wilbur Van Horn Bennett, the Canadian Immigration agent in Omaha, Nebraska, who had found American buyers for other surrendered lands. Another participant, apparently new to speculating in former reserve land, was Crown Prosecutor James Thomas Brown from Moosomin, Saskatchewan. Brown was appointed to the Supreme Court of Saskatchewan in 1910 and then named chief justice to the Court of King's Bench in 1918. He would remain on the Saskatchewan bench until his 1956 death at the age of eighty-six.

With Grant serving as secretary, the men around the table divvied up the lots, agreeing among themselves who would buy particular parcels to

Some Saskatchewan Liberal officials and politicians who bought surrendered land were members of Regina's exclusive Assiniboia Club. Among them was Saskatchewan Crown prosecutor J.T. Brown who would later serve as chief justice to the Court of King's Bench. (Provincial Archives of Saskatchewan)

avoid bidding against one another. They also knew in advance, thanks to leaked information from Indian Affairs, the estimated value of the land. Grant apparently provided these upset prices, based on the incriminating evidence found in his office files.[47] Fifty-eight of the eighty-two parcels (29,000 acres) sold over the two-day auction went to four men at the meeting: Atkins, Brown, Grant (with Preston), and Kenning. Newly appointed Liberal senator and former Battleford mayor Benjamin Price purchased a half-section. Perhaps one of the most surprising participants in the sale was John Henderson Lamont, puisne judge of the Supreme Court of Saskatchewan. He might even have travelled from Regina to Battleford with Brown. The future Supreme Court of Canada justice (1927) acquired over four sections. There were also American buyers from Maine and Michigan, who may have been linked to Grant.

The last auction sale in 1909 was held at Ponoka, Alberta, on November 10 for the Bobtail and Samson lands (over 19,000 acres). Inspector Markle supervised the sale. Indian Affairs, at Minister Oliver's urging, had doggedly pursued surrenders from the Hobbema bands on the grounds that they had too much land and that the reserves were too close to the Calgary-Edmonton railway. At the auction, though, only one-third of the lots sold, many to local buyers, at an average $13.53 per acre. The Ontario speculator tandem of Grant and Preston successfully bid on nineteen quarter-sections.

At a second sale the following June, even less land was sold, leaving close to another 9,000 acres to be marketed. Markle tried to explain away the poor results, saying there was "too much land to sell at once and buyers weren't interested in scruffy sections."[48] But the lack of interest served to underscore how Indian Affairs under Oliver was blindly committed to securing surrenders, even if the land in question wasn't needed or even wanted by local white settlers at the time.

Speculators continued to be accommodated by the Laurier government. On November 11, 1909, Pedley made another change to Indian Affairs land sales policy that was designed to help Liberal friends. Acting on a suggestion from an unnamed person, he decided that the department would henceforth "furnish when requested the upset price of lands . . . I do not see any objection to this."[49] If buyers knew the upset prices, though, they would be more circumspect about how high they would be willing to go at auctions. Or they could collude beforehand to fix the bidding, as had been done for the Moosomin/Thunderchild sale. This formerly confidential information would now be readily available, if and when asked for. It would eventually be included in little sales booklets prepared in advance of auctions.

At the combined The Key and Keeseekoose auction at Kamsack, Saskatchewan, on December 1, 1910, Graham arranged to have the upset prices sent beforehand to a number of individuals and companies. Up for sale were 19,500 acres, and the availability of upset prices, ranging from $3 to $8 per acre, seemed to expedite bidding at the auction. Seventy percent of the land (103 of 143 parcels) was sold to the usual mix of local and outside buyers, including William Frank, a Winnipeg real estate broker with Liberal credentials.[50] Within a few years, though, Chief Andrew Quewezance complained to the department about how little the Keeseekoose people had received from the sale of their reserve lands and how they had been misled by the inspector into making the surrender. "Mr. Graham did . . . make a bargain with us," Quewezance declared. "I don't know how the Indians [will] get along."[51]

The Keeseekoose band wasn't alone in believing that their surrender agreements, especially the promised cash payments for their lands, hadn't been honoured by Indian Affairs. The prices realized at the sales were sometimes lower than what had been anticipated. Nor did the land always get sold at the first auction. The most vexing problem, though, was delinquent payments. As of December 1906, buyers only had to provide 10 percent of the total cost of their land purchase on the condition that they would thereafter meet nine instalment deadlines. These payments were often in arrears and dragged out over years, if not decades. In the case of the Cowessess/Kahkewistahaw sale, some final payments weren't made until the late 1920s. Some buyers had their purchases cancelled when they defaulted on their payments. That happened to Saskatchewan judge J.T. Brown and his Moosomin/Thunderchild lands.

The other complication was buyers assigning their purchases to someone else, sometimes within days of the auction, and that only further delayed payments in several instances. The Enoch auction was probably one of the worst examples of a sale gone awry. On June 24, 1909, Markle sent a triumphant telegram to Ottawa, happily reporting how he had "sold all Enoch Land [for] over ninety-three thousand dollars."[52] The accompanying land file is overflowing with an avalanche of documentation — over 2,400 pages of missed deadline notices, ownership transfers, insufficient payments, department warnings, and special pleading. It took Indian Affairs until the 1940s to secure full payment for some of the lots purchased that day.[53]

Indian Affairs treated two delinquent land speculators quite differently after the December 1906 Michel auction — even though both were Liberals. Christopher Fahrni and Frederick W. Grant had put down $6,000 and $5,000, respectively, as down payments at the time of the sale. The same amount, as instalments, was due annually from both men. By the start of 1910, though, no money had been submitted. The pair had missed three consecutive instalment payments.[54]

Indian Affairs dutifully contacted Grant after every missed instalment deadline. The lawyer responded that he would pay soon, then said he had been ill, and then didn't respond. Fahrni ignored the first reminder notice in December 1907, only to be issued a second letter a few months later threatening cancellation. The Manitoba farmer replied that he had been told "that the government would not push payments if they were well secured" and asked for more time.[55] That was granted, probably because of the intervention of Fahrni's friend John Crawford, the Liberal MP for Portage la Prairie. The matter, though, had been brought to the attention of Minister Oliver and his deputy Pedley and not simply handled by a senior clerk.[56]

Four years after the Michel sale, Indian Affairs tried to pry money out of Grant by sending two stiff warnings, one in December 1910 and the other in January 1911, that his purchases would be cancelled. When Grant continued to stall, the department sent him an ultimatum by telegram: he had to make a payment by March 13 or he would lose his land. The day of the deadline, Liberal MP Manley Chew informed secretary McLean that Grant was travelling to Ottawa to get things resolved. The substance of the meeting isn't known, but Grant didn't make a payment.[57]

Fahrni, on the other hand, was forced to scramble to find the necessary funds to pay off his debt. Fearing cancellation of his purchase, Fahrni suggested that his down payment be applied to two quarter-sections and that patents be issued for them. The department said no. Then, in January 1910, Indian Affairs learned that Fahrni was desperately negotiating with a Winnipeg investment company to finance his purchases — if only to pay the interest due. Pedley initiated a cancellation order: unless Fahrni paid $5,000 within thirty days, he would forfeit his Michel land and his down payment.

When Fahrni ignored the notice, Pedley countered with a much-shortened instalment schedule that would have required payment in full for all the land by the end of the year. The day after the first new instalment deadline was missed, Fahrni frantically notified Pedley that he was close to finding a buyer for the land. When no payment was received by the end of April, McLean told Fahrni that a cancellation order was being prepared. Pedley signed the document on May 10 and the sale was entered as withdrawn in a department register on June 1.[58] That was six months before Grant received his first cancellation warning.

Fahrni was soon thrown a lifeline. On June 3, 1910, John J. Anderson, manager of Edmonton's Union Bank of Canada, asked Indian Affairs for the addresses of Fahrni and Grant. He then approached Fahrni with an unsolicited offer to buy all his Michel land. It was too good to be true, after all of Fahrni's failed attempts to unload the land and minimize his loss. As the Fahrni family recalled that moment, "We were under very great pressure . . . from the Government . . . naturally we were ready to clutch at anything . . . we were prepared to sell at a sacrifice if necessary, provided we could give title."[59]

That was the sticking point. On June 2, McLean had formally advised Fahrni that the Michel sale had been cancelled. Then, five days later, McLean issued another letter to the effect that the sale had amazingly been reinstated. That could only have been done with Pedley's say-so, and probably not before informing the minister. It was also unprecedented. There was no provision in the regulations — not even a mention — for reinstating a cancelled sale. With this reprieve, something he never requested, a relieved Fahrni at last found a way out of his troubles. He sold his Michel land to Anderson for roughly $4,900. That was about $1,000 less than Fahrni's December 1906 down payment. It was better than losing his down payment and title to the land if the cancellation hadn't been lifted, but still, it was a huge loss. The Edmonton banker had coolly acquired Fahrni's 3,080 acres for about $0.63 per acre. The average price of western land in 1911 was $13.59 per acre.[60]

Anderson didn't try to pull the same stunt with Grant and his Michel land, probably because of the Midland lawyer's cozy relationship with the Laurier government, including Indian Affairs officials. But his days of evading a second payment wouldn't last forever, and in November 1911, Ottawa lobbyist Robert Abercrombie Pringle visited the Indian Affairs offices on Grant's behalf to discuss a possible extension of his obligations — approximately $20,000. Acting deputy minister Duncan Campbell Scott took a principled position, observing that "the lands are held in trust for the Indians, and in order to carry out obligations incurred . . . the Department is obliged to ask for a payment of at least a portion of the arrears."[61] What Scott wanted was $5,000 immediately and another $5,000 in three months. Indian Affairs received $5,000 a few days later — not from Grant, but his old Midland business associate James Playfair. In early December, Pringle sent Indian Affairs a formal transfer agreement between Grant and Playfair for the Michel lands.

Playfair was just as derelict as Grant in paying for the Michel land. Despite Scott's terms, the Midland entrepreneur didn't make another payment until March 1914, and that was only $1,000. Pringle told Indian Affairs to expect something "substantial" soon from Playfair, but the department had to wait until January 1918 to get another payment of $5,000. Thereafter, Pringle and Indian Affairs engaged in a saw-off through the 1920s.[62] Payments were received for certain parcels, while the sales of other lots were cancelled.

Grant, for his part, became front-page news in January 1913 for another one of his shady money-making schemes. In applying for a federal dredging contract, Grant had apparently forged signatures and submitted tender bids from more than one company.[63] He led a charmed business life, though, and brushed off the controversy. Two decades later, he headed up a plant on behalf of the department of munitions and supply, manufacturing alloy steel for gun barrels and other armaments during the Second World War.

Anderson, by contrast, paid off the Michel land he had bought from Fahrni by the end of 1911. Patents for approximately 3,600 acres were issued to Anderson in the early new year. The banker then bided his time until November 2, 1914, when he quietly transferred title to Oliver, then a Liberal backbencher in the House of Commons and Anderson's father-in-law. He was married to Dora, one of Oliver's five daughters. Anderson had paid roughly $28,500 for the land — $4,900 to Fahrni and $23,600 to Indian Affairs. In making the formal transfer to Oliver, though, he estimated its value to be $71,460. Anderson's 1910 investment had increased a whopping 250 percent.[64]

The former Indian Affairs minister's real estate windfall didn't remain secret for long. Former Edmonton mayor William J. McNamara, a declared enemy of the former Laurier government and especially Oliver, learned about the scheme during a visit to Ottawa and told the Fahrni family. A distressed Stanley Fahrni wrote Oliver on behalf of his ill father in early March 1915, just months before the elder Fahrni's death. A copy of the letter found its way into the hands of William James Roche, the Conservative minister of Interior and Indian Affairs, who read it aloud on the floor of the Commons. The younger Fahrni described in detail how Oliver had orchestrated "a very infamous conspiracy . . . through fraud and misrepresentation with the connivance of the Department." Anderson was the "blind," Fahrni fumed, his father the "victim." The letter ended with the threat of legal action unless there was "some restitution of this damage."[65]

Nothing was done about the swindle. Oliver was never called to account, not even censured by the House. He continued to represent Edmonton until his defeat in the December 1917 general election. Oliver had no shame. It had always been known that the newspaper publisher and editor was vehemently opposed to the presence of First Nations in the Edmonton area. He had consistently maintained that these reserves and their occupants stood in the way of settling and developing the West and bringing about a greater future. Like other Indian Affairs officials, though, Oliver couldn't resist helping himself to the Michel land for personal gain. He was no different from other speculators and certainly just as resourceful as men like Grant, but more cunning given how he had "buncoed [Fahrni] out of his lands."[66]

Perhaps that's why, in September 1915, the deputy minister of Alberta's department of municipal affairs asked Ottawa for a complete list of surrendered land sales in the province.[67] Like his counterpart in Saskatchewan a few years earlier, he apparently wanted to know who had bought former reserve land and how much. He may also have wondered how many Andersons were out there playing at the same game.

Notes

1. *Library and Archives Canada (LAC)*, RG10, v. 4007, f. 241,354, J.N. Bayne to J.D. McLean, November 20, 1909; Bayne to McLean, January 19, 1910; McLean to Bayne, February 17, 1910.
2. The legal careers of Lamont and Brown are examined in D. Mittelstadt, *The Court of Appeal for Saskatchewan: The First Hundred Years* (Regina: University of Regina Press, 2018).
3. *LAC*, RG2, P.C. 1787, September 15, 1888. One-fifth of the purchase price was due at the time of sale and the balance was to be paid in four equal annual instalments at 6 percent interest. "Actual occupation and improvement of the land" was also a condition of any

sale. The buyer had to settle the land within six months of purchase and break a prescribed amount of land and build a dwelling within a three-year period.

4. Tyler and Wright Research Consultants Ltd., "The Alienation of Indian Reserve Lands during the Administration of Sir Wilfrid Laurier, 1896–1911: Michel Reserve #132," unpublished report, 1978, p. 180; P. Martin-McGuire, *First Nations Land Surrenders on the Prairies, 1896–1911* (Ottawa: Indian Claims Commission, 1998), pp. 458–9, 481; *LAC*, RG10, v. 4007, f. 241,354, W.A. Orr to J. Perrie, September 29, 1905, "Statement re Lands sold from the surrendered Alexander Reserve (134), 3rd October 1906."

5. Regina *Leader-Post*, October 18, 1906.

6. Martin-McGuire, *First Nations Land Surrenders*, p. 129.

7. Miller was apparently working for the Grand Trunk Pacific, buying up land along the proposed route before the steel was laid. *Montreal Gazette*, October 18, 1906.

8. *LAC*, RG10, v. 4007, f. 241,354, J.D. McLean to J.N. Bayne, February 17, 1910, "Statement showing the lands sold in Pasqua Indian reserve on the 17th of October 1906."

9. Martin-McGuire, *First Nations Land Surrenders*, pp. 492–3.

10. J.R. Miller, *Shingwauk's Vision: A History of Native Residential Schools* (Toronto: University of Toronto Press, 1996), p. 188.

11. Tyler and Wright, "Michel Reserve #132," pp. 170–3.

12. *LAC*, RG10, v. 56, Shannon File 14(a), J. Gibbons to R. Smith, November 14, 1906.

13. Indian Affairs insisted on a careful record of the auction sales. The presiding official would be sent a plan and description of the land, as well as a small book which listed the legal description for each quarter-section lot and the upset price. The name, occupation, and address for every parcel sold were to be entered, followed by the purchase price and amount paid. Receipts were also to be issued. These materials, along with a report about the sale, were to be returned to Ottawa. See, for example, *LAC*, RG10, v. 4035, f. 304,072, S. Stewart to W.M. Graham, October 12, 1909; RG10, v. 4037, f. 316,676-1, F. Pedley to J.A. Markle, June 1, 1909.

14. *Edmonton Bulletin*, December 6, 1906.

15. "Biography of Christian Fahrni," Memorable Manitobans, Manitoba Historical Society. http://www.mhs.mb.ca/docs/pageant/20/fahrni_c1.shtml.

16. *Edmonton Bulletin*, December 8, 1906.

17. "John Crawford," Memorable Manitobans, Manitoba Historical Society. http://www.mhs.mb.ca/docs/people/crawford_j.shtml.

18. Tyler and Wright, "Michel Reserve #132," p. 183.

19. House of Commons, *Debates*, May 25, 1905, pp. 6481–9.

20. Before any auction, a surveyor would carefully assess the quality of the land and arrive at an expected price per acre (upset price) for every quarter-section parcel. If this minimum price was not met or exceeded during the sale, then the lot was not sold.

21. Martin-McGuire, *First Nations Land Surrenders*, pp. 362, 406, 464, 481, 493; *LAC*, RG10, v. 4007, f. 241,354, M. Chew to J.D. McLean, April 12, 1911.

22. *LAC*, RG10, v. 6667, f. 110A-4-1, v. 2, F.W. Grant to J.D. McLean, December 5, 1906.

23. *LAC*, Wilfrid Laurier papers, pp. 159222–3, George D. Grant to W. Laurier, August 26, 1909.

24. Martin-McGuire, *First Nations Land Surrenders*, p. 352.

25. Ibid., pp. 360–1.

26. *LAC*, RG10, v. 3994, f. 195126/2, W.M. Graham to J.D. McLean, November 17, 1906.

27. See *LAC*, RG10, v. 4007, f. 241,354.

28. Martin-McGuire, *First Nations Land Surrenders*, pp. 64, 368–9.

29. Indian Claims Commission, "Inquiry into the 1907 Reserve Land Surrender Claim of the Kahkewistahaw First Nation," unpublished report, 1997, pp. 47–8.

30. *LAC*, RG10, v. 3732, f. 26623-1, M. Miller to J.D. McLean, December 17, 1909.

31. *LAC*, RG10, v. 4007, f. 241,354, J.D. McLean to J.N. Bayne, February 17, 1910, "Statement showing the lands sold in Crooked Lakes reserve on the 25th of November 1908."

32. *LAC*, RG10, v. 3086, f. 279,222-1, F. Pedley, "Notice," January 24, 1910.

33. *LAC*, RG10, v. 4007, f. 241,354, J.D. McLean to J.N. Bayne, February 17, 1910, "Statement showing the lands sold in Crooked Lakes reserve on the 25th of November 1908."

34. *LAC*, RG10, v. 4037, f. 316,676-1, J.A. Markle to J.D. McLean, June 28, 1909.

35. Martin-McGuire, *First Nations Land Surrenders*, pp. 151, 388, 459.

36. Ibid., pp. 64, 151, 390–1.

37. Ibid., p. 355.

38. Ibid., pp. 151, 376–7.

39. *LAC*, RG10, v. 4035, f. 304,072, J.K. McLean to F. Pedley, June 2, 1909.

40. *LAC*, RG10, v. 6683, f. 114A-2-2, "Draft Advertisement, Muscowpetung Land Sale, 3 September 1909."

41. *LAC*, RG10, v. 4035, f. 304,072, W.M. Graham to J.D. McLean, October 28, 1909.

42. Ibid., W.M. Graham to F. Pedley, November 22, 1908.

43. *LAC*, RG10, v. 4007, f. 241,354, J.D. McLean to J.N. Bayne, February 17, 1910, "Statement showing the lands sold in Muscowpetung Indian reserve on the 27th of October 1909"; Martin-McGuire, *First Nations Land Surrenders*, pp. 63, 104, 151, 393–6, 459, 465.

44. *LAC*, RG10, v. 4041, f. 335,933, W.W. Smith to F. Pedley, October 20, 1909.

45. Ibid., J.D. McLean to W.W. Smith, October 28, 1909.

46. Martin-McGuire, *First Nations Land Surrenders*, pp. 477, 485.

47. D. McMahon, "The Surrender and Sale of Moosomin Indian Reserve No. 112," unpublished report for Federation of Saskatchewan Indian Nations, 1985, pp. 49–51; Martin-McGuire, *First Nations Land Surrenders*, pp. 405–6.

48. Martin-McGuire, *First Nations Land Surrenders*, pp. 401–2.

49. *LAC*, RG10, v. 4007, f. 241,354, F. Pedley to W.A. Orr, November 11, 1909.

50. Martin-McGuire, *First Nations Land Surrenders*, pp. 397–9.

51. Quoted in ibid., p. 399.

52. *LAC*, RG10, v. 4037, f. 316,676-1, J.A. Markle to Dept. Indian Affairs, June 24, 1909.

53. Martin-McGuire, *First Nations Land Surrenders*, pp. 374, 406; *LAC*, RG10, v. 6668, f. 110A-6-1A, "Stony Plains Land Sale General."

54. Tyler and Wright, "Michel Reserve #132," pp. 176–7, 182.

55. *LAC*, RG10, v. 6671, f. 110B-4-14, C. Fahrni to J.D. McLean, May 17, 1908.

56. Tyler and Wright, "Michel Reserve #132," pp. 182–3.

57. Ibid., pp. 183–4.

58. Ibid., pp. 191–3.

59. Quoted in *Debates*, April 14, 1915, p. 2566 (S.H. Fahrni to F. Oliver, March 9, 1915).

60. Tyler and Wright, "Michel Reserve #132," pp. 194–9; *Debates*, April 14, 1915, p. 2550.

61. *LAC*, RG10, v. 6671, f. 110B-4-8, D.C. Scott to R.A. Pringle, November 9, 1911.

62. Tyler and Wright, "Michel Reserve #132," pp. 187–9.

63. *Calgary Herald*, January 24, 1913.

64. Tyler and Wright, "Michel Reserve #132," pp. 195–6.

65. *Debates*, April 14, 1915, p. 2566 (S.H. Fahrni to F. Oliver, March 9, 1915).

66. *Debates*, April 14, 1915, p. 2566.

67. *LAC*, RG10, v. 4007, f. 241,354, J. Perrie to J.D. McLean, September 24, 1915.

-◄- *Ten* -►-

A GREAT DEAL OF MISCHIEF

They are "the most intractable Indians on the North American continent." That's how Indian Affairs minister Frank Oliver justified his department's failure to secure a surrender from the Niitsitapi (collectively known as Blackfoot) of southern Alberta. "I do not want to say the task is impossible," Oliver told the House of Commons in February 1909, "but . . . it is one of very extraordinary difficulty."[1]

This surprising admission came on the heels of a string of successful reserve surrenders since Oliver had assumed the Indian Affairs portfolio in the spring of 1905. Indeed, several Cree, Nakoda, and Saulteaux bands in the three prairie provinces had reluctantly agreed, sometimes under duress, to forfeit reserve lands to the Crown. The Niitsitapi tribes (Piikani or Peigan, Kainai or Blood, and Siksika or Blackfoot) had evaded that fate largely because of their uneasy, at times testy, relationship with Canada.

Nothing was "impossible," though, once the department decided to take reserve land. Just six months after Oliver's public hand-wringing about "intractable" Indians, the Piikani surrendered part of their reserve. The Siksika followed in June 1910. And even though the Kainai refused to co-operate, Oliver plowed ahead and amended the Indian Act so that Canada had the right to acquire reserve land if it was in or near a town with a population of more than 8,000.

Oliver's single-mindedness of purpose as Indian Affairs minister would have been impressive, if not admirable, except that he was actively working against the interests of the very people he was supposed to serve.

≺≺∙∙≻≻

The Niitsitapi had warily agreed to Treaty Seven in September 1877. A proud, fiercely independent people, they were masters of present-day southern Alberta for much of the nineteenth century. Anyone who dared enter their territory could expect a swift armed-and-mounted response. But by the early 1870s, after Canada had assumed control of the western interior, the once powerful Niitsitapi were a shell of their former selves. Weakened by disease, hunger, and warfare, they had succumbed to the worst excesses of the whisky trade. American traders from Fort Benton, Montana, had set up business in Niitsitapi country dealing in alcohol, more commonly known as "firewater" because it was often laced with tobacco, pepper, molasses, and ink to produce powerful and debilitating concoctions. In 1874, the North-West Mounted Police marched into the region, closing the whisky posts and chasing the traders back across the border.[2] Thereafter, the Queen's soldiers, as they were called, enjoyed a special relationship with the Niitsitapi.

Canada attempted to take advantage of this goodwill between the Blackfoot and the police by concluding the last of the numbered prairie treaties in September 1877. David Laird, the new lieutenant governor and Indian commissioner for the North-West Territories, was dispatched to bring the Niitsitapi and their territory into treaty. He was under strict instructions to limit government commitments and curtail the distribution of gifts. There was one concession, though. The planned treaty meeting at Fort Macleod was moved to Blackfoot Crossing at the request of Chief Crowfoot (Isapo-Muxika).

During the deliberations, commissioner Laird told the Niitsitapi that the Queen would protect them — "hold them in the palm of her hand" — in the same way that the mounted police had vanquished

Chief Crowfoot (centre) insisted that the Treaty Seven meeting be held at Blackfoot Crossing in 1877. (McCord Museum)

the whisky trade.[3] This offer of security, reinforced by the heavy police presence at Blackfoot Crossing, appealed to Niitsitapi leaders. They looked upon Treaty Seven as first and foremost a peace agreement.

The Niitsitapi didn't take up reserves until the start of the 1880s. They stubbornly hunted the last remnants of the northern bison herds, often spending long stretches of time across the border in Montana, before accepting the painful reality that they had to settle on traditional lands and adopt a new way of life. The Kainai reserve, running southwest from Lethbridge and bounded by the Belly, Oldman, and St. Mary rivers, was almost 550 square miles. It was the largest in Canada. The Siksika reserve (470 square miles) was located east of Calgary along the Bow River and immediately south of the new Canadian Pacific Railway main line. The comparatively small Piikani reserve (180 square miles) was higher in the foothills, west of the Blood reserve, with Fort Macleod to the northeast and Pincher Creek to the southwest, and the Oldman River running through it.

All three reserves, rich in grass and water, were ideal for stock raising. But the Department of Indian Affairs doggedly pursued a one-size-fits-all policy and insisted that the Niitsitapi break ground for raising crops and growing gardens. Not only were the Niitsitapi ill-equipped to bring the land under cultivation, but their fledgling attempts at farming ended in failure and demoralization. They never achieved any semblance of self-sufficiency and were heavily dependent on government rations well into the early twentieth century.[4] Even then, disease, malnutrition, and poverty took a grim toll. In the sixteen-year period from 1886 to 1902, the Kainai and Piikani lost more than 40 percent of their population. The Siksika decline was even more precipitous — from 2,147 to 942 people.[5]

Life under treaty became especially bleak when Manitoba Indian agent John A. Markle was transferred to the Siksika reserve in July 1900. Determined to reduce the huge volume of food supplied to the Siksika every budget year, Markle introduced a "work or starve" policy for the able-bodied in 1901. The removal of names from the "free rations list" led to significant government savings, which in turn probably facilitated Markle's promotion to inspector of Indian agencies in 1904. But the Siksika deeply resented the Indian Affairs cutbacks, insisting that rations had always been a treaty right and that government parsimony was a betrayal of the 1877 agreement.[6]

This sense of grievance and alienation was exacerbated by CPR operations in the region. Because the main line skirted the northern boundary of the Siksika reserve, trains frequently killed livestock, while hot cinders from steam locomotives sparked grass fires. The railway also ran pipelines across reserve land to collect water from the Bow River. The Siksika sought compensation — and fencing along the railway right-of-way.

The same set of problems arose with the building of a new, government-backed CPR branch line from Lethbridge to Kootenay Landing, British Columbia, in 1897–98. The Crowsnest Pass Railway bisected the Piikani reserve, thereby obstructing access to the Oldman River. Again, Niitsitapi complaints were little more than acknowledged, rarely acted upon.

The same story was repeated in 1902 when the St. Mary River Railway was routed across the southeast corner of the Kainai reserve on its way to Cardston. As Indian Affairs secretary J.D. McLean informed Laird, government policy dictated that railway companies "are not to be interfered with."[7]

Ranchers posed another threat. Under federal grazing policy, effective December 1881, prospective ranchers could lease up to 100,000 acres for a twenty-one-year period for the ridiculously low sum of one cent per acre per year, provided they had one head of cattle on every ten acres within three years. These closed leases — homesteading wasn't permitted on the land — encouraged the flow of British and eastern Canadian capital to the Alberta range country south of Calgary, and in only a few short years, ten large companies controlled two-thirds of all stocked land.

Because these cattle operations effectively surrounded the three Niitsitapi reserves, it was only a matter of time before some began to encroach on Niitsitapi land, all the more because there were no fences. It appeared to be open range. The Cochrane Ranche, for example, regarded the bordering Kainai reserve "as a natural extension of their own grazing lease."[8] Smaller ranchers, scrambling to survive in the corporate landscape, brazenly grazed their animals on reserve pasture. By 1893, Indian agent R.N. Wilson was reporting that parts of the Kainai reserve were overrun with outsider cattle.[9]

In the past, the Niitsitapi would never have allowed these incursions into their home territory. Now, their repeated attempts to drive settler cattle from reserve lands only aggravated their uneasy and sometimes fractious relationship with the ranching community. Nor did it end the trespassing. Ranchers generally believed that the Niitsitapi had been given too much land under treaty and what they had wasn't being utilized.[10]

These challenges to reserve boundaries made the Niitsitapi only more determined to protect their treaty lands, especially after they began to build their own herds. In the mid-1890s, the Niitsitapi began trading horses for heifers under a government program to cull the horse populations on each reserve. These cattle didn't end the pressing Niitsitapi reliance on government rations, but they marked a significant shift in reserve economies to raising stock.

The obvious solution to keeping rancher cattle from illegally grazing on Niitsitapi lands was to fence the reserves. But Indian Affairs dithered on the matter. J.B. Lash, a former Indian agent serving as secretary to the Indian commissioner, attributed the department's reluctance to the power and influence of the ranching community. "If these reserves were fenced," an exasperated Lash wrote in a letter to Ottawa, "the Indians would derive a large income from grazing privileges which at present time they are unable to collect." But until that time "there will be very little change" as stockmen regard the reserves as "public property."[11]

The alternative was to charge a fee for grazing privileges — something that was initiated on the Kainai reserve in 1895. Under these annual permits, ranchers were charged fifty cents per head. The arrangement was a mixed success. The Cochrane Ranche grazed up to 3,000 head for seven years without complaint. Some smaller ranchers, though, balked at paying their dues, while a few didn't bother securing a permit, insisting that the unfenced Niitsitapi land was free range.[12]

The new century brought with it new grazing agreements. In late 1902, the Piikani agreed to a long-term reserve grazing lease with the Maunsell Brothers, a ranching company based in Fort Macleod. The Irish-born Edward Maunsell, called "Freckled Face" by the Piikani, was an original mounted policeman who had taken up ranching upon discharge from the force. He was also an unsuccessful Liberal candidate.[13] A few months later, in May 1903, the Kainai concluded an exclusive grazing contract with the McEwen Company of Brandon, Manitoba. No such arrangement was struck by the Siksika.

The Piikani leased some of their reserve to grazing outfits. (Glenbow Archives)

The Kainai apparently took the initiative with the McEwen lease. All existing grazing permits with local ranchers were cancelled in favour of a ten-year deal for 220,000 reserve acres for $5,000 per year, on the understanding that McEwen would place a minimum of 7,000 head on the land. The deal was justified on the grounds that it would be "easier" and "more profitable" for the Kainai to "lease excess reserve grazing capacity to one or two companies."[14] In exchange for monopoly access to the Kainai reserve, the company was to confine its cattle to certain areas of the reserve — so as not to mix with Kainai herds — and build fireguards, construct water dams, and keep intruders at bay. McEwen was also never to sublet to another party without department approval. Indian Affairs, meanwhile, could use the lease revenue to purchase more stock and move the Kainai closer to the goal of self-sufficiency.

It wasn't long before the McEwen grazing contract came under scrutiny because of who was involved. Donald McEwen may have been a wealthy Brandon farmer with extensive business interests across the

West, but his grazing lease with the Kainai raised suspicions. The fact that McEwen, the master of the stately country mansion Tullichewen, was a Sifton acquaintance was too much of a coincidence.

Manitoba Conservative MP William J. Roche questioned the propriety of the exclusive arrangement in the House of Commons in July 1903. Roche claimed that the Kainai would have done better if the lease had been advertised and gone to tender. Sifton coolly countered that the Kainai didn't lose in the deal, especially because they had been able to negotiate the terms.[15] The minister was on his feet about the matter again in May 1904 — this time, to provide the names of all the applicants for the Kainai lease. Sifton also briefly reviewed the terms of the McEwen lease, noting that Indian Affairs had ratified the agreement on June 6, 1903, and that the grazing privileges couldn't be transferred to another party without his authorization.[16]

Behind the scenes, it was another story — something stumbled upon by accident by assistant Indian commissioner James McKenna. In mid-November 1903, dominion lands commissioner John Gillanders Turriff advised Sifton that a group of Mormons from Cardston wanted to lease 3,000 acres of Kainai land along the southern boundary of the reserve. The request had the wholehearted backing of Frank Oliver, who insisted in having a finger in all such matters, especially when First Nations reserves were involved. "He [Oliver] says that the Indians are agreeable," Turriff noted, "and that the Agent in charge is favourable."[17]

It wasn't so straightforward. The land that the Mormons wanted to rent was part of the McEwen grazing grant. McKenna was dispatched from the Winnipeg office to see whether the Kainai would allow the Mormons to farm a portion of their reserve. If they agreed, Indian Affairs would seek a revision of McEwen's grazing privileges; at this point he still hadn't put any cattle on the land.

The news wasn't good. The Kainai were visibly "annoyed" by the request from the Mormons — they didn't want "white men . . . to secure

. . . the use of the land." When McKenna and Indian agent Wilson probed further, trying to understand why they were so upset, the Kainai angrily complained about the grazing lease and wanted it cancelled immediately. They felt duped by Thomas Page Wadsworth, the inspector of Indian agencies who had accompanied Donald McEwen to assist with the lease negotiations. Wadsworth had apparently tried to bribe the Kainai by promising bonus money, above and beyond the grazing fee, and a trip to Ottawa for some of the Kainai leaders. Maybe that's why one Kainai speaker intimated that the lease arrangement was "crooked." McKenna warned Sifton that the Kainai weren't prepared to consider "the use of any portion of their reserve. The Blood Indians are extremely sensitive on this point."[18]

Sifton decided to ask McEwen to surrender the lease and sent McKenna to take care of it. At a meeting in Brandon in early February 1904, McKenna told McEwen that the Kainai were now regretting the agreement, as was the minister for granting it. McEwen wanted to co-operate, but given his Liberal party support, "did not think he should be asked to make such a sacrifice." He'd already had to wait several weeks after the agreement was signed before he learned from Sifton that "the lease would stand." Then, and only then, did he start to buy stockers from the Cochrane Ranche, and he didn't see how the cattle could simply be returned. There was a bigger stumbling block, though: his secret partners.

McEwen had never planned to enter into a grazing agreement on the Kainai reserve. He said he'd been approached by Peter Ryan, registrar for the city of Toronto and another well-connected Liberal. Ryan knew both Sifton and Frank Pedley, the deputy minister of Indian Affairs who had taken up his position mere months before the Kainai grazing agreement. McEwen liked Ryan's pitch, and together they formed a syndicate with Winnipeg's Gordon, Ironside, and Fares, Canada's largest cattle-exporting business. Even though the agreement document was in McEwen's name only, he couldn't now step back, he told McKenna, because "he is one of many, and to do so would . . . be 'traitorous.'"[19]

Sifton took this response in stride, as if the involvement of other players were no surprise or any concern. Before deciding what to do about the Kainai lease, though, he asked McEwen to confirm what financial obligations had already been made.

The more immediate concern was Kainai opposition to the agreement. It wasn't just a handful of tribe members who wanted the grazing deal declared null and void. Indian agent Wilson reported in late March 1904 that a straw poll had been taken and the vote was "almost unanimous."[20] He asked McKenna, and by extension, Indian Affairs, for some clarity on the issue — McEwen's cattle were expected to arrive in two weeks.

Sifton likely huddled with his deputy Pedley, who had awarded the lease in the minister's absence. There's no record of what might have been said between the pair — or what Sifton knew or wanted to know — but they closed ranks.[21] The signed agreement was considered binding on the Kainai. The McEwen group did its part to backstop this decision by paying the $5,000 annual grazing fee. In July 1904, the *Macleod Advance* noted that the Kainai "visited the town en masse last week . . . as the [grazing fee] money is being spent in town we are satisfied."[22]

A Kainai family, probably near the St. Mary's River Railway that cut through the reserve. (Library and Archives Canada)

The McEwen Company had no sooner started to graze cattle on the Kainai reserve when it was realized that the St. Mary River Railway cut off roughly 3,000 acres from its lease area. That was the same southeast section of reserve land that the Cardston Mormons had unsuccessfully tried to rent from the Kainai. McEwen asked that his lease agreement be revised, and Indian Affairs offered the parcel to the Mormons — without consulting the Kainai. Pedley took the dubious position that the department had a free hand to do as it pleased because of the lease.[23] Reading between the lines, it seems Pedley was hiding something. Ottawa, though, eventually gave up its secrets at a time when political points were to be scored.

The first hint of trouble for the government came on March 30, 1906, when Oliver was yet again called upon in the House of Commons to defend the decision not to tender the Kainai grazing lease. The Conservative Opposition used this opening to suggest that "McEwen and Company were only stalking horses in whose name the deal was made" and that Liberal operative Peter Ryan was at the reins. Oliver feigned ignorance, claiming that his department had "no knowledge" of anyone else connected to the lease.[24]

The Conservatives wouldn't so easily be fobbed off. Two months later, on June 1, 1906, members of the House were debating the Liberal administration of Crown lands. William Bennett, the Conservative representative for Simcoe East, began his remarks by going after Oliver for enabling Liberal friends to buy islands in Georgian Bay at bargain prices. One of the properties on the block was Giants Tomb Island, now part of Awenda Provincial Park. Bennett told the House that Toronto "carpetbagger" Peter Ryan had his sights on the island — and that he had gotten his way in the past.

That's when the Conservative member pivoted to the Kainai grazing lease and how Ryan had orchestrated "a steal of such gigantic proportion . . . carried out in the light of day."[25] He then proceeded to read a number of Indian Affairs letters into the record — letters that are not part of the Kainai lease agreement file today — while stitching together the story of how Ryan scored the grazing concession.

Ryan wasn't the only Liberal competitor for the lease. In a letter dated December 11, 1902, J.F. McLaughlin, a real estate superintendent with Toronto's Title and Trust Company, thanked Pedley for recently meeting with him and then outlined the terms he was willing to offer for "the exclusive privilege of grazing cattle on the Blood reserve." It's not known why a Toronto professional, who'd probably never had cow shit on his dress shoes, wanted to get into ranching in southern Alberta — though he probably just wanted to cash in on the great western settlement bonanza. It's also unknown who tipped him off about the opportunity, given that Indian Affairs never advertised the lease.

The fact that McLaughlin met with Pedley before submitting his application suggests that they probably knew each other through their Toronto or Liberal circles. But when Pedley turned down the proposal, McLaughlin persisted and sent another letter before the end of the year that provided the names of several American Midwest investors who were prepared to fund the ranching operation. Department secretary McLean replied this time, indicating that the application would be given "careful consideration."[26]

By early March 1903, according to Bennett's incriminating file of letters, McLaughlin and Pedley seemed to have reached an understanding about the Kainai lease. McLaughlin told the deputy minister that Toronto lawyer Charles Millar would be representing his interests.[27] On April 2, 1903, Millar sent Pedley papers for the incorporation of the Alberta Cattle Company, in the expectation that a lease agreement was pending and that cattle could be placed on the reserve later that spring. Again it fell to McLean to report that the matter was still under consideration.

"At this stage," Bennett dramatically recounted to the House, "Mr. Peter Ryan appears on the scene and . . . hypnotized Mr. Pedley."[28] On April 23, 1903, the Ottawa legal firm of Latchford, McDougall, and Daly had submitted a formal lease proposal on behalf of Donald

McEwen. Bennett pointed to the correspondence as evidence that the fix was in. On the one hand, Francis Robert Latchford, a former attorney general of Ontario (1904–05) in the George Ross Liberal government, was a friend of Ryan and was secretly representing his interests in the Kainai reserve. On the other, McEwen was already in Fort Macleod when the proposal was submitted under his name and seeking authorization to negotiate a grazing agreement with the Kainai. The permission was quickly forthcoming from Pedley, and a deal was concluded.

That wasn't the end of the story, though. Bennett had more "bomb-shell" material. Sifton was in Europe when the lease was awarded, and on his return in late July 1903, apparently in response to a complaint from McLaughlin, he asked the Department of Justice whether Pedley had proper authority to award the lease.

A few weeks later, in mid-September, McLaughlin's Toronto solic-itors, Millar and Ferguson, asked for a copy of the Justice opinion as a prelude to possibly seeking damages for costs incurred. It fell again to McLean to make an official reply. The department secretary told the Toronto lawyers that Indian Affairs had no record of a lease application from the Alberta Cattle Company. Nor was the department obliged to turn over any Justice opinion. McLean disdainfully claimed that "the department has no knowledge or responsibility" in the matter.[29] Charles Millar's damning paper trail, turned over to the Conservatives, suggested otherwise. Pedley had kept his own department in the dark and only used McLean to insulate his behind-the-scenes chicanery.

At the conclusion of his remarks, and with the concurrence of the Leader of the Opposition, Bennett censured the Liberal government for granting Peter Ryan such a lucrative deal. Pedley's "suspicious con-duct" deserved to be formally investigated — much like the recent inquiry into the Liberal government contract with North Atlantic Trading Company.

Hugh Guthrie, the Liberal MP for Wellington South and a future minister of Justice, responded on behalf of the government. Guthrie offered a completely different reading of the letters, accus-ing the Conservative benches of engaging in a "covert smear" and "miserable insinuation." He also stoutly defended Pedley, who "assures me that he did not know nor did anybody in his department know . . . that Mr. Peter Ryan of Toronto had any interest . . . in the McEwen Ranching Company, nor do they know yet." In the end, there would be an investigation into what Guthrie admitted "would be a very high offence if the official were guilty of it."[30]

Little did he realize that Pedley had secretly accepted six shares in Ryan's enterprise as payment for his co-operation. Millar's future partner, Thomas Roberts Ferguson, wouldn't forget, though, how the Liberal government had sandbagged their law firm and the McLaughlin group. He also put Pedley near the top of his Liberal enemies list. Years later, Ferguson would get at the truth — and gain a measure of revenge — when he headed a Conservative inquiry into the Wilfrid Laurier government's administration of the Departments of the Interior and Indian Affairs.

What got lost in the partisan dust-up over the Kainai grazing lease — what Oliver would later call the "alleged scandal"[31] — were the demands to open Niitsitapi lands. As early as September 1904, when the Cardston Mormons were negotiating with Indian Affairs to farm the southeast corner of the Kainai reserve, it was recommended the tribe simply surrender the 3,000 acres and sell the land in lots to local settlers. Two years later, in June 1906, John Herron, a Pincher Creek rancher and MP for Alberta (later Macleod), asked that the Piikani turn over reserve land for a townsite along the Crowsnest Pass Railway.

These requests were grounded in the popular belief that the Niitsitapi occupied valuable agricultural land at a time when settlement was booming in the new province of Alberta. And if one member of the Niitsitapi confederacy could be convinced to surrender part of their reserve, it was assumed that the other two would likely follow. It didn't seem to matter that the Niitsitapi regarded surrenders as a violation of their treaty agreement.[32]

One of the most coveted sections of the Kainai reserve was that bordering Cardston along the southeast boundary. The town's main street literally bumped up against the reserve fence. While paying lip service to the "importance of the government keeping faith with the Indians," Herron confessed on behalf of his Macleod constituents that "I don't know what obstacle is in the way" in getting a portion of the reserve surrendered.[33]

Oliver promised in the spring of 1906 that efforts would be redoubled to secure the land in question. But those negotiations, handled by Markle, now inspector of Indian agencies for Alberta, failed miserably. The Kainai refused to give up any reserve land and had even hired their own legal counsel, Colin McLeod, to ensure that their treaty rights were upheld. When a vote was taken in May 1907, after several tense days of Kainai objections, the surrender was soundly rejected.

A chagrined Markle blamed this rebuke on the influence of Chief Crop Eared Wolf and called for his removal for drunkenness. The department trod warily, worried that the Chief's deposition might be wrongly equated with his opposition to the surrender. The situation became even more complicated when Crop Eared Wolf and

Chief Crop Eared Wolf (on horseback) led the Kainai resistance to any reserve surrender. (Library and Archives Canada)

Indian agent Wilson levelled charges and countercharges against one another. The Chief accused Wilson of badly mistreating the Kainai after the negative vote, while the agent called out the Chief for being "a chronic kicker and mischief maker." Markle's investigation of the complaints came down in favour of Wilson. Crop Eared Wolf was denounced as "an egomaniac."[34] The feud sidetracked the surrender question for more than two years.

In February 1909, Charles Alexander Magrath, the newly elected Conservative MP for Medicine Hat and former mayor of Lethbridge, raised the Kainai surrender during a debate over the Indian Affairs budget. Magrath had been ruminating over reserve statistics for southern Alberta and concluded that the Kainai had surplus land because their population had declined since treaty. Would it not be, he queried Frank Oliver, "in the interest of the settler and . . . the Indian as well, that the land should be sold?" Magrath then recommended that Oliver personally take on the task. He said the surrender "could be accomplished" if the minister made time to visit the Kainai.

Flattered by the suggestion, the minister spoke about the value of the land and how he wanted it to become productive, but then warned, "I do not know that it is a thing that will be advanced very much by being spoken about." A bemused Magrath replied, "The Indians do not read 'Hansard.'"[35] Oliver reiterated that no amount of talking would make any difference to Kainai resistance and that continued attempts might end in failure as well.

He was right. Oliver glumly informed the House in April 1910 that "the prospect of securing a surrender there [the Kainai reserve] is rather remote."[36]

Markle's negotiations with the Piikani and Siksika were more fruitful, but only because he pursued the surrenders with a singleness of purpose. His meetings with the Piikani, starting in 1908, were like a sparring match. The Piikani members assumed a defensive stance, refusing to consider a surrender, while the inspector kept jabbing, insisting that agricultural equipment could only be secured by selling some of their land. Markle's strategy, in meeting after meeting, was to wear down Piikani resistance — if only to get them to identify what part of the reserve might possibly be surrendered.

At a meeting in May 1909, the Piikani put forth terms: thirty sections of land (19,200 acres) southeast of the Crowsnest Pass line for a minimum $20 per acre, farming implements and stock, and rations "forever." Markle countered that the proposed land sale price was too high — $10 per acre was more realistic — and called for a larger surrender, forty-five sections (28,800 acres). There was further refinement by the department, especially over how much could be expended for working outfits and how rations were to be funded and for how long.[37]

On June 14, 1909, Pedley authorized Markle to take a surrender, but at the inspector's request, sent blank forms in the event that any changes and additions had to be made to the draft terms to secure Piikani agreement. Markle held straw votes the second and third week of July that failed to carry. He ascribed some of the resistance to the presence of Colin McLeod, the same lawyer who had worked for the Kainai. Markle's mission was saved, though, when some Piikani members suggested that a surrender of marginal land in the northwest part of the reserve might be more palatable. That vote was held August 18 and resulted in the release of 23,500 acres (36.5 sections), about 20 percent of the reserve. Out of a possible voting group of 108, only 40 supposedly approved the agreement, but Markle kept no record of the proceedings.[38]

Piikani Chief Butcher at once protested the surrender vote, as did McLeod, who sarcastically suggested that Markle was prepared to "take a vote on this question every day in the week and report upon the first impression that is favourable."[39] The lawyer advised Oliver to look into what happened before the courts did.

Pressed for more details, including a personal plea from the minister, Markle insisted that surrender provisions had been fully observed and cobbled together information about the vote that satisfied anxious department officials. The surrender was confirmed and the sale of the land was set for November 24, 1909. One week before the auction, surrender advocate John Herron stood in the House on "a case of urgency" and recounted the stories he had heard about Markle's tactics. "Perhaps they may be serious," he almost whispered.

Oliver seemed ready for the question and insisted that Parliament shouldn't be approving "large sums of money" to provide agricultural equipment to the Piikani when they had "ample means" to meet their requirements. He also argued that the surrender was good for the Piikani given that the land was of "practically no value" to them. Then, as if daring anyone to contradict him, Oliver solemnly vowed, "there is no foundation for any suggestion of impropriety on the part of the department."[40]

Markle also secured a controversial surrender from the Siksika in June 1910. This surrender had been brewing since Markle was promoted to inspector for Alberta agencies. In 1907, Siksika Head Chief Running Rabbit had asked visiting artist Edmund Morris to take a message to Ottawa: "They do not want any part of the reserve sold."[41] Markle, though, playing the long game, was willing to outwait the Siksika, while reminding them that the tribe's needs could be met only if the Siksika parted with some land.

Markle convened a series of informal discussions over the next two years to come to an appreciation of what it might take to win over the Siksika. Even though the Siksika asked for an assortment of items, including implements, work animals, fencing, and housing, the main concern was food. The Siksika wanted a guarantee of rations.

The Department of Indian Affairs recoiled at the prospect, but both Markle and Indian agent J.H. Gooderham knew that providing rations was a deal-breaker. Besides, Markle believed that rationing would be better than cash payments to tribe members and that the cost could be covered from the land sale proceeds.[42]

Markle was given the go-ahead to try to take a surrender in the spring of 1910. Even though he was once again provided with blank surrender forms, he was ordered to follow the statutory requirements strictly in light of the Piikani controversy a year earlier. When Markle revealed that his surrender strategy was "to try and get them

[Siksika] . . . to agree on some stated condition and then to quickly take a vote," secretary McLean was stunned. The department "does not wish to obtain a snap verdict from the Indians," he told the inspector. "Everything in connection with the proposed surrender must be done openly and above board."[43] Pedley offered similar caution, pointedly telling him to ensure that all eligible members were notified of the day and time of the meeting and to "keep a careful record of all procedures taken."[44]

Markle continued his negotiations right up until the vote on June 15, 1910, when the Siksika, by a 69–64 count, surrendered 115,000 acres (almost 40 percent of the reserve) south of the Bow River.

When the land sales failed to generate the expected income, the department cut back on rations in June 1915. The Siksika considered the action yet another Indian Affairs betrayal. "They were promised rations, not only for themselves, but for succeeding generations,"

The town of Cardston, Alberta, coveted the southeast portion of the Kainai reserve. (Library and Archives Canada)

Gooderham reminded the deputy minister. "They have been assured of the certainty of this over and over again."[45] A nonplussed inspector Markle, on the other hand, insisted that the Siksika had understood that the fulfillment of the agreement would depend on the available funds, but also admitted that he didn't explicitly tell them about this possibility because "they would have refused to agree to the proposed release of land in question."[46]

Securing parts of two Niitsitapi reserves in southern Alberta — nearly 140,000 acres — was undoubtedly a coup for Oliver and his department. But Indian Affairs soon faced a rearguard action in Saskatchewan. Frustrated and disillusioned by Canada's failure to keep its treaty promises, especially its handling of surrender agreements, Louis O'Soup from Cowessess spearheaded an ever-widening pro-test movement that started with the Crooked Lakes and spread to the Fishing (Qu'Appelle) Lakes and other Treaty Four bands.

A series of organizational meetings through the summer and fall of 1910 culminated in the dispatch of eight delegates to Ottawa in January 1911. Their trip east on the CPR was laden with "heavy griev-ances," backed by letters and petitions they carried with them. They even brought their own translator, Alexander Gadie.

Agent Matthew Millar of the Crooked Lakes reserves, who had bought surrendered land at the November 1908 auction, downplayed the unrest. "They will come back wiser although probably disappointed men," he confidently predicted before the start of the meetings. "The results of their going should have a beneficial effect."[47]

The Treaty Four representatives met with Oliver and Pedley over five days, sometimes twice a day, from January 24 to 28, 1911. The minis-ter and his deputy tried to be as accommodating as possible, according to the transcript. On the third morning, for example, Laird, who had served as one of three commissioners for Treaty Four, attended the meeting at the request of the delegates.

The first day was largely taken up with opening statements. The men all thanked the government for meeting with them and explained who they represented; some handed over papers from other bands. O'Soup, who had been a "very young" man at the Treaty Four signing in 1874, spoke about how the "bargain" had failed his people. "When I heard what was said," he remembered, "I thought to myself, 'Oh, we will make a living by the promises that are made to us.'" But they had not been "looked after." Joe Cote from Cote's band also emphasized the non-fulfillment of the treaty: "It is . . . what was promised [that] I want. My wish is to know why has an Indian nothing. I am just like as if I was a prisoner."[48]

The delegates raised a wide range of issues over the next few sessions — there was no formal agenda — but the discussion invariably came back to reserve surrenders. They all asked the same questions. They wanted to know what the land was sold for, how much money was made, and most importantly, where was that money? They placed great faith in the surrender agreements, as if they were a form of treaty, and expected the promises to be honoured. The problem, though, was that they were never informed about the surrender sales, just that they could expect money.

In January 1911, Louis O'Soup (far left) led a Treaty Four delegation to Ottawa. The meeting with the Indian Affairs minister and deputy minister failed to resolve any of the First Nations grievances. (Provincial Archives of Saskatchewan)

Oliver remained uncharacteristically silent for the first three days of meetings, but on the Friday morning, after hearing yet another query about what had happened to "the money on the land sale," he took over the discussion. Oliver began by reporting that the department deducted 10 percent from sale proceeds as a land management fee. "When the Indian sells his reserve somebody — that is, the Govt. — has to take care of the books, collect the money, and see that the accounts are paid," he said.

This administrative grab didn't sit well with the delegates.

Oliver then turned to something he suggested might be "a little hard to explain." He said that buyers had ten years to pay for their reserve land and that the interest collected on any deferred payment meant that bands actually got more for their land in the long run. This positive spin on land sales was undone by what Oliver said next: "But some of the purchasers have not paid up . . . are behind in their payments, so we didn't really get the money when we should have got it."[49]

Oliver didn't want to leave things hanging by admitting that Indian Affairs had mishandled the land sales. "Now, you have come down here and you want to go back with something," he said, trying to reassure the delegates. "We will turn our pockets inside out, and you will have everything that is yours."[50]

What Oliver actually meant was that the delegates would get a full accounting of the surrender sales — how many acres were sold, the average price, the total sale proceeds, the uncollected balance, and any interest. That's how the last two sessions were spent on Saturday, January 28. Oliver meticulously reviewed the details of several Treaty Four land sales, noting when further payments to band members might be forthcoming. He offered little more, except for copies of the financial statements.

On the return home, the delegates stopped over briefly in Winnipeg and told a *Free Press* reporter, through interpreter Gadie, that they were "very well satisfied with their treatment."[51] Securing action, though, was another matter, especially when the Indian Affairs department's 1911 annual report depicted the representatives as "a few misguided discontents."[52]

Three days after the Ottawa meetings concluded, while the delegates were on their way home, Indian Affairs instructed Indian agent Thomas Borthwick to take a surrender of Mistawasis land.

This action would have been unimaginable to Chief Mistawasis, a senior Plains Cree Chief in the Carlton district. Mistawasis had been a forceful advocate for Treaty Six. At the treaty deliberations at Fort Carlton in August 1876, he told the assembled Cree that the treaty offered the best protection against the loss of the bison and that the great Queen Mother (Victoria) had their best interests at heart. "Have you anything better to offer our people?" he passionately challenged any dissenters. "I for one will take the hand that is offered."[53]

Mistawasis led by example and was one of the first Chiefs to ask for treaty land in the Snake Plains area, southwest of present-day Shellbrook, Saskatchewan. Once the reserve (seventy-seven square miles) was surveyed in 1878, the band tried its hand at mixed farming, but its efforts were stymied by the lack of animals, implements, and other promised agricultural assistance. Chief Mistawasis stood by the treaty, though, and remained loyal during the 1885 North-West Rebellion. He always did his best to make the treaty relationship work in the genuine belief that Canada would reciprocate.

By 1910, settlement had surrounded the Mistawasis reserve, while a Canadian Northern branch line ran through its southeast corner. The band, now headed by Chief George Dreaver, wanted to fence the reserve to keep stray animals from wandering onto Mistawasis land and looked for a way to pay for the materials, estimated to cost $1,500.

Borthwick, who had served as commissioner for Treaty Ten in northern Saskatchewan in 1907, suggested that the 118 acres cut off from the reserve by the CNoR line be surrendered. Indian Affairs officials countered that a larger portion of the reserve should be taken — 1,607 acres — and that any surrender proceeds be paid to the band only after the land sale.[54] Clearly, the department had learned, albeit belatedly, that land auctions didn't generate enough funds to cover cash advances, especially when buyers didn't pay their instalments on time or simply defaulted on their purchases.

On February 22, 1911, Borthwick reported that a surrender agreement had been reached with the Mistawasis band. The details of the meeting are sketchy at best. There were two key provisions, though: that the land be valued at a minimum of $15 per acre, and that 50 percent of the sale proceeds, the maximum allowable, be paid to band members.

The Indian Affairs department rejected both terms and instructed Borthwick to take another surrender, minus the objectionable clauses. The band voted again on March 20, 1911, this time agreeing that the sale proceeds would be used to pay for the reserve fencing and some farm implements. In submitting the documentation to the department, Borthwick recommended — without consulting the Mistawasis men — that one of the key provisions be modified. He advised Secretary McLean that the agency, not the band, purchase the machinery and that reserve farmers be required to pay to use it. This change appeared in the order-in-council, dated April 20, 1911, that confirmed the surrender.[55]

Borthwick's unilateral change to the Mistawasis surrender document, together with Markle's contentious handling of the Piikani and Siksika surrenders, signalled how far Indian Affairs was willing to go to secure reserve land. No matter what was said or promised, formal surrender meeting or not, the minister and his department were prepared to accept and defend the signed agreements.

Oliver, though, wanted an even freer hand and sponsored an amendment to the Indian Act in the spring of 1911 that gave Canada the right to acquire reserve land if it was near a town with a population of more than 8,000. It was "a radical departure," Oliver noted, made necessary by Canada's galloping population growth. "It is not right that the requirements of the expansion of white settlement should be ignored," he said in defence of the legislation in the House of Commons, "[or] that the right of the Indian should be allowed to become a wrong to the white man."[56]

When asked to provide an example, Oliver pointed to the Songhees reserve in British Columbia, which had to be moved from Victoria to

Esquimalt. He said that similar cases were going to arise in the future and he wanted a general rule on the books to deal with these situations.

Opposition leader Robert Borden denounced the amendment for overriding Indigenous rights secured through treaty agreements. He testily warned, "The breaking of treaties with the Indians of this country — because you cannot put it lower than that — is . . . a very extreme step." Another member found the change "too arbitrary": it gave the Indian Affairs minister too much power to do away with reserves, while leaving bands with little recourse. Conservative back-bencher J.E. Armstrong was also worried about the force of the amendment, but for an entirely different reason. He hinted that Oliver was simply looking for another way to get reserve land into the hands of government friends.[57]

The most devastating critique came from Clifford Sifton — not in the House, where he rarely spoke or attended the sessions, but in a letter where he denied any responsibility for what was happening. "Providence," Sifton wrote, "put an incompetent mischief maker in the position to do a great deal of mischief."[58]

Prime Minister Laurier spoke in support of the necessity of the legislation. Rising in his seat in answer to Borden's fault-finding, he acknowledged that it was "an exceptional bill" that would interfere with treaty rights "to a certain extent." But Laurier stood by the principle behind the Indian Act amendment: growing cities shouldn't have to coexist with reserves.

Several members of the House rallied to the prime minister's position, some wanting to go even further. Medicine Hat MP Magrath, who had been calling for a surrender of part of the Kainai reserve, said that Cardston wouldn't be helped by the legislation because of its size. "If the presence of ten thousand white people are not good for the Indian," he reasoned, "it seems to be that the same idea holds as to a smaller population." Magrath wanted the limit lowered to 2,000. Another member questioned why there had to be a limit at all.

Yet even though Oliver believed that the presence of a reserve is "ordinarily a detriment" to a town, he was only willing, with the verbal concurrence of House members, to lower the limit to 8,000. He didn't

want to push the matter beyond what he considered "perfectly justifi-
able" at the time.[59] Further changes to the Indian Act could be made in
a year or so, probably after the Liberals had secured another mandate.

That general election seemed imminent in the spring of 1911. In
late January, Liberal finance minister W.S. Fielding had gleefully
announced in the House that Canada had reached a broad trade
agreement with the United States, starting first with the removal of
duties on most natural products. Once formally approved by both
governments, the deal was expected to eventually lead to full reciprocity. Prime Minister Laurier believed the agreement would serve as the
capstone to his fifteen years in office.

Conservative leader Robert Borden, once he found his feet on the
issue, came out swinging, claiming that reciprocity would weaken ties
with Great Britain and lead to commercial absorption by the United
States. His spirited attack was bolstered by Canadian business leaders
and manufacturers, including Liberal party supporters, who greatly
feared what the deal would mean to their livelihood. Even former
cabinet minister Clifford Sifton broke with his party, as did several
other prominent Liberals.

Through the late winter into the spring of 1911, the Conservative
Opposition filibustered passage of the reciprocity resolutions. Laurier
chose not to dissolve Parliament, but adjourned the session on May
19, 1911, in order to attend the Imperial Conference in London. An
election was on the horizon, though. The adjournment motion was
preceded by an announcement by the Speaker that over seventy bills
had received royal assent, including the Indian Act amendment.

The House of Commons resumed business on July 18, but the two-
month hiatus only delayed the inevitable. Laurier endured another
ten days of Conservative obstruction before calling on the electorate
to decide the matter on September 21, 1911. Laurier was confident that
reciprocity, in combination with the Liberal record, would carry the day.
So were many of his ministers. At the end of the session, agriculture
minister Sidney Fisher mused, "Reciprocity will be interesting, I think."[60]

It was a tired Liberal government, bereft of new ideas and headed by an aged leader, that went to the polls. Borden's linking of reciprocity with Canada's demise, by contrast, tapped into popular fears of American aggression, particularly in older regions. His questioning of Liberal naval policy in the lead-up to the Great War also found appeal. When the votes were tallied, the overwhelming support of Ontario translated into a national Conservative victory.

Oliver's mischief-making at Indian Affairs had come to an end.

Notes

1. House of Commons, *Debates*, February 12, 1909, p. 1009.
2. See H.A. Dempsey, *Firewater: The Impact of the Whisky Trade on the Blackfoot Nation* (Calgary: Fifth House, 2002).
3. Quoted in S. Krasowski, *No Surrender: The Land Remains Indigenous* (Regina: University of Regina Press, 2019), p. 264.
4. V.K. Jobson, "The Blackfoot Farming Experiment, 1880–1905," unpublished M.A. thesis, University of Calgary, 1990, pp. 13–21.
5. D.J. Hall, *From Treaties to Reserves: The Federal Government and Native Peoples in Territorial Alberta, 1870–1905* (Edmonton: University of Alberta Press, 2015), pp. 117, 120.
6. Hall, *From Treaties to Reserves*, pp. 186–8; Jobson, "The Blackfoot Farming Experiment," p. 25.
7. *Library and Archives Canada (LAC)*, RG10, v. 3968, f. 155036, J.D. McLean to D. Laird, March 13, 1902.
8. W.K. Regular, "'Trucking and Trading with Outsiders': Blood Indian Reserve Integration into the Southern Alberta Economic Environment, 1884–1939, A Case of Shared Neighbourhoods," unpublished Ph.D. thesis, Memorial University of Newfoundland, 1999, p. 85.
9. Ibid., p. 91.
10. Ibid., p. 76.

11. *LAC*, RG10, v. 3968, f. 155036, J.B. Lash to J.D. McLean, July 22, 1899, *Tribune*.

12. Regular, "Trucking and Trading with Outsiders," pp. 95–110.

13. H.A. Dempsey, "Maunsell, Edward Herbert" in R. Cook, *Dictionary of Canadian Biography, v. XV, 1921–1939* (Toronto: University of Toronto Press, 2005), pp. 722–3.

14. Regular, "Trucking and Trading with Outsiders," pp. 111–13. See also *Debates*, June 5, 1906, p. 4665 (R.N. Wilson to J.D. McLean, March 11, 1903).

15. *Debates*, July 20, 1903, pp. 7197–9.

16. Ibid., May 4, 1904, pp. 2554.

17. *LAC*, RG10, v. 3571, f. 130, pt. 19, J.G. Turriff to C. Sifton, November 19, 1903.

18. Ibid., J.A.J. McKenna, memorandum to Superintendent General of Indian Affairs, January 5, 1904; J.A.J. McKenna to C. Sifton, January 5, 1904.

19. Ibid., J.A.J. McKenna to C. Sifton, February 6, 1904.

20. Ibid., R.N. Wilson to J.A.J. McKenna to C. Sifton, March 25, 1904.

21. Sifton had a file on the Piikani reserve in his subject file papers. It's the only band file in his collection.

22. *Macleod Advance*, July 26, 1904.

23. *LAC*, RG10, v. 3571, f. 130, pt. 19, J.A.J. McKenna to J.D. McLean, July 22, 1904; F. Pedley to J.A.J. McKenna, July 27, 1904.

24. *Debates*, March 30, 1906, pp. 956–9.

25. Ibid., June 1, 1906, p. 4400.

26. Ibid., June 1, 1906, p. 4401; June 5, 1906, pp. 4663–4.

27. Millar would gain international notoriety for a clause in his will that gave the majority of his estate to the Toronto woman who had the most children in the ten years after his 1926 death.

28. *Debates*, June 1, 1906, p. 4401.

29. Ibid., p. 4408–9. Millar was then partners with T.R. Ferguson's brother.

30. Ibid., June 1, 1906, p. 4410; June 5, 1906, pp. 4663–72.

31. Ibid., July 11, 1908, p. 12745.

32. Jobson, "The Blackfoot Farming Experiment," p. 43; P. Martin-McGuire,

First Nations Land Surrenders on the Prairies, 1896–1911 (Ottawa: Indian Claims Commission, 1998), p. 317.

33. *Debates*, March 30, 1906, p. 955.

34. *LAC*, RG10, v. 4018, f. 274096, "Report from J.A. Markle to Secretary Indian Affairs," January 30, 1908; v. 3949, f. 121698, "Report from R.N. Wilson to the Indian Commissioner," June 28, 1908.

35. *Debates*, February 12, 1909, pp. 1007–8.

36. Ibid., April 22, 1910, p. 7855.

37. Martin-McGuire, *First Nations Land Surrenders*, pp. 149, 314–16.

38. Ibid., pp. 150, 316–21.

39. Quoted in ibid., p. 318.

40. *Debates*, November 16, 1909, pp. 119–22.

41. Quoted in Jobson, "The Blackfoot Farming Experiment," p. 41.

42. Jobson, "The Blackfoot Farming Experiment," p. 44; Martin-McGuire, *First Nations Land Surrenders*, pp. 154, 238–9.

43. *LAC*, RG10, v. 7543, f. 29120, pt. 1, J.D. McLean to J.A. Markle, March 10, 1910.

44. Quoted in Martin-McGuire, *First Nations Land Surrenders*, p. 323.

45. *LAC*, RG10, v. 3702, f. 17537, pt. 3, J.A. Gooderham to D.C. Scott, May 1, 1915.

46. Quoted in Martin-McGuire, *First Nations Land Surrenders*, p. xxxix.

47. *LAC*, RG10, v. 4053, f. 379,203-1, M. Miller to J.D. McLean, January 10, 1911.

48. Ibid., "Notes of representation made by delegation of Indians from the West," January 1911.

49. Ibid.

50. Ibid.

51. *Manitoba Free Press*, February 3, 1911.

52. Quoted in S. Carter, *Lost Harvests: Prairie Indian Reserve Farmers and Government Policy* (Montreal: McGill-Queen's University Press, 1990), p. 257.

53. Quoted in P. Erasmus, *Buffalo Days and Nights* (Calgary: Glenbow Museum, 1974), pp. 247, 249.

54. Martin-McGuire, *First Nations Land Surrenders*, pp. 242, 325.

55. The bulk of the surrendered land was sold at auction on August 2, 1911, to two real estate agents who defaulted on their payments. Indian Claims Commission, "Mistawasis First Nations Inquiry 1911, 1917, and 1919 Surrenders," 2002, pp. 13–19.

56. *Debates*, April 26, 1911, pp. 7826, 7851.

57. Ibid., April 26, 1911, pp. 7833, 7835, 7842.

58. Quoted in D.J. Hall, *Clifford Sifton, v. 2: A Lonely Eminence, 1901–1929* (Vancouver: University of British Columbia Press, 1985), p. 217.

59. *Debates*, April 26, 1911, p. 7829–30, 7851–2.

60. Ibid., July 28, 1911, p. 10590.

⊰ *Eleven* ⊱

HIRED THUG

Prime Minister Robert Borden and the Conservative front benches were waiting for the right moment. For the past several weeks, as the spring 1915 session of Parliament was winding down, the Liberal Opposition, led by former prime minister Wilfrid Laurier, had been hammering at Conservative mishandling of military procurement contracts for the Canadian war effort. Over 3,000 contracts, worth an estimated $50 million, had been awarded since the start of the Great War in August 1914, and the cry of scandal echoed through the Commons almost daily.

Then, on Wednesday, April 14, just minutes into the start of the day's business, Cabinet Minister William James Roche launched the Conservative counterattack. With his colleagues baying for blood, Roche electrified the House for several hours with his methodical accounting of the explosive findings of the Ferguson Commission, an official inquiry into the handling of public and First Nations lands under the Liberals since 1896. The tandem of Arthur Meighen and Richard Bedford Bennett, two western MPs and future prime ministers, then carried the raucous debate past midnight, alternately deriding and mocking the Liberals for betraying the public trust during their years in office.

The revelations — and the way the Conservatives had stunned the Opposition — seemed to breathe new life into the Borden government as it prepared to fight a possible general election in the coming months. The next day, when the prime minister was once again being pilloried over the purchase of war supplies, Borden replied to his Liberal inquisitor, "Might I ask him to turn his gaze upon the inferno of the Ferguson report?"[1]

⤛⤜

The Ferguson Commission was all about payback. The Conservatives resented missing out on the profits from the great settlement and development boom in western Canada, whether it was timber berths, ranching leases, or First Nations reserve surrenders. And they wanted a measure of revenge. What better way than establishing a federal commission to investigate Liberal malfeasance and corruption at Interior and Indian Affairs departments during Laurier's fifteen years in office?

The inquiry was largely the doing of Robert Rogers. The former minister of Public Works in Rodmond Roblin's Conservative government in Manitoba was sworn in as Interior and Indian Affairs minister in October 1911. His appointment to the Borden cabinet was widely disparaged by Liberals as odious. The *Saskatoon Phoenix* denounced the "unsavoury" Rogers as unacceptable to the West and the region's aspirations.[2] Clifford Sifton, who had once held the same position in the Wilfrid Laurier government but had defected and helped get Borden elected, "feared" that Rogers "will set about building a [patronage]

*Prime Minister Robert Borden was expected to clean up Ottawa governance after the Conservatives won the 1911 general election. (*Edmonton Journal, *April 17, 1915)*

machine to capture the West, just as he has . . . branded Manitoba."[3] Even some veteran Conservatives wondered if Borden had forgotten his "clean" principles in appointing someone so "politically immoral and offensive."[4]

Rogers, though, had earned a seat at the cabinet table. A master organizer and party manager, he had orchestrated the Conservative campaigns in the prairie west for the 1904, 1908, and 1911 general elections while serving in the Roblin government. Indeed, Rogers reportedly ran "the best political machine in Canada" and helped carry Manitoba for the Tories.[5] He was now expected to handle party matters for the Borden government. His departure for the federal arena so upset Premier Roblin that he predicted his "weakened" provincial government faced "defeat . . . at next election."[6]

What made Rogers's politicking so successful and yet so loathsome was his lack of inhibition when it came to doing whatever was necessary, including buying votes, to win. Nothing was beneath him. Perhaps the most generous assessment of the "legendary" Bob Rogers was that he was Manitoba's "unique contribution" to the Borden government.[7]

One week after entering cabinet, Rogers met with his Liberal predecessor Frank Oliver in his new Langevin Block office. Sifton was also present. According to reporters, the men were all smiles during their fifteen-minute chat.[8] That was quite a departure for Rogers and Sifton. The two former Manitoban politicians had been bitter foes for political control of the province. Their grudging respect for each other's organizational skills only intensified the rivalry. Before the election, though, the word had been put out among Conservatives "to leave Sifton alone."[9]

Sifton had become increasingly alienated from Laurier and his Liberal government since his abrupt resignation from cabinet in 1905. His four-square stand against reciprocity had made him a welcome guest in the Borden Conservative camp. The new prime minister also admired Sifton's intellect and judgment and sought his advice on the makeup of his first cabinet.[10] That's why Rogers and Sifton could spend some time together in the same office, albeit briefly, shaking hands and not wringing each other's throats.

Rogers and Oliver, on the other hand, had been engaged in a long, simmering feud over politics and policies. The strained relationship between the two western politicians would take a decidedly nasty turn after Rogers entered cabinet and was tasked with running Conservative party machinery in western Canada. Oliver, with his Alberta stronghold, would have to be taken down. As a Liberal rival observed, "Mr. Rogers played the game hard and with success."[11]

Oliver would give as good as he got. From his new perch on the Opposition benches in the House of Commons, the Edmonton MP constantly criticized the new Borden government, aiming his razor-sharp barbs at Rogers and his handling of his dual portfolios.

No sooner had Rogers been appointed to the Borden cabinet than there were rumours in Conservative newspapers of a possible investigation into the Interior department and how "the people's resources have been squandered."[12] The call for an inquiry was likely a response to the "scandal sessions" in the House of Commons from March 1906 to July 1908, when the Conservative Opposition used every opportunity to probe corruption in Liberal ranks.

There was nothing stopping the new Borden government from sponsoring such a commission — except for other, more pressing demands. It had been fifteen years since the Conservatives had last been in power, and there was only so much a new administration could do in its first few months, especially when there were seemingly irreconcilable internal differences over Canada's naval policy. These divisions over how best to meet imperial obligations prompted Borden's Quebec lieutenant Frederick Debartzch Monk to resign in late October 1912.

Rogers was asked to take over Public Works. There was no better portfolio for his brand of pork-barrel politics, all the more so once the Great War started in August 1914. In the first six months of the conflict, Rogers was "the one most responsible" for the 10,000 patronage appointments.[13]

Rogers's replacement at Interior and Indian Affairs was Dr. William James Roche, who had represented the western riding of Marquette

Conservative W.J. Roche led the attack on the Liberals during the debate on the Ferguson report in April 1915.
(Parliament of Canada webpage)

since 1896. Roche had entered the Borden cabinet, one of two ministers from Manitoba, as Secretary of State. His qualification for his new post seemed to be that he was from western Canada — just like many of his predecessors, beginning with fellow Conservative Thomas Mayne Daly in 1892. He had also been a persistent critic of Liberal policies, regularly challenging Sifton and Oliver in the House over some Interior or Indian Affairs matter or other, especially those that seemed to favour Liberal friends.

Roche did however share the Laurier government's interest in opening reserves to settlement, and once asked about a surrender from the Crooked Lakes reserves in southeastern Saskatchewan.[14] In March 1913, just five months after he landed at Interior and Indian Affairs, there were concerns that Roche might have to step down from cabinet and resign his seat because of ill health. April found Roche at the Mayo Clinic in Rochester, Minnesota, for kidney surgery. His leave denied him a front seat to an ugly row between Rogers and Oliver on the floor of the House of Commons.

On April 17, 1913, at the beginning of House of Commons business that afternoon, Frank Oliver introduced a motion of censure against Rogers, seconded by William Martin, the MP for Regina and a future Saskatchewan premier. For the past two House sessions, whenever addressing government policy, Rogers had taken a swipe at Oliver and his past handling of Interior affairs. The Edmonton MP tired of the constant sniping — he saw it as a personal attack on his integrity — and used his connections to gather evidence that Rogers had awarded a parcel of reserved land within the Prince Albert city limits to the son of a Conservative member of the Saskatchewan legislature.

Rogers bristled at the accusation and fought back by charging that Wilfrid Laurier, acting on Oliver's recommendation, had awarded a timber tract to Liberal supporters almost two weeks after their September 1911 election defeat. To bolster his case, Rogers used the Commons supper break to slip over to his government offices and return with the incriminating documentation, which he insisted on reading into the record. "Just sit quiet and take your medicine," Rogers said, taunting the Opposition benches. "You will get it."

Martin mockingly congratulated Rogers on his two-hour speech, suggesting that it was a master performance in obfuscation. The only thing the minister had proven, Martin sarcastically quipped, was that some former government officials "were just as bad as he is himself." Incensed Liberals, including former prime minister Laurier, then demanded that the letters be tabled. When Rogers insisted the information in the files was confidential, Martin countered that the minister possessed stolen material taken from the office of a Liberal organizer.

The Conservatives rallied around Rogers by going after Oliver and accusing him of favouritism in department decisions during his tenure. The supercharged debate finally ended when Oliver's motion was defeated by a vote along party lines.[15] Rogers sought revenge.

Five days later, Thomas Crothers, the acting minister of the Interior, informed his deputy by memo that he wanted a federal commission, headed by Winnipeg lawyer Thomas Roberts Ferguson, to investigate the Liberal administration of natural resources in western Canada.[16]

It's doubtful that Crothers acted on his own, since he also held the Labour portfolio and was only serving in the absence of Interior minister Roche. According to a short notation along the side of the appointment document, a copy was sent to Robert Rogers, and interestingly not the minister of Justice. That Rogers was behind the move was confirmed by the choice of "Tommy" Ferguson as commissioner.

Thomas Ferguson was a Conservative party organizer and platform advisor, but most importantly a friend of the so-called minister of elections, Robert Rogers. Born in Ontario and educated at Upper Canada College, University of Toronto, and Osgoode Hall, Ferguson moved to Winnipeg in 1902 and became a fixture in police court, defending petty crooks, bootleggers, and small businesses that found themselves on the wrong side of the law.

His clientele contrasted sharply with his standing in the Winnipeg community. He lived in an exclusive neighbourhood and belonged to several clubs and organizations, in particular the Orange Lodge. It

Winnipeg lawyer and Conservative T.R. Ferguson investigated the Laurier government's administration of the Interior and Indian Affairs departments.
(Manitoba Historical Society)

might have been Rogers, as a member of the Manitoba government, who had a hand in Ferguson's 1908 appointment as a King's Counsel. There were also rumours that Ferguson was being considered for a judgeship after the 1911 Conservative election victory. One Liberal newspaper called him "a thorough-going partisan . . . one of Hon. Robert Rogers' fighting men."[17]

That was kind compared to Ferguson's treatment in the *Winnipeg Tribune*, which was published by Robert Lorne Richardson, a Liberal. He was skewered for being fat, having greasy hair, and being a simpleton masquerading as a third-rate lawyer. "Tommy Ferguson returned to the city today," the *Tribune* reported, "looking as young and as chipper as he did half a century ago when he was all the rage."[18]

The Borden government empowered the Ferguson Commission to investigate any and all aspects of the Laurier government's administration of the Interior and Indian Affairs departments.[19] It was open season on Liberals, and the inquiry had more firepower than it would ever likely need. Sifton was certainly worried. Prime Minister Borden wrote in his diary entry for July 25, 1913, that Sifton had complained to Sam Hughes, the minister of Militia, "that [the] Ferguson Commission is directed against him and that Rogers is desirous of attacking him."[20] The Sifton-owned *Winnipeg Free Press* also claimed that Ferguson, "a warm supporter of Hon. Robert Rogers," was on the "hunt for scandals . . . to substantiate pre-election charges of graft against the Laurier administration."[21]

It was a fair assessment. The proposed investigation perfectly suited Rogers's other, seamier role running the Conservative party machinery. Whatever dirt Ferguson unearthed could have useful political purposes, especially in an election campaign. It could also help Rogers settle some scores with Liberal opponents.

The commission was well-funded. Ferguson was paid $50 per day on inquiry business — over $1,200 in today's economy — plus his travel expenses. He had a full-time secretary, C.L. Simmonds, as well as reporters and stenographers in various cities to take evidence and prepare transcripts. There was even money for witness fees and hiring local agents for "making searches."[22]

Ferguson started work in Ottawa, scrutinizing Indian Affairs files. Before he officially assumed his duties, Ferguson had written Secretary Francis H. Gisbourne of the Justice department that one of the ministers, probably Rogers, suggested Ferguson "should investigate the circumstances connected with the acquiring . . . of a tract of land of considerable size." Department officials, according to the unnamed source, were "improperly" involved.

Ferguson took the hint and reviewed the tenders for the two Nakoda reserves that had been sold in November 1901. He found that three Toronto lawyers — R.B. Beaumont, J.W. Marsh, and E.C. Mackenzie — had acquired 298 of the 308 parcels at Moose Mountain under forged signatures. He also interviewed W.Λ. Orr of the Lands and Timber branch, who had handled the tender sale and the subsequent disposition of the lands. He then travelled to Montreal and Toronto to take evidence from several people of interest — in particular former deputy minister of Interior and Indian Affairs James Smart and lawyer Alban Cartwright Bedford-Jones.[23]

It didn't take much detective work for Ferguson to determine that Smart, Deputy Minister of Indian Affairs Frank Pedley, and William J. White, inspector of United States immigration agencies, had fraudulently secured 45,000 acres with the connivance of Bedford-Jones. Or that the Pheasant Rump and Ocean Man bands had been duped into surrendering their reserves.

Ferguson didn't bother to investigate reserve surrenders, no matter how questionable. He didn't look at auction sales for surrendered lands, even if there were large purchases by a select Liberal few or apparent collusion among the buyers. He was only interested in reserve lands sold by sealed tender, and only when the bids were fraudulent. Even there, Ferguson missed the unsuccessful attempt by Smart, Pedley, and White to secure Enoch land by rigged tender in 1902.

News of Ferguson's findings was splashed over the front page of the *Ottawa Evening Journal* on September 15, 1913. The article stated that Ferguson had submitted "revelations of a startling character," but did not provide any specifics. The remainder of the story, based on information from "an authoritative source," reported that "several well known government officials" faced serious graft charges and were to be dismissed and likely prosecuted.[24]

Two legal opinions, though, recommended against laying criminal charges. In late September 1913, Ottawa prosecutor William Drummond Hogg was asked to review two interim reports that Ferguson had submitted to the government. The first, dated August 1, 1913, detailed how Pedley had accepted a bribe in awarding an exclusive grazing lease on the Piikani reserve to the McEwen Cattle Company in May 1903. Bedford-Jones testified that he had held this money in trust until 1908, when he turned over $900 to Pedley and kept $100 for his services. The second interim report, dated August 2, dealt with the sale of the two Moose Mountain reserves and how Smart, White, and Pedley had used their insider positions to secure most of the land.

In considering both reports, Hogg concluded that, even though the officials' actions were "perhaps somewhat unfortunate," the evidence did not support "any case of fraudulent dealings or serious misconduct."[25]

A second, internal opinion, likely provided by Edmund Leslie Newcombe, deputy minister of Justice and a future Supreme Court of Canada judge, was more deprecatory. Newcombe had regularly offered legal advice on government matters to both Smart and Pedley and probably felt betrayed. The men, he sternly observed, had breached their duty as public officials. But because of the passage of time and the difficulty in securing a criminal conviction, Newcombe recommended that the government pursue compensation in civil court.[26]

Neither lawyer commented on whether the two Nakoda bands should be compensated. It was apparently never even considered. First Nations were no more than flotsam in the Ferguson maelstrom.

Although never identified in the Ottawa newspaper story, Pedley submitted his resignation on Saturday, October 11, 1913. The matter was discussed at the federal cabinet that same day. Minister of Trade and Commerce George Foster, who had first been elected in 1882 and served as finance minister for five consecutive Conservative prime ministers, vehemently recommended against leniency. Prime Minister Borden accepted the deputy's resignation with the caveat that it didn't preclude the Crown taking future action.[27] Pedley was also allowed to keep his pension, valued at nearly $1,900 after fourteen years of government service.[28] He had made more than ten times that much in profit from the Nakoda lands.

Pedley's departure made the Monday headlines across the country. Although Roche, who had resumed his Interior and Indian Affairs duties, refused to comment on the deputy's resignation, most newspapers connected the dots between Ferguson's investigation and Pedley's "retirement" from government service.

Robert Rogers also continued to stir the pot and feed confidential information to the press. Pedley's partners, Smart and White, were mentioned in several of the stories, as was the fact that the trio made $80,000 in one transaction (Pedley's salary was $4,000). The *Toronto World* even knew that Ferguson had interviewed Peter Ryan, the Liberal operative who had offered Pedley a share of the profits from the McEwen Cattle Company, and Charles Millar, the Toronto lawyer who had handled the competing bid for the same Piikani grazing lease. The *Victoria Daily Colonist* and *Ottawa Evening Journal*, meanwhile, reported that Ferguson was delving into some shady "deal" involving John Gillanders Turriff, the Liberal MP for Assiniboia. If the Conservative papers were to be believed, Pedley's activities were only the tip of the "Liberal graft" iceberg.[29]

The question of what to do about Ferguson's preliminary reports, though, continued to dog the Borden government. Three days before Pedley resigned, Justice deputy minister Newcombe advised the prime minister that Ferguson had failed to observe two sections of the Inquiries Act: those who gave evidence weren't represented by counsel or given the opportunity to be represented by counsel, and no charges were made or notice given of any pending charges. Ferguson appeared to be acting in such a manner, Newcombe speculated in his memorandum, because he was only gathering facts from the documents and witnesses, not submitting findings or making charges.[30]

This approach — essentially letting the evidence speak for itself — roiled Roche. The Interior and Indian Affairs minister wanted Ferguson to lay charges, or at least submit findings, so that there might be trials, and told him that his way of running the commission was out of step with the Justice department. A miffed Ferguson, travelling on inquiry business, replied with a lengthy letter to Roche, defending his way of proceeding and "leav[ing] it to you and Council [cabinet] or Parliament, or the public to draw its own conclusions, from the evidence submitted."[31]

When he returned to Ottawa in early November 1913, Ferguson conferred with Newcombe to settle any doubts about the discharge of his duties. The pair agreed that the "course [Ferguson was taking] was quite open to him."[32] It was certainly not what Robert Rogers and company had wanted or expected, especially from a fellow Conservative who was given the power to rattle the Laurier Liberals.

Ferguson's volatile behaviour in Regina also raised concerns about whether he was able to carry out his mandate with gravitas. On Tuesday, October 7, the start of the hearings in the Saskatchewan capital, Ferguson had created a local stir by initially barring Liberal MP William Martin and reporters from attending. "We do not wish one witness to know what evidence has been given by other witnesses," he explained.[33] Three days later, Ferguson complained to Royal North-West Mounted Police commissioner A.B. Perry about "some disturbances and improper conduct" and asked that a constable be present at the next hearing.[34]

What Ferguson didn't mention was that he was largely to blame for the kerfuffle. The Friday session had started badly. Richard Edward Albert Leech, who had served in various capacities for the Liberals in Manitoba, including handling the 1901 census before being named inspector of dominion lands agents by Oliver, was called as a witness. Leech was the kind of special political operative that would have been admired by Robert Rogers, if not for the fact that he was a Liberal. Even Sifton, who had made good use of his talents, questioned Leech's grubby methods, especially when it came to helping himself. "I am afraid Leech is a shyster," Sifton confided to an aide.[35]

Leech appeared before Ferguson accompanied by his lawyer James Albert Cross, a Regina Liberal and future Saskatchewan attorney general. Leech asked that Cross be recognized as his counsel, a request Ferguson denied. Cross couldn't resist, though, objecting to the questions put to Leech and even challenging Ferguson's impartiality because of past bad blood between the two political foes in Manitoba.

At one point during his questioning, Ferguson asked Leech how he came to hold an interest in a timber berth. When Leech refused to co-operate, Ferguson pulled out a letter from a file, handed it to the witness, and ordered him to read it aloud. Leech declared the letter to have been stolen from him, along with other personal papers, and wouldn't give it back. A flustered Ferguson grabbed Leech and tried to wrest the letter from him. Cross broke up the scuffle, forcing the commissioner to let go of his client.

Once he had collected himself, Ferguson asked through clenched teeth for the letter. When Leech said no, Ferguson threatened prosecution. Leech held his ground, declining to answer any more questions without the benefit of his counsel. Ferguson angrily picked up the Regina phone book and barked at his secretary to get him the number of the city police chief. Leech remained defiant, prompting the commissioner to adjourn the hearing until the next morning.[36]

The *Regina Leader*, a Liberal newspaper, had a field day with Ferguson's antics. The Saturday morning edition accused the commissioner of using "star chambers" methods, more in keeping with medieval courts where due process was arbitrarily trampled by authoritarian judges.[37] The Conservative counterpart, the *Regina Province*, scrambled to rescue Ferguson's reputation, dismissing the claim that Leech had been "assaulted" as "utterly false."[38] The truth was somewhere between the two partisan extremes.

When the hearing resumed Saturday morning, Ferguson and Leech resumed their tête-à-tête before a quick adjournment was declared. The commissioner was more composed at the next session on Monday. He began his remarks by reminding Leech that his "gross misconduct" had placed him in contempt of the court, but he was still expected to answer some questions. Leech asked yet again about being represented by counsel. Ferguson approved the request this time, but then added that it could be anyone except for Cross — as he had ruled at the start of Leech's testimony.

The session quickly dissolved into more acrimony, and a heated warning from Ferguson that he was close to arresting Leech. This outburst sent a wave of murmuring through the courtroom. As Ferguson admonished the spectators to remain silent, it became painfully apparent that the Leech hearing had reached an impasse. The damage had been done, though. Ferguson was pilloried in the Liberal press as Rogers's "Handy Man," hired to persecute witnesses. "Manitoba methods do not go down in Saskatchewan," the *Leader* sanctimoniously proclaimed, "as Bob Rogers and his hirelings should have come to realize before now."[39]

Ferguson planned to convene inquiry sittings in Alberta in late October. But before he left Regina for Medicine Hat and then Lethbridge, Roche asked Ferguson to interview White about his land dealings with Smart and Pedley. The minister wanted it done as soon as possible. Ferguson balked at abandoning his travel plans and recommended that his brother William Nassau Ferguson, a Toronto lawyer and future Supreme Court of Ontario judge, be deputized to take White's testimony. As the commissioner explained to Roche, he had regularly confided in his brother about the inquiry and his findings. He was also prepared to give his brother access to all his papers and exhibits, which he kept in a safety box at the Toronto General Trust Company.[40]

Roche chose not to take up the offer, probably because it would have raised more questions about the integrity of the inquiry. The examination of White would have to wait until Ferguson returned to Ottawa in November. It's noteworthy, though, that Ferguson was compelled to safeguard his commission materials under lock and key in Toronto to keep them from falling into the wrong hands.

Before the end of the year, Ferguson submitted another interim report about a cozy Saskatchewan land deal involving Premier Walter Scott and Lieutenant Governor George W. Brown. In 1900, Scott, then a Liberal backbencher, had lobbied J.G. Turriff, the federal commissioner of dominion lands, to allow his friend Brown to purchase 1,000 acres around Craven. Because Brown, a Rose Plain farmer and Regina lawyer, maintained that the land was marginal at best, he got it for only $1 per acre. Several years later, Brown's parcel was expropriated for the construction of the Craven dam at the bottom of Long Lake. He pocketed $25 per acre. On reviewing the evidence in the report, Prime Minister Borden's acting private secretary Loring C. Christie, a lawyer by training, remarked, "This is in every respect a very remarkable transaction."[41]

In mid-February 1914, a news story suggested that Ferguson's report would be presented at the fall sitting of Parliament. In April, though, the commissioner was busy gathering evidence in Calgary and told the *Herald* newspaper that he didn't know when he would be reporting to the government.[42]

The Conservatives tried to keep the investigation from disappearing from the political radar and arranged for a backbencher, Herménégilde Boulay, to ask Roche in the House of Commons whether Pedley had been dismissed from his position. When Roche reported that Pedley had "resigned after an investigation," Boulay then moved that a copy of the evidence against the deputy minister be tabled.[43]

This request, forwarded to Indian Affairs, elicited a long-delayed non-answer in June 1914. Secretary J.D. McLean pretended to know nothing: "The Department has no particulars on file with regard to these investigations."[44] The evasive response ensured that the Ferguson report would be released in its entirety, when completed and when the Borden government could make best use of its findings. It also signalled that Indian Affairs had moved on from Pedley.

The deputy minister position was immediately filled by Duncan Campbell Scott, a long-time accountant who had started as a temporary copy clerk in 1879. One of Scott's first acts was to issue new, detailed surrender regulations. For years, Pedley and his boss Oliver, among others, had maintained that a reserve surrender required a majority vote from only those male members attending the meeting. A 1914 department circular now explicitly stated that a majority of all qualified male voters had to approve a surrender and that every effort must be taken to ensure a good turnout at the meeting.[45]

Ferguson submitted a multi-volume inquiry report a few days before Christmas 1914. His findings provided plenty of ammunition to go after the Laurier Liberals and their record in office. The political situation, though, had undergone a profound shift with the start of the Great War in August 1914. Former prime minister Laurier had solemnly committed his party to supporting the national war effort. "In view of the critical nature of the situation," he announced the day that Great Britain declared war on Germany, "there should be a truce to party strife." The Liberal leader expanded on his position during a special parliamentary session. Laurier vowed in the House of Commons, "We shall offer no criticism as long as there is danger at the front."[46]

This cry for Canadian unity, for putting country above party, effectively undermined Conservative plans to call a general election and punish the Liberals for their obstructionist tactics leading up to the war. It also called into question what to do with Ferguson's investigation. Until that question had been internally resolved, the Borden government patiently sat on the commission findings. That included stalling a formal request from Manitoba Liberal backbencher Robert Cruise for the report to be laid before the House in February 1915. The former Dauphin merchant may have been caught in Ferguson's net, but the Conservatives weren't ready to show off their catch.

Tommy Ferguson, in the meantime, faced problems of his own. In mid-March 1915, Ferguson's wife Etta, a favoured and much-followed darling in Winnipeg's society pages, began proceedings in Ottawa to secure a separation allowance of $15 per day and support for their daughter, Edith. These actions were in response to a Toronto court application by Ferguson for custody of the child. The couple had been living apart for the past two years — he had left her before the commission appointment — and their daughter was caught in the middle.

Ferguson didn't shrink from publicly discussing the breakup. When the *Winnipeg* alleged that Etta Ferguson had suffered "brutal treatment" and was suing for divorce, an irate Ferguson responded by letter, accusing the newspaper of "malice" and calling on the editor to refrain from expressing "any opinion prejudicial to me" until the courts had spoken. The paper publicly acknowledged that Ferguson had "some fair ground of complaint."[47] It was quite the admission coming from the *Tribune*, but what Ferguson really wanted was to see his daughter, Edith, who was living and travelling with his wife.

It's not known if Ferguson was in Ottawa on April 14 when his report was finally debated in the House of Commons. The newspaper coverage doesn't mention him being there, let alone giving any interviews.

It was Robert Rogers's show. The very idea of a political truce with the hated Laurier Liberals smacked of heresy to him. The rabid partisan had wanted an election in the fall of 1914, and he wanted an election even more in the late spring or early summer of 1915 now that Ferguson had provided fodder for the Conservative campaign. He also believed, as did many of his beleaguered colleagues, that the sanctimonious Liberals had violated the political ceasefire.

The Opposition took every opportunity to vilify the Borden government for botching the purchase of war supplies and military equipment. The Conservatives were desperate to change the focus and punish the Liberals in the process. That's why the government introduced the Ferguson report in the House of Commons on the cusp of the proroguing of Parliament. Now that the Canadian Expeditionary Force seemed destined to play an auxiliary role in the Great War, an election was deemed acceptable. It was also necessary given that the customary four-year life of Parliament was about to expire. An election would determine which party should be entrusted with directing the national war effort.[48]

Ferguson's report was introduced in the House of Commons in two instalments. The first two parts appeared Saturday, April 9, as sessional papers. One dealt with the McEwen grazing lease, the other the Riding Mountain Forest Reserve. Someone in the government, most likely Rogers again, ensured that the Conservative press was fed copies. On Monday, the same day the other nine reports were tabled (five volumes in total),[49] the *Edmonton Journal* announced that "startling revelations" had "blown up" the plan to prorogue the House that week and that the Liberal ranks were racked with "considerable nervousness."[50] The Tory newspapers pounced on why Pedley had suddenly resigned his position — how the deputy minister had "feathered [his] own nest" in awarding the grazing lease instead of "looking after the interests of the noble aborigines."[51]

The better part of the coverage, though, dwelled on what the *Winnipeg Telegram* called "the gory details [of] one of the coarsest pieces of land-grabbing 'villainy' ever pulled off in Canada."[52] In 1906, when the boundaries of Riding Mountain Forest Reserve were redrawn, thousands of acres in Manitoba's Dauphin district became available for settlement. Forest ranger W.A. Davis, a Liberal appointee, had homestead applications printed, signed them, and then gave the blank forms to two Liberal workers, Albert McLeod and Sam Cohen, to shower local party supporters with quarter-section parcels. Fitzroy Dixon of the dominion lands department became suspicious about the applications and asked R.E.A. Leech to pay a visit to Oliver Herchmer at the Dauphin land office. Leech found nothing amiss, but was sent back by Dixon a second time, only to confirm that everything was okay.

Commissioner Ferguson interviewed Davis and Herchmer about the boondoggle as part of his investigation. Both openly admitted that 60 to 80 percent of the homestead grants were fraudulent. Davis said he had been "used for the benefit of the party," while Herchmer pointed the finger at Oliver, who had personally told him to accept any application carrying the Davis signature.[53] One of those so blessed was Robert Cruise, the Liberal MP for Dauphin, who had borrowed some cattle from a friend to make his homestead claim look legitimate.

The *Edmonton Journal* reported that the other nine Ferguson reports contained more salacious examples of Liberal corruption.[54]

On Tuesday, April 13, former prime minister Laurier briefly alluded to the five inquiry volumes that had now been tabled in the Commons, feigning ignorance about what they were about and not even mentioning Ferguson's name.

The next day, shortly after 3 p.m., with the business of the session winding down, former Liberal cabinet minister Oliver asked permission to discuss the report. He spoke for more than an hour with little

HON. FRANK OLIVER
CAUGHT IN ACTION
BY THE CARTOONIST

*Frank Oliver dismissed the Ferguson report as a partisan smear job, while stoutly defending his tenure as Interior and Indian Affairs minister. (*Edmonton Journal, *April 15, 1915)*

interruption from the government benches. That seemed to be the Conservative plan, as if they were setting a trap.

Oliver claimed that $40,000 had been spent on a report solely for "petty partisan advantage." The sad irony, he maintained, was that the "investigations have added very little in the way of information to the public" except to confirm that "under our Liberal administration our lands in all departments were administered as honestly as they were efficiently." Oliver also complained that there hadn't been adequate time to examine the hundreds of pages of documents, but then said there were reasonable explanations for all of Ferguson's examples of so-called Liberal wrongdoing. He also took umbrage at the suggestion that Liberal friends got special favours. "As far as I have been able to gather from a glance through these reports," Oliver steadfastly insisted, "there is no suggestion that these people got anything they did not pay for." He added that "it has yet to be shown that the public interest suffered in any degree."[55]

Oliver also couldn't understand why Frank Pedley had been dragged into the spotlight. The former deputy minister no longer worked for Indian Affairs, no longer had anything to do with the government. In Oliver's estimation, he was an "honest citizen." Oliver had spoken to Pedley a few days earlier and been assured that there was no substance to the report. "I am [as] prepared to take his word," Oliver told the House, "as that of Mr. Ferguson, or any other hired thug such as he is."

He also proclaimed that Pedley, with Smart and White, had done absolutely nothing wrong in buying First Nations lands: "They paid dollar for dollar for everything they got . . . the Indian got what was coming to him." According to Oliver, Ferguson had wasted his time — and taxpayers' money — by failing to uncover "something more serious than the mere fact that these gentlemen bought Indian lands, by tender, taking their chances."

A dismayed W.J. Roche shot back, "If the hon. gentleman thinks that is all right we have a different idea of the propriety of things." He added, "I am quite willing to allow the people of this country to judge . . . these transactions."[56]

Roche, as minister of the Interior and Indian Affairs, responded on behalf of the Borden government. He began by explaining that the Ferguson report had been submitted to the House "at the earliest possible moment under the circumstances," and more importantly, that the government had every right to examine the Liberal administration of lands and resources — just as the Liberal Opposition was at present putting government war purchases under the microscope. Roche also dismissed Oliver's claims of innocence, coolly informing the former cabinet minister that if he read the report "carefully, or even hurriedly," there was no denying the seriousness of the disclosures.[57]

Roche then walked the aggrieved Oliver through some of the findings, quoting sections of the report, including witness testimony, while members of the House looked on. It was found, for example, that the Grand Trunk Pacific Railway had invested $15,000 in Oliver's *Edmonton Bulletin* newspaper at a time when he was making decisions on railway matters. It was also found that Leech, along with Rocky Mountains Park superintendent Howard Douglas and others, had secured a western timber berth at one-eighth the estimated value. And it was found that Alan Joseph Adamson, the former Liberal MP for Humboldt (1904–08), and James Duncan McGregor, a Sifton associate who once served as mining inspector and then liquor commissioner in the Yukon, used a Montana friend, H.B. Brown, to secretly apply for a 28,000-acre grazing lease on their behalf. But when the lease was granted by Adamson's brother-in-law J.G. Turriff, it had miraculously increased to 60,000 acres.

Roche saved his big bombshell for the evening sitting. He told the House about the sorry case of Manitoba farmer Christopher Fahrni, who had bought 3,000 acres of Michel reserve land in 1906, only to lose it to Edmonton banker John Jamieson Anderson in 1910 when he couldn't meet the payments. Anderson didn't keep the land, but quietly transferred it in 1914 to his father-in-law Oliver. It was an outright gift to the former minister, valued at $71,460.

This shady arrangement would never have come to light if Fahrni's son Stanley hadn't written to Oliver about how the family had been hoodwinked. A copy of the letter was slipped to Roche, prompting some digging in the Michel file and the discovery of other incriminating correspondence. The Anderson swindle was never part of the Ferguson investigation. And there was probably much more that he missed. Roche told the House that the report "merely scratched the surface . . . we [the Borden government] could unearth very many more things without referring to Mr. Ferguson at all."[58]

Roche's accusation that Oliver was up to his neck in a cesspool of corruption sparked an exchange of insults. When Roche recoiled at the government's members being called thieves, blackmailers, and porch climbers, Oliver sneered, "I was too flattering." Roche ignored the provocation, mentioning further scandals to come and the need for restitution, before declaring that the "country did not get rid of the late Government any too soon . . . [it] has frittered away the public domain, scattering it out amongst its own political friends."

Laurier immediately got to his feet, denying personal involvement in any dubious transaction and asking "in the name of fair play" why Ferguson hadn't called on him to give evidence. A remorseless Turriff took a different tack, stating in his defence that he hadn't read the "bulky reports" and that "it is a rather difficult matter [to] understand them on so short a notice." He also didn't see the point of discussing the findings because "it is all ancient history."[59]

Robert Rogers didn't utter a word during the debate. Instead, he left it to the western tag-team of Arthur Meighen and Richard Bennett to follow Roche's lead and carry the debate into the late evening. Meighen, the solicitor general of Canada, suggested that any Opposition request to extend the life of the session to discuss the report "will be met in the friendliest spirit by us." He added, "There will be no hurry; we can stay here for a week if the hon. gentleman wishes."

There was nothing friendly, though, about Meighen's demeanour or tone. Known for his cold-blooded debating style, Meighen called out Oliver for being the most partisan member of the House, "who has addressed himself with assiduity to that task." Meighen also swatted aside the suggestion that the Ferguson report was a patronage smear job. The Laurier government had "resisted motions, resisted resolutions, resisted every effort . . . to have the very subjects which are here revealed," and yet, he argued, the Liberals now cry foul.[60]

Meighen's most acid comments went to the heart of Oliver's credibility — namely, his unqualified support of Pedley. With shouts of "go on" echoing in the chamber, Meighen painstakingly read into the record Pedley's tight-lipped testimony about his involvement in the Moose Mountain land sale and the McEwen grazing lease. He then contrasted the former deputy minister's evasive answers with the evidence provided by other, more forthcoming witnesses. When mercilessly badgered by Meighen whether he still believed his former deputy, a somewhat contrite Oliver confessed that he had taken Pedley at his word.

Near the end of his remarks, Meighen took a swipe at Liberal William Pugsley, the former minister of Public Works in the Laurier cabinet, who had been a fierce and unrelenting critic of Borden's war policy, employing the same courtroom skills that had made him a successful Fredericton lawyer. Meighen suggested that Pugsley would probably resort to his "wrecking-tug" tactics to derail the Ferguson report.

"Slippery Bill," as Pugsley was nicknamed, rose to the challenge, claiming that the Conservatives had fallen into a deep hole during the session and that nothing, not even the Ferguson findings, could save them from their scandalous handling of war supplies. "They are trying to divert the minds of the people of this country," said Pugsley, playing to the House, "by seeking to revive not only ancient history but ancient romance."

He then reviewed the instances of so-called Liberal wrongdoing, intimating Ferguson was more concerned with justifying his $40,000 fee when he actually found "very little to complain of."[61] If Pedley had used his position for personal gain, Pugsley submitted, then Sifton would have sacked him. Pugsley, though, wasn't so innocent. He had speculated heavily in western lands and railways as a promoter of the Saskatoon and Western Land Company and President of the Qu'Appelle, Long Lake, and Saskatchewan Railway.

Pugsley had no sooner finished speaking than R.B. Bennett, the Conservative MP for Calgary, was called upon to sum up the Conservative argument. It was well past 11 p.m. and Bennett proposed not "to trespass for any considerable time upon the patience of the House." But he couldn't resist the opportunity to take the high moral ground in his condemnation of the Liberals. Rising in righteous indignation, he let forth with a speech that could have easily been mistaken as a sermon. Bennett had a rolling, rapid-fire way of speaking, repeating phrases and emphasizing words to drive home his argument.

He started slowly — "more in sorrow than in anger" — saying it gave him no pleasure to speak to the Ferguson report. But he had to say something to defend the honour of government and public service against Liberal corruption. "Everything," he fulminated, "that could be done to alienate the public resources of Canada by conspiracy . . . was done . . . graft is the proper word to describe the situation."

For the next hour, steadily building momentum, he detailed Liberal sins and shamed the men who committed them, all the while asking if they could ever be trusted again. Reaching the climax, Bennett called on Laurier to stand in his place before Parliament prorogued and "give to the people of Canada some encouragement or some word" that he regretted what happened during his tenure as prime minister. It was the kind of speech that had helped him earn his reputation as "bonfire" Bennett.

What was particularly remarkable about it, though, was that Bennett was the only member that day who recognized that First Nations were also "victims of the conspiracy." Their rights were sacrificed by the very people entrusted to protect them and look after their interests. "Lo, the poor Indians," Bennett lamented, "they must suffer!"[62]

When the session resumed the next day — Thursday, April 15 — it was on the understanding that there would be a few remaining housekeeping matters before Parliament was prorogued. The first item of business was a damaging report from the Public Accounts Committee about continuing problems with the purchase of war supplies and the need for measures to prevent similar problems in the future. Prime Minister Borden promised that "irregularities and frauds" would be fully investigated and if necessary prosecuted, implying that the Liberals had failed to do the same, as evidenced by the "inferno" Ferguson report.

Wilfrid Laurier couldn't let the comment go unchallenged and supported the need for an inquiry, just not the way Ferguson had conducted his commission. "If we are to . . . purify public life," the Liberal leader said, "then I insist . . . that these investigations shall take place with open doors, and that every man . . . shall have the opportunity to give his own version." Laurier also used his time to muse about a possible general election, while claiming that "we on this side of the House have endeavoured . . . to forget . . . that we are party men." This self-serving comment elicited howls from the Conservative benches, but Laurier persisted, noting that "the only thing which should engross our attention at this time is the war in which we are now engaged."[63]

The House of Commons debate on the Ferguson report generated front-page coverage in Canada's daily newspapers. The dominant story was how three government officials — Pedley, Smart, and White — had "made a clean-up" speculating in reserve lands.[64] It generated more ink than all the other parts of the Ferguson report — not only what the men made, but how they did it. It was all there in gritty detail, including how Smart and Pedley personally prepared the tenders in their Ottawa offices and then took them to Bedford-Jones for submission, how a stenographer, A.S. Manary, was called upon to sign tenders for one of the reserve sales, and how Pedley didn't deposit his "earnings" in the bank but kept the money in a safe at home, or in his pockets.

The Conservative press also chose to villainize Oliver, even though Sifton had served as Indian Affairs and Interior minister when the trio of government officials made their "big profits."[65] It was a replay of what had transpired in the House of Commons when Sifton's name was mentioned in passing only three times during the debate on the report. The once powerful Liberal minister was untouchable because of his influence with Prime Minister Borden and the key role he had played in helping the Conservatives win the 1911 election.

The Liberal press, on the other hand, understanding all too well what the Borden Conservatives were doing, took a more calculated approach to the Ferguson report. In an editorial first carried in the *Toronto Star* and then reprinted in the *Winnipeg Free Press*, Ferguson's findings were said to be no more than "campaign pamphlets written by a Winnipeg lawyer, a worker and a stomper for the present Government, who has been told to find out something which would serve as campaign material for the Government. . . . They might as well have been written by Mr. Rogers himself." The editorial also called on Ferguson to appear before a parliamentary committee, make his charges there, and see whether they stood up to public scrutiny. Until that time, he had as much credibility as "a Liberal lawyer [conducting] an inquiry of his own into the war graft." Any investigation of the Liberal running of Interior and Indian Affairs had to be handled in a "fair, regular way."[66]

A new or expanded investigation took a back seat to crass political needs. The Conservative caucus, especially the prime minister and his cabinet, were elated by the drubbing of the Laurier Liberals in the House. Rogers had delivered, and it was only a question of when, not if, the electorate would head to the polls. Any resistance to calling a general election while Canada was at war had evaporated as the Liberals floundered about during the debate, trying to put up a brave front while distancing themselves from the sensational evidence in the Ferguson report. "No fight in them," was how Borden summed up the Opposition's lassitude in his private diary on April 14.[67]

Conservative election preparations were blindsided by the first major German offensive of 1915. On April 22, one week after Parliament was prorogued, German artillery pounded the Canadian and Allied trenches along the Ypres salient in Belgium. The heavy shelling was followed by the release of deadly chlorine gas — the first time it was used on the western front   that silently seeped into low-lying defensive positions. The Germans expected to meet no resistance as they moved forward, but the Canadians stubbornly held the line at a terrible cost.

Prime Minister Borden planned to used the Ferguson report against the Liberals in an expected summer 1915 general election. (Library and Archives Canada)

Four days of fierce fighting left 6,000 dead, wounded, or taken captive. One lucky survivor of the carnage said "many [were] blown to eternity," never to be found, never to have a known grave.[68] Others suffered burned lungs that shortened their lives or left them permanently impaired. The long casualty lists, reproduced in local papers or read at church services across the nation, shocked the Canadian public. There would be no shrinking, though, from what one minister called the "baptism of blood."[69] Canadians became ever more determined to take the fight to the enemy, even if it demanded more and more sacrifice.

The Second Battle of Ypres caused the Borden Conservatives to lose their appetite for a general election — except for Rogers, who was ready to launch the campaign. In Montreal in early May 1915, while the country was still digesting the losses in Belgium, Rogers demanded a national vote to "clear the air."[70] Liberals and Conservatives alike were offended by the speech — the more urgent need was reaching an agreement to extend the life of Parliament so that the country and the government could concentrate on winning the war. The negotiations between the two parties lasted through the second half of 1915.

Rogers had to find another way of making political life uncomfortable for the Liberals and pushed for a new inquiry that would not only continue Ferguson's investigation of Interior and Indian Affairs but be expanded to include Railways and Public Works. His choice for commissioner was David Marr Walker, an old Conservative warhorse from Winnipeg who had served as Manitoba attorney general, district judge, and police commissioner. Rogers brought the inquiry proposal to cabinet on September 9, but Prime Minister Borden found the choice of Walker distasteful. The prime minister jotted in his diary, "Afraid of methods."[71] Before making a decision, Borden sought the advice of several colleagues and asked for a summary statement of Ferguson's findings.

On October 16, 1915, after two days of discussion at the cabinet table, Rogers got his new inquiry. An order-in-council was prepared, under Borden's signature, appointing Walker as royal commissioner.[72] It was done with some reluctance. Borden apparently preferred the highly respected Conservative lawyer Edward Ludlow Wetmore, the former chief justice of the Supreme Court of Saskatchewan and chancellor of the University of Saskatchewan.[73]

By late October, Borden was still unsure about another investigation and was seeking guidance. According to his diary entries, the decisive meeting was November 2, 1915, when he huddled with Rogers and Sifton about the political situation. Borden then met them individually later in the day, presumably to tell them of his decision.[74] Rogers's brand of politics was no longer palatable to the prime minister at this point. The "minister of elections" had effectively politicized the Ferguson inquiry by appointing, in the words of the Liberal press, a "notorious partisan" to conduct a "secret investigation."[75]

It might have been different if Ferguson had convened public hearings, allowed witnesses to have counsel, conducted himself with a modicum of impartiality and independence, and, above all, been seen to be acting in Canada's interest. But as it stood, because Ferguson was in Rogers's pocket, the report had questionable integrity and compromised significance.[76] Any new investigation might be just as defective.

Rogers was also under a cloud because he had mixed Conservative politics with the public interest during his time as minister of Public Works in Manitoba. His Liberal foes were so convinced that Rogers was crooked that they hired a detective agency to follow and report on his movements, especially those he met with. Rumours circulated that he'd been involved in a political kickbacks scheme in the construction of the new Manitoba legislative building. The scandal had forced the Roblin government to resign in May 1915. Because of lingering questions about Rogers's role in the sordid affair, his credibility with Borden was in tatters.

Sifton, in contrast, was one of the few Canadian politicians who appreciated at the outset that the war would be "most awful" and could last for years.[77] And he likely urged Borden, who had been profoundly affected by his visits with the Canadian wounded in English hospitals

Because former Liberal Interior and Indian Affairs minister Clifford Sifton had helped the Conservatives win the 1911 general election, he was not caught up in the Ferguson investigation. (Musée national des beaux-arts du Québec)

that summer, to do everything possible to support the Canadian Expeditionary Force in Belgium and France. There was also a personal reason for his plea. Four of Sifton's five sons had enlisted, two of whom had been wounded. It wasn't the time, then, to play political games, especially when the Conservatives were trying to come to an agreement with Laurier about continuing the political truce and avoiding an election for the foreseeable future.

What that meant, from Sifton's perspective, was that there should be no new inquiry into past Liberal practices — or himself for that matter. That would only poison the inter-party negotiations. Nor should the Liberals feel threatened by the Ferguson report and how it might be used in the future. It too had to be set aside — moved on from — if both parties were to focus their energies on the war. The proposed Walker inquiry consequently never got off the ground because the government order was never approved.

The Ferguson report became yesterday's news. When Parliament was recalled in mid-January 1916, there was no resumption of the debate that had brought the last session to a raucous ending and sullied the reputation of several members. It was as if the inquiry — despite its explosive findings — had never happened.

The one and only time the report came up again in the House of Commons was February 1916, when Liberal backbencher William Chisholm asked whether Ferguson was still working for the government and how much had been spent on the commission.[78] The Liberals seemingly wanted to embarrass the Conservatives about sponsoring the investigation, especially after the prime minister had sombrely pledged in late December 1915 to "fight to the end" no matter the cost.[79] The Borden government also took no steps to follow up any of Ferguson's findings or pursue prosecution of those who committed fraud.

Sadly, the malfeasance of Pedley, Smart, and White had nothing to do with being Liberal or Conservative, or fighting the Great War for that matter; they had cheated First Nations bands out of their reserves. It was pure and simple graft, and the civil servants would get away with it.

Notes

1. House of Commons, *Debates*, April 15, 1915, p. 2610.

2. Reproduced in the *Victoria Daily Times*, October 9, 1911.

3. Quoted in D.J. Hall, *Clifford Sifton, v. 2: A Lonely Eminence, 1901–1929* (Vancouver: University of British Columbia Press, 1985), p. 270.

4. M. Bliss, *Right Honourable Men: The Descent of Canadian Politics from Macdonald to Mulroney* (Toronto: Harper Collins, 1994), p. 74.

5. J.M. Beck, *Pendulum of Power: Canada's Federal Elections* (Scarborough: Prentice-Hall, 1968), p. 128.

6. Quoted in W.L.R. Clark, "Politics in Brandon City, 1899–1949," unpublished Ph.D. thesis, University of Alberta, 1976, p. 107.

7. J. English, *The Decline of Politics: The Conservatives and the Party System, 1901–1920* (Oakville: Rock's Mill Press, 2016), p. 16.

8. *Calgary Herald*, October 19, 1911.

9. R.C. Brown and R. Cook, *Canada 1896–1921: A Nation Transformed* (Toronto: McClelland and Stewart, 1974), p. 182.

10. See Hall, *Clifford Sifton, v. 2*.

11. Quoted in K. Nicholson, "Rogers, Robert," *Dictionary of Canadian Biography, vol. 16*, University of Toronto/Université Laval, accessed April 8, 2020. http://www.biographi.ca/en/bio/rogers_robert_16E .html.

12. Ibid.

13. English, *The Decline of Politics*, p. 101.

14. *Debates*, July 18, 1904, p. 6951.

15. See Ibid., April 17, 1913, pp. 7892–8013.

16. *Library and Archives Canada (LAC)*, RG15, v. 1106, f. 2923465, T.W. Crothers to W.W. Cory, April 22, 1913.

17. *Winnipeg Free Press*, April 20, 1915.

18. *Winnipeg Tribune*, April 21, 1906.

19. The Ferguson Commission was established by order-in-council (P.C. 1109) on May 10, 1913. Under the provisions of the federal Inquiries Act, Winnipeg lawyer Thomas Roberts Ferguson was asked "to investigate and report upon all matters connected with the sale, lease, grant, exchange or disposition by any means whatsoever, since the First day

of July 1896, of (a) Dominion Lands; (b) Timber and Mineral lands and mining rights and privileges, including coal, petroleum and gas lands and rights; (c) Water powers and rights." It was a broad mandate, clearly intended to ferret out any and all manner of wrongdoing and corruption during the Laurier Liberals' lengthy tenure in office. It overlooked, though, a significant area of federal jurisdiction — namely, Indian Affairs. Five weeks later on June 19, 1913, another order-in-council (P.C. 1589) was approved. Noting that "it is expedient to enlarge the powers conferred upon him [Ferguson]," the government order added First Nations lands and reserves to the list of inquiry topics. It also gave Ferguson, for good measure, the authority to investigate "the acts or proceedings of any person, or corporation, in relation to the matters aforesaid [the four areas of inquiry]." *LAC*, RG2, series 1, v. 1252, P.C. 1109/1913; v. 1258, P.C. 1589/1913.

20. *LAC*, R.L. Borden papers, diaries, July 25, 1913.

21. *Winnipeg Free Press*, May 21, 1913.

22. Canada. *Sessional Papers*, n. 1, 1915, "Report of the Auditor General of Canada for 1913–1914," p. K75.

23. Tyler and Wright Research Consultants, "The Alienation of Indian Reserve Lands During the Administration of Sir Wilfrid Laurier, 1896–1911: Addendum, The Royal Commission of Thomas Roberts Ferguson," unpublished report, May 1977, appendix F.

24. *Ottawa Evening Journal*, September 15, 1913.

25. Department of Justice, HQOLD 9-713 (Y-320-592475), "Ferguson Appointment," W.D. Hogg legal opinion, September 29, 1913. (This file, henceforth called File 713, had not been processed by *LAC* at the time of access.)

26. File 713, Newcombe to W.J. Roche, October 7, 1913.

27. Borden diary, October 10 and 11, 1913.

28. *LAC*, RG10, v. 3059, f. 253,792, J.G. Macfarlane, "memorandum re Frank Pedley," October 2, 1929.

29. *Ottawa Evening Journal, Victoria Daily Colonist*, and *Ottawa Evening Journal*, all October 13, 1913.

30. File 713, E.L. Newcombe to R.L. Borden, October 8, 1913.

31. File 713, T.R. Ferguson to W.J. Roche, October 17, 1913.

32. *LAC*, RG13, section A-3, v. 158, E.L. Newcombe to W.J. Roche, November 7, 1913.

33. Quoted in *Canadian Annual Review*, 1913, p. 331.

34. *LAC*, RG18, section A1, v. 450, f. 562/1913, T.R. Ferguson to A.B. Perry, October 10, 1913.

35. Quoted in W.L.R. Clark, "Politics in Brandon City, 1899–1949," unpublished Ph.D. thesis, University of Alberta, 1976, p. 50.

36. *Regina Leader*, October 11, 1913.

37. Ibid.

38. *Regina Province*, October 13, 1913.

39. *Regina Leader*, October 14, 1913.

40. File 713, T.R. Ferguson to W.J. Roche, October 17, 1913.

41. Borden papers, v. 144, pp. 77036–38, L.C. Christie to R.L. Borden, n.d.

42. *Calgary Herald*, May 5, 1914.

43. *Debates*, February 16, 1914, p. 817; *Journals of the House of Commons*, March 23, 1914, p. 293.

44. *LAC*, RG10., v. 2911, f. 185,723-9B, J.D. McLean to T. Mulvey, June 25, 1914.

45. Martin-McGuire, *First Nations Land Surrenders*, p. 160 (*LAC*, RG10, v. 7995, f. 29103-1/1) 1914 circular.

46. English, *The Decline of Politics*, pp. 89–90.

47. *Winnipeg Tribune*, March 20 and March 30, 1915.

48. English, *The Decline of Politics*, pp. 90, 98–101.

49. Collectively, the following reports made up five volumes: Blood Indian Reserve and acquisition of certain Indian Lands by Smart, Pedley, and White (sessional paper n. 266); Riding Mountain Forest Reserve (n. 268); Ferguson Report (n. 281); Timber Berths 550½ and 528 (no. 282); Kananaskis Coal Company (n. 283); Southern Alberta Land Company (n. 285); The Bulletin Company, Frank Oliver, and Grand Trunk Pacific Company (n. 286); Aylwin Irrigation Tract (n. 287); Timber Berths 1107 and 1108 (n. 288); Grazing Ranch No. 2422 (n. 289); Craven Dam (n. 290); and Ferguson orders-in-council (n. 291).

50. *Edmonton Journal*, April 12, 1915.

51. *Winnipeg Telegram*, April 12, 1915.

52. Ibid.

53. Ibid.

54. *Edmonton Journal*, April 12, 1915.

55. *Debates*, April 14, 1915, pp. 2540–1, 2548, 2551.

56. Ibid., pp. 2548–50, 2560. Roche's comments on the Ferguson report were published in a forty-two-page pamphlet for Conservative party distribution.

57. *Debates*, April 14, 1915, p. 2551.

58. Ibid., p. 2567.

59. Ibid., pp. 2568, 2570, 2572.

60. Ibid., pp. 2573–5.

61. Ibid., pp. 2583–4, 2589.

62. Ibid., pp. 2592–3, 2601.

63. Ibid., pp. 2608, 2610, 2621, 2623.

64. *Montreal Gazette*, April 14, 1915.

65. *Toronto Daily News*, April 14, 1915.

66. *Winnipeg Free Press*, April 20, 1915.

67. Borden diary, April 14, 1915.

68. T. Cook, *The Madman and the Butcher* (Toronto: Allen Lane, 2010), p. 190.

69. Ibid., p. 199.

70. English, *The Decline of Politics*, p. 102.

71. Borden diary, September 9, 1915.

72. *LAC*, RG2, v. 47, 1915, PC#2439, October 16, 1915.

73. The prime minister sent a telegram to Sir Douglas Hazen, the former Conservative premier of New Brunswick, about Wetmore, who was born in the province and served there before moving to the North-West Territories. Borden diary, October 16, 1915.

74. Borden diary, November 2, 1915.

75. *Winnipeg Free Press*, June 21, 1915.

76. The *Winnipeg Free Press* belittled the commission as "a striking illustration of how a Government investigation should not be carried on." *Winnipeg Free Press*, June 21, 1915. The *Winnipeg Tribune*, no friend of Ferguson, was even more dismissive. "Ye gods," the newspaper expressed in shock at the expense, "the investigation looks like a bigger scandal than the matters investigated. Wouldn't it jar you?" *Winnipeg Tribune*, November 5, 1915.

77. English, *The Decline of Politics*, p. 94.

78. Interior and Indian Affairs minister W.J. Roche reported that the cost of the commission was almost $64,000, including Ferguson's fee. *Debates*, February 17, 1916, pp. 885–6.

79. T. Cook, *Warlords: Borden, Mackenzie King, and Canada's World Wars* (Toronto: Allen Lane, 2012), p. 71.

⊰⊱ *Epilogue* ⊱⊰

THE HONOUR OF CANADA WAS INVOLVED

Fire razed the Centre Block of Parliament Hill on the evening of February 3, 1916. The conflagration started in the House of Commons reading room, probably caused by a carelessly discarded cigar in a wastepaper basket, and raced out of control along hallways into the Commons and Senate chambers. People scrambled for their lives. Prime Minister Robert Borden and his secretary reportedly made for the exit on their hands and knees into the cold Ottawa winter air. Others escaped out windows to waiting ladders or simply jumped. Seven perished.

Even though fire crews arrived within minutes of getting the call, the Centre Block couldn't be saved. The bell in the Victoria clock tower came crashing down before midnight, followed by the collapse of the tower less than two hours later. By morning, the once grand neo-Gothic building had been reduced to a jumbled, smouldering pile of stone and brick, broken glass, and charred wood, coated in ice from the vain attempt to douse the flames.[1]

It's been widely assumed that the Ferguson report, which Borden ironically likened to an inferno, was claimed by the blaze.[2] But did the report really go up in flames? And was the supposed loss of the report a convenient excuse for failing to act on the findings when other, more pressing political reasons were at play?

All copies of the Ferguson report were supposedly lost in the February 1916 fire that destroyed the Centre Block on Ottawa's Parliament Hill. (Library and Archives Canada)

◄◄-►►

In late October 1915, William James Roche, the Interior and Indian Affairs minister, advised his cabinet colleague Charles Joseph Doherty that he was transferring all the Ferguson investigation materials to the Justice department. "I submit them to you," Roche wrote, "for such action as the Department of Justice feels disposed to take."[3]

It had been more than half a year since the Conservative government presented the Ferguson report in the House of Commons. Nothing had been done in the interim. While the Canadian Expeditionary Force found itself at the sharp end in the Great War, and the Conservatives and Laurier Liberals hammered out a truce to extend the life of Parliament and avoid a general election, the Ferguson Commission became a casualty. The report languished in Roche's Langevin Block offices, the devastating revelations about past Liberal graft and corruption becoming more muted with each passing day.

Nor would the Justice department do anything about the investigation. Even though Justice minister Doherty promised to "have them [evidence and findings] carefully looked into," he was still waiting for the Ferguson materials in early November.[4] They appear to have gone astray. The fate of the missing inquiry documents is a mystery that remains unsolved to this day.

The eleven case studies making up the five-volume Ferguson report were prepared as separate sessional papers, each with its own number. Another sessional paper was devoted to Ferguson's appointment, including the government orders detailing the scope of his commission and his powers under the federal Inquiries Act. None of these sessional papers were printed and bound as part of the official record for 1914 or 1915. There were consequently only a few hard copies. One copy, possibly more, might have been among the journals and other papers that fuelled the fire that started in the House of Commons reading room.[5]

It's extremely doubtful, though, that all copies of the Ferguson report went up in flames that evening, much less the considerable paperwork that would have been generated by the investigation. It's known, for example, that Ferguson kept the inquiry's witness testimony in a Toronto safe. Roche never specifically mentioned whether it was part of the October 1915 document transfer to the Justice department. It might have remained among the clients' files at Ferguson's law firm and been destroyed years later as partners died or retired and the practice eventually dissolved.[6]

Borden's working office, along with those of several cabinet ministers, and the cabinet meeting room (the Queen's Privy Council chamber) were located in another building, the East Block, on Parliament Hill.[7] The prime minister probably had his own copy, given the controversial nature of the report. And surely Public Works minister Robert Rogers did, since he was the mastermind behind the inquiry who would have drooled over the incriminating evidence and how it could be used to smite the Liberals in any future election.

Both Arthur Meighen and Richard Bedford Bennett also appear to have consulted and studied the report at length. Neither Conservative could have made their incisive speeches during the Commons' April 1915 debate, given the details they knew, without having a copy to hand. As representatives for Manitoba and Alberta, they would have also wanted an accounting of how Liberals had exploited western lands and resources for their own benefit. In fact, while serving as Interior and Indian Affairs minister in March 1918, Meighen asked lawyer and senior civil servant William Francis O'Connor to provide an independent assessment of one of Ferguson's findings by "examin[ing] at this office the report."[8]

Meighen had either kept a personal copy of the Ferguson inquiry for his own political purposes, or more likely had access to a copy held at the Interior and Indian Affairs offices in the Langevin Block. It would have made sense for the two departments, the subject of the Ferguson Commission, to have retained a copy of the report, if only to compare the findings with the record on file. The departments' senior Ottawa staff might even have expected to be called on to provide an explanation for what happened — how Liberal connections overrode official policy and practice. At the very least, they would have wanted a record of what exactly Ferguson was told or found out to shield themselves from shouldering the blame.

Ferguson's findings, and the evidence on which they were based, were also well known and well publicized at the time. When the Winnipeg barrister submitted an interim report in September 1913, Rogers provided tantalizing hints to the press. And when the report was tabled in the House in April 1915, Rogers once again slipped information to friendly Conservative editors. The newspapers not only published what they had been fed, but supplemented their reporting with what had been revealed during the Commons debate. It wasn't only the evidence that was reproduced in the papers, but actual testimony given before Ferguson.

The House debate, at sixty-two pages in Hansard, also provided a comprehensive snapshot of the commission report. The Conservatives knew the odious findings could put the Laurier Liberals on the run and tried to put as much as possible on the official record. Roche even reproduced his Commons remarks in pamphlet form.[9]

But the report quickly became a political deadweight for the Borden government. When the Ferguson inquiry was established in May 1913, Canada was at peace and the only battle that mattered in Ottawa was the one between the Conservatives and the Liberals. For decades, both parties had exploited every advantage no matter how small the gain. The Great War created a new political landscape where a shared national purpose took precedence over petty partisan activity.

That was never more apparent than in the summer of 1917. As casualties mounted and recruitment sagged, Prime Minister Borden concluded that Canada could only continue to meet its military obligations and secure victory with conscripted soldiers. Such a controversial measure required the creation of a coalition government with the support of the Laurier Liberals. But Laurier balked at the proposal, questioning the need for conscription. He also feared that any Liberal involvement in a union government would effectively alienate Quebec, which was already seething over the prospect of compulsory military service.

Borden's proposal also faced a formidable challenge from within Conservative ranks from none other than Rogers. The popular, resourceful minister of Public Works was apoplectic that power was to be shared with the Liberal enemy and tried to lead a caucus revolt against coalition. Undeterred, Borden offered to step aside in favour of someone more palatable to the Liberals. This threat spooked wavering Conservatives and they rallied to their leader. The politically savvy Rogers was now a liability.

While Borden shored up his own party support for coalition, Clifford Sifton actively worked on bringing prominent western Liberals into the union fold. These provincial heavyweights included agrarian leader

Prime Minister Robert Borden, in front of Public Works minister Robert Rogers, visiting members of the Canadian Expeditionary Force in England during the Great War. (Library and Archives Canada)

Thomas Crerar from Manitoba, deputy Saskatchewan premier and political fixer James Calder, and Clifford's older brother, Arthur Sifton, the premier of Alberta. The involvement of these Liberals critically hinged on the withdrawal of Rogers, a move that Borden finessed by dropping him from cabinet in August 1917. Rogers's surrender appeared complete when he didn't contest the December general election that validated the union government experiment.[10]

The departure of Rogers — and the reasons for it — also doomed the Ferguson report. Both coalition partners had to believe they were on the same side, working in the national interest. That would be possible only if the Ferguson sword weren't hanging over the heads of Liberal members — if the report became, in the words of Liberal J.G. Turriff, "ancient history."[11] Union government was consequently the death knell of the partisan inquiry.

Rogers, being a political animal, didn't remain on the sidelines for long, but his career thereafter amounted to a series of retreats. In 1920, following Meighen's assumption of the prime ministership at the head of the Unionist government (National Liberal and Conservative Party), Rogers called for a return to strict party lines and the old reliance on patronage. The former Manitoba MP despised the boy wonder Meighen's rise in the party, believing there could be only one Conservative star from western Canada. As a veteran political observer commented on the feud, "Rogers makes no bones of his determination to get Meighen."[12]

The two men didn't reach a public rapprochement until 1923, when Conservative fortunes were on the wane. Rogers returned to the House of Commons in 1925 as part of a minority government, only to lose his seat the following year. Although elected one more time in 1930 when Bennett, then Conservative leader, swept to power, Rogers was by then a broken man in ill health. The death of his wife, Aurelia, in 1934 after nearly fifty years of marriage pushed him over the edge, and he spent the last two years of his life at Homewood Sanitarium in Guelph. His only son auctioned off his father's possessions and demolished the family mansion on Roslyn Road in Winnipeg.

Obituaries praised Rogers for his affable personality, a partisan more suited to the hustings and party backrooms than serving as a minister of the Crown. In retrospect, his passion for his party often went too far. A satirical rebuke in *Saturday Night* magazine suggested that "had Canada progressed somewhat further towards fascism . . . we can imagine him as a highly successful Fuhrer."[13]

Sifton, Rogers's bête noire, continued to play an influential role in federal politics. Unlike Rogers, who could only contribute by absenting himself from the political scene, Sifton helped the Conservatives, now running under the Unionist banner, win the December 1917 wartime election. "He was the coxswain," one feature article declared, "and he did the steering."[14]

Sifton chose not to participate in the union experiment but had great hopes that coalition would cleanse party government in Canada and put an end to the kind of cutthroat politics he'd once mastered. He was greatly dismayed, though, as the Canadian ship of state drifted, seemingly rudderless, by the end of the war. Sifton retired to Toronto in 1919, where he lived out the last ten years of his life. Mistrusted by Liberals and Conservatives alike, he was a "lonely eminence" at the head of a Canadian newspaper empire, in the words of his biographer.[15]

Sifton would be remembered for completing the settlement and development of the prairie west. The Conservatives insisted that there was a sleazy side to the settlement and development story — that Liberal friends and associates greatly profited from western lands and resources, and that Sifton may even have quietly helped himself. Ferguson's focus, though, was distorted by Borden's admiration of Sifton, and the investigation had to circle the bull's eye without hitting home.

Even then, the damning evidence of patronage wheeling-and-dealing in the Ferguson report was subsumed by the Great War and its increasing demands on the country. Sifton may have argued that the war and only the war mattered, but there was a side benefit to his stance. He had escaped unscathed in the Ferguson report and then saw to it that there would be no further questioning of his record in office. He would never answer for the special treatment that fellow Liberals enjoyed during his tenure as Interior and Indian Affairs minister.

The two deputy ministers, James Smart and Frank Pedley, who worked under Sifton, were also spared any reckoning, including returning the profits they had made in reserve land sales.

Smart had left his government position in late 1904 to set up a lucrative immigration and labour service, specializing in domestic workers, with offices in Winnipeg and Montreal. His new endeavour was tainted by scandal. The same year he resigned as deputy minister, a nineteen-year-old Swedish housemaid who worked in the Smart home abruptly left her position and jumped from a train as it crossed a bridge over the Richelieu River. No one could explain why the young immigrant had leapt to certain death.[16]

Smart was questioned in the Ferguson inquiry and co-operated by giving details on how he and his co-conspirators had manipulated the tender process. After the Ferguson report was released, though, Smart was never held to account. He resided in Montreal, living comfortably off his various entrepreneurial exploits, until his death at age eighty-four in 1942.

Pedley saved himself from the embarrassment of dismissal by resigning his government position before Ferguson submitted his official report. Aside from his ignoble exit from the civil service, he was treated as largely blameless. The general consensus was that it had happened over a decade ago and wasn't worth pursuing.

This treatment was unconscionable. Not only had Pedley earned a top-tier salary during his tenure as deputy minister of Indian Affairs, but he had pocketed a cash windfall from the sale of reserve lands. Pedley's retirement present to himself was a world tour with his much younger wife. He also continued to speak at Liberal meetings and rallies. Pedley was living in Ottawa at the time of his death in 1920 at age sixty-three.

The most reviled Liberal on Robert Rogers's most wanted list was Frank Oliver, Sifton's successor at Interior and Indian Affairs. Since the 1911 election, the Edmonton MP had acted as if the Conservative government were an aberration and was forever telling the House how the Laurier Liberals would have handled things better. Rogers consequently turned Ferguson loose on Oliver and then had his Conservative colleagues crucify the former minister for his lame responses during the April 1915 House of Commons debate on the Ferguson report.

But because of the war and the Conservatives' need to work with the Liberals, Oliver eluded any kind of punishment for his reckless abuse of power. He wasn't even censured when Parliament resumed sitting in early 1916.

Oliver's swindling of Christopher Fahrni, though, wasn't completely shelved or forgotten. During the December 1917 general election, when

Oliver chose Laurier over conscription and coalition, his Unionist opponent told a campaign rally about "Honest" Frank Oliver's "duplicitous" acquisition of Michel reserve land. The story was repeated the next day in the *Edmonton Journal*, along with a venomous cartoon featuring Laurier, Oliver, and other Liberal candidates playing instruments on behalf of the German band overseas.[17]

It appears to have been the only the time, apart from initial April 1915 newspaper coverage, that Oliver's dubious transaction was held against him. It was only raised to garner support for the Union cause and compulsory military service in a close fight for the Edmonton seat. Following his defeat in two consecutive elections, Oliver was named to the Board of Railway Commissioners in 1923, which was, most appropriately, a patronage appointment. The University of Alberta also granted him an honorary degree in 1931, two years before his death at eighty.

Edmonton commemorated Oliver's legacy by naming a school, park, and neighbourhood after him. Long-time staff at the Interior department also fondly recalled Oliver's "most kindly and generous nature" during his years as minister.[18] It was as if Rogers and Ferguson had gone after the wrong man, the accusations against him groundless.

Those who had worked most closely with Oliver at Indian Affairs remained in place at department headquarters through the Great War years. As the new deputy minister, Duncan Campbell Scott continued to be guided by the two watchwords that informed his lengthy career as department accountant: restraint and accountability. His jaundiced rival for the deputy minister position, J.D. McLean, hung on to his position as department secretary, gatekeeper, and taskmaster.

Both men had exercised considerable authority under the Liberals, especially decision-making power, and continued to do so after the 1911 Conservative election victory. In fact, the Ferguson inquiry made no difference to Canada's Indian Affairs policies and practices, even though Richard Bennett had lamented the Laurier government's shabby treatment of First Nations during debate on the report.

McLean retired in 1930, receiving a presentation of silver in a small farewell ceremony at the Indian Affairs offices. Scott and Indian commissioner W.M. Graham followed in 1932, taking with them their knowledge of how the Laurier government had met its treaty responsibilities, especially when it came to reserves.

T.R. Ferguson moved on from his Conservative political work to other interests and causes in the middle war years. After his scandalous separation and alimony battle with his society wife, he left Winnipeg in 1916 to replace his brother at the Toronto law firm of Millar, Ferguson, and Hunter. W.N. Ferguson had been elevated to the bench. Coincidentally, the brothers' sister, Emily Ferguson Murphy — the popular author "Janey Canuck" — was also named a judge in 1916, becoming the first female police magistrate in the British Empire.

Once ensconced in Toronto, Tommy Ferguson began to earn new headlines for all the wrong reasons. He continued to defend liquor interests, even though Canada had adopted prohibition for patriotic purposes. A fervent Orangeman, he also sought to block grants to certain Catholic-led charities. Then there was Ferguson's extraordinary claim at an Orange Day celebration at the Toronto exhibition grounds in July 1920 that Roman Catholics were seeking to take over the Imperial Order Daughters of the Empire.[19]

Three years later, while arguing a case before the Supreme Court of Ontario on June 19, 1923, the fifty-eight-year-old Ferguson suffered a massive stroke and died at home that evening without regaining consciousness. His funeral was a who's who of the Ontario legal establishment, including senior judges from both sides of the political divide. W.J. Roche, now serving as chair of the Civil Service Commission, was there, but not Rogers, who had retreated to Winnipeg. The base of Ferguson's gravestone was inscribed "And when a standard bearer fainteth Isaiah x:18."

Ferguson's obituary notices invariably mentioned his inquiry into Liberal management of the Interior and Indian Affairs departments. But the commission was forgotten until the 1970s, when First

Nations bands and their organizations started to challenge and seek compensation for reserve surrenders.

Canada's First Nations had a treaty right to reserves, a solemn promise by Indian commissioner Alexander Morris that they were "inviolate so long as the grass grows and the sun shines."[20] But the Laurier government broke this treaty promise by embarking on a concerted campaign to take away reserve land. Twenty-one percent of prairie reserves (one in five acres) was surrendered between 1896 and 1911.[21] It's a dubious record that has never been matched by any subsequent Canadian government.

First Nations reserve surrenders were justified on the grounds that Canada was quickly running out of homestead land and that western settlement would be stalled, if not discouraged, unless "underutilised" prairie reserves were made available to meet the demand. The excuse that First Nations bands had been given too much land at treaty or had more land than they needed served to further justify taking away some or all of their reserves.

It didn't matter that reserves represented only a minuscule percentage of the total land available for settlement. If the reserve occupied good land, then it rightfully belonged in the hands of immigrant farmers.

Surrenders, though, were more than simple land transfers to the Crown. Sifton wanted to minimize the First Nations presence because he firmly believed that they could never be part of the modern, progressive society taking shape on the western prairies. His successor Oliver shared this uncompromising attitude, but was even more extreme in zealously condemning First Nations as a blight on western Canada and its great future. He wanted them moved away from white settlement to isolated regions where they could eke out a marginal existence and not depend on government assistance.

Both men regretted how Canada's treaty obligations interfered with their other duties as minister of the Interior. They viewed the treaty relationship as an unwanted burden and wanted a free hand to deal with First Nations as they saw fit — doing the minimum possible, while managing and directing their lives. It was an attitude that reflected popular thinking in Canada at the time. First Nations were regarded as an irrelevant, inferior minority, and any time, energy, and money spent on them was a colossal waste.

The call for reserve surrenders echoed throughout the prairie west in the late nineteenth century — from politicians to business people to farmers. The Laurier government moved cautiously at first, securing surrenders for reserves that were abandoned or never occupied. But by the early 1900s, Indian Affairs began to actively encourage full or partial surrenders from First Nations bands, especially those occupying prime agricultural land near booming towns or railway branch lines. Surrenders not only became a department priority, especially under Oliver, but acquired a momentum. Any surrender, whether there was actual demand or not, was aggressively pursued.

Indian Affairs also failed to respect the mandated provisions of the Indian Act in securing surrenders. Even though a majority of adult male band members were required to approve a reserve surrender, the

Prime Minister Wilfrid Laurier's government embarked on an ambitious plan to take away reserve land from treaty bands. Those who fraudulently benefited were never held to account. (McCord Museum)

department accepted a vote from only those at the meeting — in some cases, no more than a handful of people. Legal doubts about this practice were either downplayed or ignored. Indian Affairs representatives also kept poor or incomplete records, sometimes revised the agreed-upon terms during the meeting, asked for more land to be forfeited, brought along bags of cash, held multiple votes, and even resorted to threats and intimidation.

Whereas there had been only one reserve surrender before 1896, the Laurier government accepted more than two dozen in a fifteen-year period. The prime minister wasn't exaggerating when, in reflecting on his government's fifteen-year administration of Western lands, he spoke of the "radical change in the attitude of the Government."[22]

None of the surrendered land was actually made available for homesteading. Former reserves were quickly surveyed into quarter-section parcels and then sold by private tender and later by public auction. A few farmers seeking to expand their operations bought land, but the majority of the lots went to speculators, intent on holding on to their investment or flipping it to another buyer to cash in on the great land boom. Purchasers included local merchants, real estate agents, lawyers, bankers, politicians, and government officials — even Indian Affairs employees and their families.

Over time, the auction sales came to be monopolized by a few well-connected Liberals who received advance notice of the sales, including in a few cases the upset prices for the land. Buyers also colluded with one another to avoid competitive bidding. Some speculators acquired large swaths of land because of the easy terms, including instalments stretching over several years. Indian Affairs was also lax in chasing down delinquent payments, while the land sat unoccupied. Large purchasers were generally more concerned with finding a market for their land, in most instances in the United States, than fulfilling their payment obligations.

Bands, meanwhile, got much less than they expected, despite the promises made at surrender meetings. For many First Nations, reserve surrenders were yet another broken treaty promise.

Only a small part of this sorry saga was told in Ferguson's report. One of the eleven case studies dealt with the fraudulent purchase of the two Nakoda reserves at Moose Mountain by civil servants Smart, Pedley, and White. Another detailed how Pedley was paid off for awarding the Kainai grazing lease to the McEwen Cattle Company. That was it. Not even Frank Oliver's secret acquisition of Michel land was included in the investigation.

The Ferguson Commission wasn't at all concerned with the extraordinary number of reserve surrenders between 1896 and 1911. Nor was it much interested in how surrendered parcels were marketed or how the treaty right to reserves was sacrificed for the benefit of speculators. Ferguson sought out Liberal corruption, the more egregious the better.

Patronage appointees Smart, Pedley, and White had used their government positions to commit fraud. That's why they were exposed — not because they had cheated First Nations.[23]

Canada's contradictory approach to treaty rights and reserves was best encapsulated by Oliver. In March 1931, he reflected on the larger meaning of treaties in an article on Treaty Seven in *Maclean's* magazine. Oliver said it had been "my privilege" to attend the treaty signing at Blackfoot Crossing in 1877 and "Canadians may well be proud, both as to the means, method and achievement" in settling western Canada.

He then challenged anyone who believed that "treaties were only made to fool Indians . . . that the bargains made were not carried out." He refused to accept this "accusation," insisting that "the honour of Canada was involved."[24]

What the elderly Oliver conveniently forgot was his defining role as the main driver of reserve surrenders in the early twentieth century. While readily acknowledging Canada's relationship with its treaty partners, Oliver did everything within his power as Indian Affairs minister, including amending the Indian Act, to appropriate First Nations land. He also violated his sworn duty to the Crown by using his position and influence to secretly acquire reserve land near Edmonton.

Oliver's corrupt behaviour was unforgivable. But what was truly appalling was that he was only one of many who wilfully preyed on First Nations and their lands. So much for the honour of Canada.

Andrew Littlechief, dressed in his regalia and holding a red ensign flag, at a powwow in the Moose Mountain district of southeastern Saskatchewan, circa 1915. (Adrian Paton Collection)

Notes

1. Miraculously, paintings and other valuable items were rescued from the blaze. The Library of Parliament also survived untouched because of the closure of its iron fire doors. J.H. Marsh, "The Parliament Hill Fire of 1916," *The Canadian Encyclopedia*, https://www.thecanadianencyclopedia .ca/en/article/fire-on-the-hill-feature.

2. Tyler and Wright Research Consultants, "The Alienation of Indian Reserve Lands During the Administration of Sir Wilfrid Laurier, 1896–1911: Addendum, The Royal Commission of Thomas Roberts Ferguson," unpublished report, May 1977, p. 5.

3. *Library and Archives Canada* (*LAC*), Department of Justice, HQOLD 9-713 (Y-320- 592475), "Ferguson Appointment," W.J. Roche to C.J. Doherty, October 30, 1915. (This file, henceforth called File 713, hadn't been processed by *LAC* at the time of access.)

4. Ibid., C.J. Doherty to W.J. Roche, November 1, 1915.

5. It's possible that the Ferguson report might have been removed, effectively taken out of circulation, because of the sensitive negotiations between the two parties over continuing the 12th Parliament beyond 1915. When the new session convened on January 12, 1916, three weeks before the catastrophic fire, Liberal members would have been disgruntled to know that the report, with its damaging findings, could still be consulted in the reading room.

6. Following the deaths of Charles Millar and T.R. Ferguson, the firm was renamed Millar and Hunter and then Millar, Hunter, and Milne until 1956 when the firm folded. The practice's old records were probably destroyed at the time of A.W. Hunter's death in 1956. The Law Society of Ontario confirms that no client records exist today.

7. The Leader of the Opposition's office — in this case, former Liberal prime minister Wilfrid Laurier — was located in the Centre Block. It was completely destroyed by the fire.

8. *LAC*, W.F. O'Connor papers, v. 2, f. Meighen, A. Meighen to W.F. O'Connor, March 14, 1918.

9. W.J. Roche, "The Ferguson Report on the Alienation of the Public Domain in Western Canada," Federal Press Agency, Ottawa, 1915.

10. J. English, *The Decline of Politics: The Conservatives and the Party System, 1901–1920* (Oakville: Rock's Mill Press, 2016), pp. 103, 138–57.

11. House of Commons, *Debates*, April 14, 1915, p. 2572.

12. Quoted in W.L.R. Clark, "Politics in Brandon City, 1899–1949," unpublished Ph.D. thesis, University of Alberta, 1976, p. 182.

13. *Saturday Night*, August 1, 1936.

14. H.F. Gadsby, "Has Canada a Political Boss?" *Maclean's*, March 1, 1918.

15. D.J. Hall, *Clifford Sifton, v. 2: A Lonely Eminence, 1901–1929* (Vancouver: University of British Columbia Press, 1985).

16. *Ottawa Journal*, April 20, 1904.

17. *Edmonton Journal*, December 5, 1917.

18. Quoted in D.J. Hall, "Oliver, Frank" in *Dictionary of Canadian Biography, v. 16*, http://www.biographi.ca/en/bio/oliver_frank_16E.html.

19. Toronto *Globe*, July 14, 1920.

20. Quoted in S. Krasowski, *No Surrender: The Land Remains Indigenous* (Regina: University of Regina Press, 2019), p. 232.

21. Of the approximately 2.7 million acres set aside as reserves in the prairie west, 576,781 were surrendered during the Liberal years in office. P. Martin-McGuire, *First Nations Land Surrenders on the Prairies, 1896–1911* (Ottawa: Indian Claims Commission, 1998), p. 27.

22. *LAC*, Wilfrid Laurier papers, "North-West Subjects: Land Administration," n.d., pp. 218669–71.

23. Reserve surrenders did not end after the Liberals' defeat in the 1911 election. In the last year of the Great War, Canada's new Union government sought to increase agricultural production for the war effort by seizing "idle" reserve land in the prairie west. The sweeping initiative empowered Canada to ignore or override band interests and either lease reserve land to non-Indigenous farmers for a fixed-term or turn over the land to government operators who would work it using non-Indigenous labour. Since the program violated treaty provisions, it required an amendment to the Indian Act. B.W. Dawson, "Better Than a Few Squirrels: The Greater Production Campaign on the First Nations Reserves of the Canadian Prairies," unpublished M.A. thesis, University of Saskatchewan, 2001, pp. 4–5, 56. In justifying the Greater Production Campaign in the House of Commons in 1918, Interior

and Indian Affairs minister Meighen said, "I do not think we need waste any time in sympathy for the Indian." Using reserve land to grow wheat, he argued, was "a lot better than a few squirrels caught by the Indian." In Meighen's words — and the sentiment behind them — could be heard the echo of Sifton and Oliver and their deputies. *Debates*, April 23, 1918, pp. 1048, 1060.

24. F. Oliver, "The Blackfoot Indian Treaty," *Maclean's*, March 15, 1931.

⊰ Acknowledgements ⊱

*C*heated began with the search for the 1913 T.R. Ferguson inquiry report into Laurier Liberal malfeasance. The "missing" investigation was said to contain damning material about First Nations prairie reserve surrenders in the early twentieth century. But an exhaustive search turned up nothing — except for a Department of Justice "Ferguson Appointment" file, still waiting to be processed at Library and Archives Canada. File 713 revealed that commissioner Ferguson was not really interested in reserve surrenders and that anything in his report on the topic had been reported in newspapers at the time.

This finding left the way open for a comprehensive study of reserve surrenders under the Laurier government. In fact, telling the larger story was justified by several Indian Claims Commission reports, in particular one by Dr. Peggy Martin-McGuire, that suggested that well-connected Liberal insiders were involved in pushing surrenders for personal gain and that taking First Nations land became a priority under Liberal cabinet minister Frank Oliver. Several — not all — surrenders are examined.

Cheated is largely based on the voluminous and detailed records of the Indian Affairs department, in combination with the official papers of several key Liberal players.

A special thank-you is owed to historian/archivist Glenn Wright and Marguerite Sauriol of Library and Archives Canada for assisting with the search for the Ferguson report, but more importantly, helping ferret out vital sources.

John English, Darren Friesen, Gerry Friesen, and Jim Miller carefully read and commented on the first substantial draft; their encouraging feedback made for a better book. Naturally, any errors or omissions are our own.

ECW Press took an immediate interest in the manuscript. Co-publisher Jack David has been an enthusiastic supporter, while Sammy Chin and her team expertly guided the book through design and production. Editor Lesley Erickson helped focus and tighten the book, improving its clarity, argument, and potential impact.

Elly Hansen and Marley Waiser read and provided unvarnished feedback at various stages along the way. They were our toughest critics but biggest fans.

As co-authors, we learned much about one another, especially our respective strengths, and about working together as a tag-team. Coco the wonder dog even started to like Bill — most days. We drew the line, though, at whiskey/whisky. Jennie likes Irish, Bill prefers Scotch. That difference was symbolic of the creative tension between us as we tried to make sense of the story and navigate the best way to tell it. Should other historians be as fortunate.

↞ Index ↠

Note: Pages in italics indicate illustrative material.

Frank, William, 226

Gadie, Alexander, 255, 257
Galician immigrants, 72–73
Giants Tomb Island (ON), 246
Gibbons, James, 110–11, 112, 115, 131–33, 134, 171–72, 213
Ginn, John C., 130
Gisbourne, Francis H., 274
Gladstone (MB), 217
Gooderham, J.H., 253, 255
Graham, William Morris ("Pegleg Bill"), 142
    Carry the Kettle lands, 142, 143, 154–55, 163
    Cote surrender, 186
    Crooked Lakes reserves, 184–85
    Fishing Lake reserve and lands, 186–89, 187–88, 221
    Fishing Lakes reserves, 168, 169–71, 199
    The Key and Keeseekoose reserves, 200–1, 226
    Muscowpetung auction, 222
    on speculation and payments, 216–17
    views on First Nations, 143
    work at Indian Affairs, 142–43, 311
Grand Trunk Pacific (GTP), 102, 169, 212, 286
Grant, Frederick W. (F.W.), 212, 214, 215–16, 223–25, 227–28, 229, 230
Grant, George Davidson, 215–16
grazing and ranchers, 240–48, 275, 276, 282–83
Great War, 306
    coalition government, 305–6, 308
    Ferguson Commission and report, 281, 282, 291–92, 294–95, 302, 308
    supplies procurement contracts, 266, 282, 289–90

Greenway, Thomas (Tom), 30, 71
Grizzly Bear's Head reserve (Nakoda), 2, 144–45, 155, 162, 166–68, 210, 221
Guthrie, Hugh, 248–49

Halpin, Henry R., 75–76
Halsey, Nicol, 220
Hansard, and Ferguson report, 305
Harkin, James Bernard, 137
Hathaway, George, 221–22
Haultain, Frederick, 104, 139, 140
Havey, A.J., 220
Henderson, David, 181
Herchmer, Oliver, 283
Heron, R.B., 212–13
Herron, John, 249, 250, 253
Hobbema (Peace Hills) agency/reserves, 173–74, 201
Hogg, William Drummond, 275
"home farm" system and program, 17, 19
homestead system, 36, 37–38, 101–2, 314
Howell, Hector, and Howell Commission, 190–91
Hudson, Dunbar H., 221
Hudson Bay railway, 183
Hughes, Sam, 180, 181, 273
Hungarian settlers, 81–83

Immigration Act, 152
immigration to Canada
    non-white, 42
    scheme in, 70, 72–74, 139
    from US, 71
Indian Act
    amendments of Oliver, 180–82, 183, 259–61
    and buying of land, 91
    First Nations as dependents, 14
    provisions for surrenders, 5, 14, 313–14
    taking over of reserves, 58–59
    transfer agreements, 61

Klondike gold discovery and goldfields, 56, 126

Laird, David
Alexander reserve, 161
background and work, 74–75, 106, 198
Carry the Kettle reserve, 155
Cote reserve, 134, 161
Crooked Lakes reserves, 106, 184
Cumberland reserve, 114–15
Hobbema agency/reserves, 173
Michel band and reserve, 131, 132
Moose Mountain reserves, 74, 75, 76, 79–80, 81, 85, 86–87, 87, 89–90, 93–94
Moosomin and Thunderchild reserves, 197–98
and Niitsitapi people, 237–38
Roseau River reserve, 129
spending estimates for Indian Affairs, 182–83
Lake, Richard S. (R.S.), 99, 103, *103*, 104–5, 167, 181–82
Lamont, John Henderson, 208, *209*, 225
land companies, settling and development of west, 37–39
Land Regulations (1888) (a.k.a. Regulations for the Disposal of Surrendered Indian Lands), 81, 163
land sales notice, example, *211*
La Rivière, Alphonse-Alfred-Clément, 128–29, 130
Lash, J.B., 90, 241
Latchford, Francis Robert, 248
Laurier, Wilfrid, *23*, *313*
as acting Indian Affairs and Interior minister, 141, 142, 154
election of 1896, 82
and Ferguson report, 287, 289, 290
and Great War, 281

on Oliver amendment, 260
on patronage, 52
provinces in west, 139
and Sifton, 137
on surrenders, 127, 314
surrenders handled, 141, 143–44
Laurier Liberals (Laurier government 1896–1911)
connections and friends as land buyers, 214–20, 246–49
criticisms and rumours, *165*
election of 1900, 84–85
election of 1904, 137–38
election of 1908, 192
election of 1911, 261–62
initiation of surrenders, 58–59
land flipping for supporters, 88–89
patronage by, 31–32, 39, 48–49, 51, 52, 54, 85, 118
in power and Indian Affairs policies, 23–24, 44–45
practices and results in surrenders, 312–16
push for settlement of western provinces, 3–4, 35–36
push for surrender of reserves, 2–5, 6–7
reserve land acquired, 202–3
sales information notices, 217–18
"scandal sessions," 191–92, 269
settling and development of west, 28–29, 35
speculation by and for, 208–9, 210–11, *214*, 214–16, 218–20, 223–26
and treaty rights, 6–7, 57, 260, 312
views on First Nations, *44*
See also ministers, MPs, and departments
Lean Man reserve (Nakoda), 2, 144–45, 155, 162, 166–68, 210, 221

Newnham, Jervois Arthur, 196
Nichol, Horatio, 212
Niitsitapi people and reserves
(collectively known as Blackfoot),
236, 237–41, 249, 255
North Atlantic Trading Company
(NATC), 40, 70, 139, 164–66
North Battleford (SK), 155
North-West Rebellion, 20–21, 43, 144,
157, 202
North-West Territories, 52–54, 56, 86,
124–25, 139
North-West Territories Council, *39*
numbered treaties (generally),
description, 12
See also individual treaties
Nut Lake reserve, 157, 186

Ocean Man reserve and people
in amalgamation of reserves, 68,
72–73, 74, 75, 78–79, 81, 85–88,
89–90
land sale, 3, 91–92, 93–95, 209, 274
sales notice for surrender, *211*
Ochapowace reserve and band, 99–100,
185
O'Connor, J.P., 216
O'Connor, William Francis, 304
O'Dwyer, Patrick Owen, 211
Office of Native Claims, 2
Ogilvie, William, 33
Oliver, Frank, *108, 152*
background and work, 107–9
Cote reserve, 159, 161
criticisms by, 145
Crooked Lakes reserves, 99, 184
delegation from Treaty Four, 1, 255,
257
end at Indian Affairs, 262
Enoch reserve surrender and sale,
107, 109–12, 113, 115, 194, 195

and Ferguson report, 5, *284*, 284–85,
286–88, 290, 309–10
Fishing Lakes reserves, 170, 199
Grizzly Bear's Head/Lean Man
auction, 167
immigration policy and beliefs,
152–53
as Indian Affairs and Interior
minister, 145, 152–54, *174*, 315–16
Kainai lands and grazing, 243, 246,
249, 251
land sales amount to First Nations
(amendment), 180–82, 183
lands transferred to, 230–31
life after politics, 310
Michel reserve and lands, 171, 213,
214, 230–31, 286–87, 309–10
Moosomin and Thunderchild
reserves, 196
and NATC, 164–65
on Niitsitapi, 236
Piikani reserve, 252–53
reserve land near towns
(amendment), 259–60, 261
R. Rogers and Borden government,
269, 271
Samson band, 174–75, 201
on speculation, 163–64, 215
St. Peter's reserve, 190, *203*
and surrenders, 5, 151–52, 153, 156,
179–81, 198, 203, *203*, 236–37, 312,
315–16
surrenders and money, 175, 182,
203–4
Swan Lake reserve, 193, 194
views on First Nations, treaties, and
reserves, 109, 111, 145, 153–54, 231,
312–13, 315
Orr, William Andrew (W.A.), 51, 63, 84,
91, 117, 132, 160, 274
O'Soup, Louis, 255, 256, *256*

as Interior minister, 35–37, 40
Kainai reserve, 243, 244–45, 248
in land flipping, 89
on Leech, 277
Moose Mountain reserves, 85–86,
  87, 94–95
and NATC, 165–66
on Oliver amendment, 260
patronage by, 31–32, 33, 34, 39, 48–49
policies on First Nations, 44–45
power and dismissals at Indian
  Affairs, 32–33, 34, 51
reorganization of Indian Affairs, 52,
  53–54, 57
replacement for Smart, 118–19
resignation, 140–41, 268
and Rogers, 267–68, 273
Roseau River reserve, 129
settling and development of west,
  35–37, 40, 42–43, 71, 308
on success in west, 28–29
and surrenders, 58, 113, 127, 145–46,
  312
and timber berths, 191–92
views on First Nations, 41, 42, 43,
  44, 312–13
western office of Indian Affairs,
  52–53
Siksika (or Blackfoot) people and
  reserve, 2, 236, 239, 251, 253–55
Simmonds, C.L., 273
Simms, Stephen Chapman, 220
Simpson, Margaret, 167
Simpson, Sidney S., 166–67, 224
Smart, James Allan, 69
  Carry the Kettle lands, 142
  Chakastaypasin reserve and lands,
    83–84, 93, 210
  as deputy minister at Indian Affairs
    and Interior, 34–35, 49–50,
    54–56, 58, 69–70, 117–18, 138–39

Enoch reserve and lands, 111, 115,
  116, 117
in Ferguson Commission and report,
  274, 275, 276, 285, 290, 309
immigration and settlement
  promotion, 69–70
in immigration scheme and NATC,
  70, 72–73, 164, 165
land purchases and flipping, 88–89,
  90–92, 95, 209–10, 274
life after politics, 308–9
in Manitoba politics, 33–34
Moose Mountain reserves, 72–74,
  75–76, 78, 79–81, 85–86, 87–88,
  89–90, 209
opening up of reserves for land,
  63–64, 65
as speculator, 65, 68, 70–71, 139
tenders as method for sale, 209–10
Smith, J. Obed, 39, 84–85
Smith, J.W., 93
Smith, M.M., 179
Smith, W.W., 223
Songhees reserve, 259–60
Speers, C. Wesley (Wes), 39, 77, 88
Speers, Robert S., 167
Staples, William, 193, 194
Stevens, J.G., 105
St. Mary River Railway, 240, 246
"Stony band of Indians," 143–44, 154
Stony Plain (AB), 109–10
Stony Plain (Enoch reserve), 194
  See also Enoch reserve and people
St. Peter's (Peguis) reserve, 189–91, 203
"scandal sessions," 191–92, 269
surrenders of reserves. See reserve
  surrenders
Swan Lake reserve and band, 127,
  193–94, 221
Swan River (MB), 193
Sweetgrass, Chief, 12